Taking the Word to the World

50 YEARS
of the

UNITED
BIBLE
SOCIETIES

Edwin H. Robertson

THOMAS NELSON PUBLISHERS
Nashville • Atlanta • London • Vancouver

Photo Credits For Jacket Photos:
  Author Photo: Margaret Smith
  "Read Any Good Books Lately?": Mediacom
  All Other Photos: United Bible Societies / Maurice Harvey

Photo Credits For Insert Photos:
  United Bible Societies

Printed in the United States of America
1 2 3 4 5 6 7 8 9 — 00 99 98 97 96

Contents

Author's Preface

When I was asked to write this Jubilee History, it seemed a straight-forward task and one which I expected to enjoy. I have enjoyed it, but it has not been a straightforward task! The United Bible Societies was born in 1946, and I had worked for it as Study Secretary from 1956 to 1962. Long before it was born, I had known of the British and Foreign Bible Society and given it support, both as a member and then minister of a Baptist church. Since 1962, I had kept a continuous interest in the UBS, and it seemed that I knew it well. After all, I had done innumerable broadcasts about its activity, both in radio and TV, and written even more articles. This was surely a subject I knew well. I approached it with confidence. Many of the leading figures in its history were still alive and most of them old friends.

Research was pleasant in New York, Stuttgart, Amsterdam, Reading, etc. The material began to grow, especially after visiting the Roman Catholics in Milan, Livorno, and Rome. That was the trouble. There was so much and no apparent shape. I found myself quietly writing about steady progress when suddenly I hit a revolution! The Second Vatican Council unexpectedly brought in the Catholics; the decision to share the funds of all the Bible Societies, with the slogan, "The work is one, let the money be one;" the opening up of the Soviet Union and of China multiplied the demands and miraculously brought in the money; a dependent Germany became a major contributor almost overnight. With all these sudden changes, there was no way in which a quiet history of the UBS could be written. Neither was it possible to treat the Bible movement like a person and the book a biography. So many people came to my aid, but their advice was not consistent one with another. A Protestant advised me on a chapter about the Roman Catholic advent; a Cardinal kindly corrected me; the Protestant said, "Edwin, the Cardinal has seduced you!" Back to the drawing board. All this help I needed, and it was kindly given. I had few minor clashes and no major ones. But the book had to find a shape. I hope that shape is now detected.

It begins with strongly independent Bible Societies discovering that God wanted them to cooperate. They were each led by strong personalities. That gave me the first clue to shape. This story was the story of people. I could not mention them all, but I could detect those who had given a major turn to events and try to describe what they were thinking and doing. From time to time that meant stepping aside just to look at and describe a person. Each time I did that I saw that the history of the UBS had progressed a little, even changed direction, under this strong leadership. There were also key moments in the history which needed to be recorded. These were not always conferences or committees and very often not even due to human intervention. There were times when God took a hand because the humans were finding it too difficult to change. Unexpected events called for original initiatives and sometimes new persons. Mistakes were made and errors had to be corrected. Enthusiasm often set goals which could not be reached. A sense of failure was often met by an unexpected success. God was not beyond using the carrot and stick method to his servants— at least it seemed like that.

But only when the whole story is told can you see what miracles have been wrought. A basically Protestant movement has been embraced by the Roman Catholic Church; Paraguay has contributed to a printing press in China; a famine of Bibles in Germany after the Second World War has given way to a German Bible Society which is a major contributor to a world Bible movement; the developments in secular translations have been initiated by staff of the UBS; the churches have been moved to think in terms of Bibles for those of other religions and none;

Bible Societies are working together with other Bible agencies, many of whom once regarded the UBS as "unsound"; a sensitive, worldwide organization has been structured which can respond to unexpected needs anywhere in the world.

That worldwide organization has proved itself in Eastern Europe, the former Soviet Union, China and Nepal. It has even responded to the chaotic needs of Bosnia and Croatia.

My judgement after writing, reading, reducing, and editing this story is that the UBS was born old already and has grown young. At its birth most of its member Societies were already over 100 years old; today, it is like a child at the beginning of life, discovering a new world and a new millennium. Its parents are still alive to guide it. It would do well to know its history but not be bound by it. There is a whole new world out there, waiting to be served with the Word of God, and that God can be trusted to see that the UBS will "never walk alone," provided it never forgets that it is required to "do justly, love mercy and walk humbly with its God."

EDWIN H. ROBERTSON
1995

Prologue

The work which is done by Bible Societies today is as old as the Christian Church, even older. The synagogues of the ancient world had to be supplied with copies of the Torah, the Prophets, and the Writings. When a large Jewish community developed in Alexandria, a community which knew little Hebrew, these Sacred Scriptures were translated into Greek. So there was Bible translation, production, and distribution even before Christ came. In the Christian Church new problems arose when Christian leaders like the Apostle Paul began writing authoritative letters to the churches he had planted. Many were too important to lose, and they were copied for the benefit of other churches. The same thing happened to other accepted writings, including the Gospels, the Acts of the Apostles, and the Book of Revelation. Before long, there was a New Testament to put beside the Old, and both had to be copied, sometimes translated, and always distributed: "The Greek-speaking Church took its cue from the Hellenistic Jews of the diaspora and 'began to produce translations of the Bible in a variety of languages so as to make sure that the gospel would be known as widely as possible.'"[1]

In the fourth century, the Latin-speaking Church followed the example of the churches of the east and began to put the Bible into the language of the people. In A.D. 383, Pope Damasus asked Jerome to revise some rather poor translations of the Psalms and give to the Church a New Testament in Latin. There was much opposition to the "vulgarizing" of the Sacred Books, but Jerome continued throughout his life to work at a translation of the whole Bible into the Latin which could be understood by the people. Eventually with other tranlators, the *Vulgate* was produced. It remained the Bible of the western Church for a thousand years, and when John Wycliffe set about putting the Bible into English, it was the Latin *Vulgate* he used as his text.

The invention of printing and the flame of the Reformation coincided. For the Reformers, the Bible was their strongest weapon in a battle to reform the Church. The Reformation period saw an avalanche of translations into almost all the languages of Europe. This was done largely by Protestant churches, who believed that the Bible should be in the hands of ordinary laymen and intelligible to them.

The Evangelical Revival of the 18th century and the birth of Protestant missionary societies towards the end of that century and into the 19th revived the need for translating and publishing the Bible. William Carey, the founder of the Baptist Missionary Society in Britain, taught himself Hebrew and Greek while still a cobbler of shoes. As a missionary in Bengal, he started a translation program at Serampore, which eventually produced thirty-five translations. Other missionaries followed. It was to serve such missionaries that Bible Societies were formed.

Dr. Laton Holmgren, in his article on "Bible Societies" in the *Oxford Companion to the Bible*, describes the formation of an early Bible Society:

> The organization of this period that most completely resembled the later Bible Societies was a direct outgrowth of the Pietistic movement, the von Canstein Bible Institute of Halle, organized in 1710 to supply inexpensive scriptures to the poor of Germany. Although the von Canstein group confined its efforts to Germany and eastern Europe, by the end of the 18th century it had achieved the remarkable record of circulating over three million low-cost Bibles and New Testaments.[2]

The first modern Bible Society, with its worldwide missionary outlook, ecumenical and serving the churches, but separated as an agency, was the British and Foreign Bible Society formed in 1804, with the stated aim, "to encourage the wider circulation of the Holy Scriptures without note or comment." From the beginning it was not intended to serve only the churches of Britain, but to extend its agencies into Europe and the British Colonies. Within a few years, the American Bible Society was founded in 1816, again serving more than the American churches, but extending its work to help American missionaries to provide copies of the Bible in the language of the people they went to evangelize. By the end of the 19th century, the British and Foreign Bible Society and the American Bible Society had spanned the world with a vast network of agencies and associations.

The Netherlands Bible Society, founded as early as 1814, and the National Bible Society of Scotland, founded in 1861,[3] both served more than their own country. These two had their own specific interests. The Netherlands Bible Society looked to the Dutch East Indies in particular and served the missionaries and churches resident there. The National Bible Society of Scotland had as its first aim the provision of Holy Scriptures to their people who went into all the world but not necessarily as missionaires. The Scots made use of the openness of the Empire and found work in distant parts. There was a nice story told by the Otago and Southlands Bible Society (now part of the Bible Society of New Zealand) about the lack of trade in Bibles in New Zealand. The National Bible Society of Scotland had thought to serve the new immigrants, but found that Scottish families in New Zealand had their own Bibles, brought from home, and that they cared for them in such a way that they never wore out. That lack of trade led the National Bible Society of Scotland to widen its field and follow its missionaries.

Many other Bible Societies were formed during the 19th century, but they were usually content to serve the churches of their own country. Inevitably there were differences of conviction. Most European Bible Societies wanted to include the Apocrypha in the Bible, while the British and Foreign Bible Society followed the Geneva Bible practice and omitted the Apocrypha as "extra-canonical."

The story told in this volume is of the United Bible Societies, formed in 1946 and celebrating in 1996 fifty years of growth from tentative moves towards cooperation to a world movement embodying the ideals of Bible Society work. The ideals are simple: to make the Bible available in a form which all can understand and all can afford. In order to accomplish this the UBS has had to develop methods of translation, techniques of printing, means of distribution, and, because no one should be deprived of a Bible for reasons of poverty, fundraising on a massive scale. To do this the UBS has drawn upon the resources and expertise of all the Bible Societies of the world, but it has also sought the closest cooperation with and strongest support of the churches; churches of all denominations.

The first task, however, was to gather the different Bible Societies into one family, and the bringing together of the two largest Societies was the initial and necessary task—the British and Foreign Bible Society (BFBS) and the American Bible Society (ABS).

CHAPTER ONE

How It All Began

———— ◇ ————

You cannot celebrate a 50th anniversary until you are quite sure about the original date of the event you are celebrating. When did the United Bible Societies begin? All agree that it was formed as the result of a conference of Bible Society representatives at the Conference Center of the Diocese of Chichester, "Elfinsward," in Haywards Heath, England. That conference was held on May 6–8, 1946. Delegates were there from the four Bible Societies most active in promoting the union: the British and Foreign Bible Society, the American Bible Society, the Netherlands Bible Society and the National Bible Society of Scotland, as well as those of Czechoslovakia, Denmark, Finland, France, Germany, Norway, Poland, Sweden, and Switzerland. The World Council of Churches (in process of formation) was also represented. The conference did not assume the right to form the United Bible Societies on the spot, but on May 9 passed a resolution that the UBS be created "upon the approval of six of the bodies eligible for membership." Each representative had to go back to his Board and seek the approval of its members. Official letters of invitation were sent out and, dependent upon the dates of Board meetings, the answers came in. By July 11, the sixth approval arrived and the UBS came into being.

Intersociety Relationships

In general terms, intersociety relationships before the formation of the UBS can be divided into three principal, historical periods:

The first was characterized by *largely independent action*. This is the period roughly from 1804 to 1900. Each Society sought to undergird the work of the missionary societies of its own country and so moved out across the world with little or no concern for the activities—translation, production, distribution, and fundraising—of other societies. During this period the BFBS and the ABS, the two largest societies, were responsible for most of the Bible production and distribution worldwide. At the outset both Societies sought to establish an ecumenical basis for their work, but received no encouragement from the Roman Catholic or Eastern Orthodox churches, and so became primarily Protestant-oriented Societies. Neither the BFBS nor the ABS were content to be merely national Bible Societies. With the British Empire at its zenith, the BFBS regarded its field as the world. The classic story of the beginning of the British and Foreign Bible Society is that of Mary Jones, the Welsh girl who walked across the mountains barefooted in order to get the Welsh Bible, a Bible in her own language and, after that long walk, could not find one. This so moved the people who received her that they set to work to prepare the Bible in Welsh and available to those who wanted it. The famous phrase then was, "If for Wales, why not for the world?" and the BFBS, right from the beginning, was "for the whole world." The ABS, although primarily concerned for the vast territory and growing population of the U.S., also sought to meet the needs of American missionaries steadily moving out across the world. In order to maintain an ecumenical balance and to widen its scope on the continent of Europe, the BFBS in 1804 appointed three general secretaries: the Rev. Josiah Pratt, from the Established Church of England; the Rev. J. Hughes, a Baptist minister; and the Rev. C. F. Steinkopff (Karl Friedrich Steinkopff), representing the Protestants of Europe.

A second period might be denoted as one of *guardedly cautious cooperation*. This is the period roughly from 1900 to 1932. Two general types of cooperation were attempted:

1. *Withdrawal agreements.*
   The ABS withdrew from Korea, and as a *quid pro quo* the BFBS withdrew from the Philippines; the ABS withdrew from Persia, the BFBS from Central America, etc.
2. *Comity agreements.*
   The ABS and BFBS agreed to share the work in Brazil, China, Japan, etc., by assigning separate geographical areas within these countries; for example, in Japan, ABS was assigned the east and north, with headquarters in Tokyo, and the BFBS in the west and south, with headquarters in Kobe.

A further example of cooperation during this period is reported by the Rev. Dr. Eric North, General Secretary of the ABS. Writing in July 1930, he tells of a recent publishing program in Russia:

Various Russian groups appealed to the ABS for aid. In 1926, without prejudice to the priority of the BFBS in that field, the Society supplied the funds through representatives in Russia, by which an entire Bible and a New Testament in smaller size were set up and plated in the government printing office in Leningrad. The action of the American Bible Society was based on a stipulation that these plates should be available to any Russian religious group which desired to print from them and could provide the funds. The "All-Russian Evangelical Christian Union," of which Mr. I. S. Prokhanoff was the president, printed from these plates an edition of 25,000 Bibles and 25,000 New Testaments. The British and Foreign Bible Society provided the funds for printing 6,000 of these Bibles, and allowed the proceeds of their sale to be applied to the publication of the New Testament."[1]

As early as 1910, the need for mutual understanding and some cooperation had become evident. In that year a conference was held in Bible House, London, at which representatives of the two societies saw the problems and proposed a standing committee of representatives to meet regularly. It was agreed by both societies that: "a Committee of Counsel, consisting of three representatives of each organization (BFBS and ABS) be appointed to meet as opportunity may admit either in London or in New York."

Such a meeting of representatives of the two societies was held in New York in October 1912 at which the problem of "territorial rights" was discussed. It came to a tentative conclusion, showing signs of disagreement and compromise. There were two points—distribution and translation. The principle of cooperation was defined as: "When either Society is in occupation of any field, and the other Society feels called upon to take up work in that field, it should not do so without consulting the one in possession."

On the question of translation: "When one Society has begun translation work in any language, the other Society should not begin work in that language without consultation."

The driving force behind this move towards cooperation seems to have come from the American Bible Society, which in March 1919, went further and proposed a "World Federation of National Bible Societies." The proposal with details of the "scheme" was very close to what later became the United Bible Societies. It was sent hopefully to the BFBS, whose General Secretary, the Rev. John Ritson, replied saying that the BFBS does not come into the category of "national" Bible Societies, adding: "From its very inception, it has been a World Society. The international character of our Society marks off its work from that of Societies which are limited to one country or section of a country, and with which you are proposing we should federate."

The BFBS General Committee thought that the American proposal was to hand over "executive powers in matters of policy and administration" to this World Federation, and preferred what the Netherlands Bible Society proposed about the same time: "occasional conferences of the leading Bible Societies for friendly and consultative purposes." These gatherings would be purely advisory, serving the valuable purpose of getting to know one another better and of understanding one another's aims and methods of working.

The rebuff to the ABS proposal showed that both Societies needed further work in overcoming their procedural differences and in pursuing their common goals. Complaints and tensions continued. North was appointed Associate General Secretary of the ABS in 1927, coming after a teaching career and with administrative and editorial experience in the Methodist Episcopal Church, followed by three years as Executive Secretary of the China Union Universities (1924–1927). In all these tasks he had learned to seek cooperation rather than competition. An early clash came when Ritson complained that the ABS had not kept to its agreements in one of the South American fields. North replied in a conciliatory tone but pointed out that the BFBS had behaved in much the same way in an adjacent field!

For some years, the proposal for a world body of Bible Societies was kept alive with polite comment, but nothing seemed to come of it. Towards the end of this period of "guardedly cautious cooperation" came the first signs of change in 1931. They were due to the efforts of three wise men. It is surprising how much great decisions by justly proud organizations depend upon the wisdom of a few individuals. When it comes to cooperation, such decisions also depend upon personal relationships.

In 1928 North was appointed General Secretary of the American Bible Society; in 1929 the Rev. Dr. Arthur Wilkinson was appointed General Secretary of the BFBS; two years later, Wilkinson was joined by the Rev. Dr. John Temple. All three men were to serve for many years, and they quickly grew to appreciate one another. Shortly after Wilkinson's appointment, he wrote to North with evident expressions of goodwill and added that he prayed for the success of the ABS. This new note led North to plan an early visit to London that he might see what this new spirit meant for inter-Society relationships. In 1931 he met Wilkinson in London to discuss certain problems arising from competition between the two major Societies in China, India, and other areas of the world. They established immediate rapport. A relationship of mutual respect and trust developed which lasted throughout their lives. The two men approached matters at issue between the two Societies with new candor and a readiness to discuss all subjects openly. It was early May 1931, and North was asked to address the BFBS annual meeting—a rare honor. In this meeting, the personal bonds between the two senior executives of the two major Societies was forged and within a few months the appointment of Temple added a third congenial member to the team. These three wise men shared the vision of a "United Bible Societies," and all three lived to see it realized.

On this 1931 trip North also visited the National Bible Society of Scotland, meeting their Board of Directors in Glasgow. This was merely a courtesy visit, except for one incident which illustrates the explosive tensions of those days. Mr. A. S. Annand, who had been NBSS agent in Japan, was present at the meeting, and spoke emotionally when the chairman asked if there was any other business. He delivered a violent denunciation of the ABS in general for its "unmoral principles," and in particular of Henry Loomis, the ABS agent in Japan during Annand's period there. North had hardly heard of Loomis, who died in 1920, and had no idea to what Annand was referring. There was little he could say but demur at the accusations.

The third historical period of Bible Society activity was one of more *orderly structured coordination*. This is the period from 1932 to 1946. The principal characteristic of this period was the creation of an increasing number of "joint agencies" and independent Bible Societies. It began with North and Temple travelling together in the Middle East to organize joint "Bible Lands" agencies all the way from Egypt and the Sudan in the south to Greece and Bulgaria in the north. Others followed in most of South America and later the Far East.

From the beginning of this period in 1932, events occurred which set the scene for the coming of the "United Bible Societies."

In July of that year an historic conference was held in London involving the ABS, BFBS, and the National Bible Society of Scotland. For two days, Board and staff members of the three Societies met in Bible House. Some of the staff meetings were held in Temple's home, and the warm fellowship of Christian workers who understood and liked each other made negotiations much easier. The ABS delegation was in raptures, declaring that no previous conference had shown "so extensive a range of matters covered, so large a degree of unanimity in the conclusions reached, so high a degree of confidence and goodwill." These proposals were almost entirely concerned with cooperative work by ABS and BFBS in Europe, the Philippine Islands, Korea, Japan, and Brazil, where it was suggested that the NBSS be invited to participate. There was a proposal for a "joint agency of the British and American Societies in uniting the entire West Indies and the Guianas." The results far exceeded their expectations, undoubtedly due in a large measure to the mutual confidence and respect the "three wise men" had already established. The importance of the rapport they maintained cannot be exaggerated. Suspicions and misunderstandings that earlier had made cooperation difficult were now largely dissolved in a common desire to enlarge the world outreach of the Bible Societies, rather than defend the prestigious position of each. The official communication, signed by these three; North, Temple, and Wilkinson; was confident and enthusiastic: "We have just completed a Conference which we believe is not only unique in the annals of the three Societies, but also rich in significance for our future history."

The formal report by the ABS representatives to their Board cannot disguise the excitement and sense of occasion they felt: "The historic conferences of 1932—as they will be called in Bible Society history—consisted of one large conference on July 26 and 27 in which the three Societies were represented (the first of its kind) and a number of Staff Conferences in which only the BFBS and the ABS were represented."

The report goes on to express thanks for the warm hospitality of London, but leaves to the end a provisional assessment of the conferences:

It is fair to say that the results have far exceeded the most sanguine hopes of any of us. We believe that we have reached bases of agreement on principles, which if supported by our Boards will eliminate confused and competitive operation in the field, greatly increase the efficiency of the work, and permeate all the workers with a fresh sense of fellowship in the cause. The Conferences have done more than prepare the way for harmonious administrative adjustments. They have envisaged a great future advance in the worldwide relationships of the work in the ultimate formation of a worldwide Federation of Bible societies which though not new in the thought of some pioneers is new in the extent of its support and in its scope. For this Federation will have as members not only the long-existing Societies, but those new Societies that may come into being in India and China and Japan, in Brazil and Mexico and Argentina and elsewhere as the churches of these lands come to carry responsibility for the Bible cause in their own lands and participate in the worldwide work.

Such an international fellowship will not only mean stronger and greater work but a more influential witness to the place, which we believe in God's providence, the Holy Scriptures are meant to carry in the life of the world.

In one of the opening prayers of the Conference we were reminded that the Master Himself had entered the Conference Room before any of us. At the close of the Conferences we were sure that He had been with us and had brought us to an outcome far beyond our hopes."[2]

A Practical Application in China

It was not surprising that the first reaction which came from the three Bible Societies in conference concerned the work in China. Both Wilkinson and Temple had served as missionaries in China, while North had quite recently been Executive Secretary of the China Union Universities. The Bible Societies had agencies in China, and all three societies at the conference had staff, who had served or were still serving, in those agencies: Carleton Lacy of the ABS China agency, G. W. Sheppard of the BFBS China agency, and A. S. Annand, formerly NBSS agent for North China. They encouraged the conference to discuss the developing situation in China. After much discussion of detail and with firsthand knowledge of the China work, it was recommended that the three Societies work together "with a view to encouraging the formation of a China Bible Society." To this end a council was soon set up in Shanghai with six representatives of each of the Bible Societies. This was at first only an advisory council, whose expenses were shared by the three Societies. Events moved quickly, and within a few months, joint staff meetings were hopefully recommending the formation of an increasing number of national Bible Societies, leading to "the vision of a world federation of Bible Societies." In the next few years, as Europe went deeper into economic depression and drifted into war, it was difficult to keep that vision at the center of concern. A new mood, however, prevailed, and an initiative of the Netherlands Bible Society led to a broader representation of Bible Societies before the war clouds broke.

125th Anniversary of the Netherlands Bible Society

The Netherlands Bible Society (NBS) was instituted in the church of the Bijdenhof (in French, Béguinage) in 1814, which at that time was being used by a congregation of the Reformed Church. It was not represented at the London Conference in 1932, but was very much concerned with the issues discussed there. It also had Bible work outside its own country, and saw the importance of being involved in this cooperative work. The NBS used the occasion of its 125th anniversary in July 1939 to invite several Bible Societies to attend a conference in Woudschoten, Zeist, in the Netherlands. There were six Bible Societies represented: ABS, by John R. Mott, one of its vice presidents, and North; the BFBS by Temple and W. J. Platt, its Home Secretary; the NBSS by R. S. Chisholm. There were, of course, several staff from the Netherlands Bible Society, but its principal representatives were Hendrick Kraemer, a layman who went to Indonesia as a translation expert on behalf of the NBS, and one of the principal lay figures of the emerging ecumenical movement, and H. C. Rutgers, NBS General Secretary. The Norwegian Bible Society was represented by L. Koren. There were also two persons representing the Bible work in France. Bible Societies from Germany, Sweden, and Denmark had been invited but were unable to send representatives.

The Place of the Bible in the Work of the Church

Professor Kraemer, with experience of the International Missionary Council and a prominent participant at its influential Conference in Madras (December 1938), opened the Woudschoten Conference with a powerful challenge to the Bible Societies to cooperate with the churches to encourage the *use* of the Bible. He made two proposals which sparked off a controversial discussion and they could not be ignored:

1. He acknowledged the important work of the Bible Societies in translating, printing, and distributing the Bible, but called for more: "a systematic and well-planned movement for teaching those who buy a Bible how to read and *use* it for private and family worship."
2. Most Bible Societies issue the Bible only. Some have additional publications. More is needed: "All Bible Societies ought to include in their activities the preparation, printing, and distribution of books with collections of tales from the Bible."

Kraemer followed this with a criticism of the quality of translations. His criticism was fundamental and questioned the instructions given by the Bible Societies to their translators, such were: "the translation of the scriptures, if possible without loss of idiom, dignity and beauty of phrase, should be made in a language that average people can understand without explanation."[3]

His attack on this phraseology was severe, and his logic seemed to lead to a proposal that Bibles should be issued with explanations. This was not what he was proposing, but rather the collection of tales from the Bible or paraphrases of certain parts. The Conference was concerned about the quality of translation, but Kraemer was cutting across the basic principles of the Bible Societies. However, he stirred up the conference and left a question as to how far the Bible Societies should be involved in helping people to use the Bibles they had bought. He seemed to some to be asking the Bible Societies to take on the task of the churches in this area. This question of how far the Bible Societies should go beyond providing the tools for the churches to do their work would arise later, but at this time it was too early to deal with adequately.

The principal concern of the Woudschoten Conference in 1939 was not use but cooperation. North, Temple, and Rutgers all spoke encouragingly of areas in which their three Bible Societies had cooperated effectively.

Common Counsel and Cooperation

Bible Societies influence and are influenced by the progress of the churches they serve and by their missionary societies. The year 1939 was a year of cooperation with the World Council of Churches waiting to be born. One man even more than Kraemer linked the Bible Societies with this ecumenical movement in the Woudschoten Conference: John R. Mott was already a veteran of the ecumenical movement. At the age of 45, he had been appointed Chairman of the Edinburgh Conference in 1910, which is accounted the origin of the movement in this century.

The seventy-four-year-old John Mott had not lost his power of oratory, nor his contact with the Source of that power. For him, every hour was the decisive hour, and at Woudschoten he pleaded for immediate action. He admitted that with war clouds gathering and dictators posturing, the time was difficult, but argued that the very complexity of the modern world demanded a greater degree of common understanding and common action. He continued:

> In face of the corroding influences in Western civilization, the hour has struck for cooperation, not only at our headquarters, but right down the line. We should only impoverish ourselves by standing alone. Cooperation makes possible having frontline men serving on the whole field. In face of the growing indigenous churches, we want the finest and widest cooperation possible, and your work is essential to undergird all other Christian activity. Moreover, there is a danger of our getting out of step, for by government and education we are making literate millions of people every year. Can you therefore delay corporate action? This is a day of God's visitation not only for our sins, but visitation by God in that He is beckoning us on and drawing us closer in this cooperation."[4]

Wilkinson, Temple, and Platt were far more influential, but Mott's rhetoric moved the conference to decision and the United Bible Societies became a glimmer in many eyes. The delegates resolved to continue to work together and encourage in each country the formation of a Bible Society working on the same principles as they were. They resolved to encourage the younger churches to share with them in a worldwide work of scripture distribution.

But that was not enough. Rutgers proposed the establishment of a Council of Bible Societies. It met with some opposition by those who thought it would be too cumbersome, but eventually he won the day, and the minutes of the conference show the prevailing view: "Impressed by the seriousness and great extent of the task before the Bible Societies, and believing in the value of common counsel and cooperation, the following resolutions were passed."

What followed was a detailed statement of a decision to form a Council of Bible Societies, according to plans outlined.[5]

The details show a defensive attitude towards any threat that the integrity of individual societies might be invaded, and the purpose is at once stated as "not superseding existing procedures of direct approach between the Societies." The business of the Council is to be carried on through a Secretary, "who shall be the Secretary of one of the Societies." The machinery is to be kept "as simple and as inexpensive as possible." The intention was that Rutgers be appointed Secretary and that the Council should become operative when three Societies approved.

It was a bold step and could have been put into operation almost immediately. But events on a larger world scale intervened. German troops marched into Poland five days after the conclusion of the Woudschoten Conference, and the Second World War became inevitable.

The Bible Societies in Wartime

By 1940 the war had become really active in Europe after a period of lull. Then it was that hundreds of thousands of prisoners of war were pouring into the barbed wire enclosures of the camps in Germany. The British and Foreign Bible Society and its agencies were cut off from these people. It was therefore necessary, either for individuals or the churches to take action, and the American Bible Society saw the opportunity of serving where Britain was no longer able to serve. North wrote to the General Secretary of the World Council of Churches, Visser 't Hooft, a most important, and as it was later called, a "fateful," letter. He asked whether an office could be set up in Geneva which would see that Scriptures were made available to the camps. The office also would have to try to maintain contact with the Bible Society agencies left without contact to London. The Ecumenical Commission for the Chaplaincy Service to Prisoners of War had just been organized with Olivier Béguin as Secretary. One of its tasks was to supply prisoners with Bibles. Béguin soon became an agent of the American Bible Society. But with Pearl Harbor, New York was also cut off from most of Europe, and the Ecumenical Commission for the Chaplaincy Service to Prisoners of War had to act without much contact with London or New York. Only cables could get through to Geneva along with funds to make possible the production of Scriptures on the spot. Somehow Bibles and New Testaments were produced and circulated, while some Scripture supplies eventually got through from overseas. From the letters from the camps one was able to perceive what it meant for a Christian to be deprived of the Word of God, and for a man on the fringe to discover the comforting and supportive power of that Word. Béguin continued to serve in that capacity as representing the work of the churches and the American Bible Society throughout the remaining years of the war. He was able to operate from neutral Switzerland. His office was in Geneva, and that later became the center of a good deal of United Bible Societies' work.

Alexander Enholc, superintendent of the BFBS Bible depot in Warsaw, gave an early example of the way in which Bible Society work went on despite and because of the destruction of war:

In the early days of the German invasion, a bomb dropped near the Warsaw Bible depot, blowing out the windows and doors. One little pane of glass only remained, on which were the words, "Heaven and earth shall pass away, but my word shall not pass away." Those words remained on that small fragment, and through the long months and years, people as they passed by took off their hats, signing the Cross and saying, "It is a miracle."[6]

By the end of the war, which was more terrible in Poland than in almost any other part of Europe, Enholc could report that 266,000 Bibles, New Testaments, and Portions had been distributed, despite great risk, during those years, and that 6,000 Bibles and 22,000 New Testaments had been printed.

Throughout the war, news came of heroic stories and determined distribution and production. Neither was the concept of a Council of Bible Societies forgotten, although international conferences were impossible. In October 1941, Wilkinson wrote to North, looking to some action when the war ended. Britain was at that time isolated and alone; America, although friendly to Britain's cause, was not yet involved as a belligerent. The initiative came from Wilkinson: "There is one thing clear in our minds, that, when work is resumed, it should be so far as possible a cooperative work of the three main Bible Societies."

A few months later, he wrote to North again, expressing his hope that they would: "get together and plan our postwar policy. I hope we shall agree to the idea of the FEDERATION with the joint title and some simple form of Constitution which will express in words what is a growing reality—mutual cooperation."

After Pearl Harbor, America was in the war, and by 1944 the Nazi Empire was collapsing. In London the Rt. Rev. G. K. A. Bell, Bishop of Chichester, was already urging the House of Lords to consider a peace treaty which would make war impossible in the future. The plot to assassinate Hitler had failed in July, and resistance had almost collapsed inside Germany. Hitler's revenge meant the destruction of Germany's future leadership. He was fulfilling his promise to bring down all Europe with him as Allied planes destroyed the cities, not only of Germany, but much of Europe. Bell's voice in the House of Lords, calling for a consideration of what these bombings were doing to the future was unheeded. Victory was in sight for the Allies, but at an awful cost. The blockade was starving enemies and friends alike. Rutgers, who had intended to resign as General Secretary of the Netherlands Bible Society, cycled out into the countryside and brought back enough food to keep the Bible Society staff alive. There was no more talk of his resignation. When all this was happening in Europe, Temple went to New York for consultation with North and the ABS Board and staff. The conversations ended with a document headed "Postwar Development of Bible Society Work in Europe."

Postwar Development of Bible Society Work in Europe

Towards the end of November 1944, Temple arrived in New York for long and valuable consultations on "the needs of liberated areas and on the policies of the two Societies in postwar work." Temple addressed the American Board and expressed his appreciation of increased collaboration. It was decided to hold a special meeting of the Board to hear the results of the two General Secretaries' conferences. The influence of North and Temple in previous conferences before the war had been considerable, and so it was now. Nothdurft (ABS Secretary in Argentina and later ABS historian) in his historical essay for the ABS, expressed it quite clearly: "Now, in this specially convened Board meeting, the influence of the two men upon subsequent—and more widespread—cooperative endeavor can easily be distinguished."

The meeting was principally a series of addresses by North and Temple. At the end, Temple dealt with "general matters including the subject of a Council of Bible Societies on a world scale, the basis of cooperative work, circulation statements, and imprints."

The meeting could not take definite action immediately, but it set a landmark. After the usual committee work on both sides of the Atlantic, the ABS Board adopted eight of the proposals made by Temple on behalf of the BFBS Board. These proposals included a statement of approval for suggestions of cooperation in postwar Bible Society work in Europe, where the BFBS had almost exclusively worked. It was obvious that the idea of cooperative work was in the air and a wholly new attitude had grown with the trust of the senior executives in ABS and BFBS.

A few months later, Temple cabled North from London: "We strongly urge calling early in May 1946 a conference in London of Bible Societies in connection with European work. Your presence essential. May we rely on it and use your name with ours in notifying other Societies?" (25 October 1945) The ABS Board approved both of the Conference and North's presence at it.[7]

The war in Europe came to an end, followed by the collapse of Japan in August and the awful shadow of an atomic bomb. Europe lay in ruins. There was unlimited work for the Bible Societies, most evidently in Europe. With boldness, the two major Bible Societies called the very first nongovernmental international conference after cessation of hostilities to meet in bomb-scarred Britain. The host was to be the Rt. Rev. G. K. A. Bell, Bishop of Chichester, in whose diocesan conference center at "Elfinsward," Haywards Heath, the historic international meeting occurred in May 1946.

◇ CHAPTER TWO ◇

"Elfinsward"

——— ◇ ———

A young man named Eugene Nida was present at this historic meeting of Bible Societies. He wrote his report many years later under the title, "'Elfinsward' Changed Us All." A few paragraphs from that report, remembered more than forty years after the event, recaptures the atmosphere:

In early May of 1946 the weather . . . was typically cold and rainy, but inside the meeting room there was the warm glow of renewed friendship by old friends who had not seen each other during the long dark years of World War II. We had all come through London and had seen the sprawling wasteland of rubble in the center of the city and realized it must be far worse in Rotterdam, Dresden, and Stalingrad. In London, St. Paul's Cathedral and the nearby Bible House were standing like symbols of hope.

Judging the mood of the conference, he adds:

We were all profoundly influenced by the sense of overwhelming urgency to meet the spiritual need of the churches in eastern Europe, the countless refugees in Asia, and the rapidly growing number of believers in sub-Saharan Africa. Colonialism was becoming a thing of the past, and the rise of two superpowers posed the threat of total atomic destruction.

Under such circumstances it was not easy to make plans, but it was also no time to be concerned about traditional ways of doing things. Old rivalries in Latin America and duplications of effort in Asia had to be forgotten.

At the end, he says: "'Elfinsward' profoundly changed the Bible Society movement and radically changed my life."[1]

Two Voices from the Darkness of Occupied Europe

Although there was urgent business to be done, recent war experiences brought many stories of how delegates had survived the horrors of Nazi occupation. The two countries involved at the outbreak of war were each represented by one delegate: Poland and Germany.

From Poland came Superintendent Alexander Enholc, who at the first session of the conference told the story of the remaining pane of glass with confidence; the "miracle." But he also told of his experiences and those of his wife:

Four times I was called to the Gestapo, and the last time I never expected to return home. I was questioned about the Society and questioned very carefully too about Mr. Haig (the BFBS Secretary for Europe, also at the conference). When I said the work had nothing to do with politics, I was asked, "Are you against Hitler?" I said I did not know but the Bible said that all governments come from the Lord. The Gestapo official replied, "That is true—now you are free."

It was much worse for his wife, and he told of her ordeal:

During the early years of the war I was transported for some weeks to Eastern Poland, and my wife took charge of the depot and was there alone through the siege of Warsaw. Later, during the insurrection, she went into Warsaw to get food, and she then helped to put into safety twelve cases of Scriptures, moulds, and typewriters. Then, owing to the state of the city, she was unable to return and for six weeks lived in a cellar. The Germans then decided to send women and children into concentration camps, and my wife was chosen to go to the mines. She made a protest, for her health was poor, and though she suffered very much physical ill-treatment, eventually she succeeded in getting away."[2]

Superintendent Enholc ended with a tribute to the Roman Catholics for their help and said that they were now asking when the depot would be reopened.

A second voice from that darkness was that of Dr. Hanns Lilje of Germany, who later became Bishop of Hannover. The conference had already convened when he came into the room. Bishop Berggrav of Norway, who was presiding, left the chair and went down the aisle to embrace him. The two friends had not seen each other since 1940. Both had suffered imprisonment. Lilje also spoke in that first session, apologizing for beginning on a personal note. Only about one year earlier he had been released by the American troops; "liberated" from his prison in Nuremberg. He spoke of his experience at the hands of the Gestapo in their special prison in Berlin:

> Three times I was nearly killed by them, having the choice of dying from hanging or starvation or being shot. It is unnecessary for me to explain that during that time, with nothing to read or write, chained up night and day, unprotected from air raids, I relied on those things that I had learnt in my youth and they kept me and many others going.[3]

Nida was especially moved by the story that Lilje told of his means of communicating with a fellow prisoner. Lilje discovered that both he and his neighbor, who had been a high-ranking Nazi official, understood the Morse code. They communicated by tapping out messages by Morse code to one another. Lilje succeeded in obtaining a Bible for his fellow prisoner, who some weeks later, before being led out to execution, tapped on the wall, "I am going out to life, not to death."[4]

Just ten years later, when the UBS opened an office for the present author as Study Secretary in Geneva, the first two visitors who signed the Visitors Book were Mrs. Enholc and Hanns Lilje. They both remembered "Elfinsward" with deep gratitude.

The Bishop of Chichester

The conference of Bible Societies was called jointly by the BFBS and the ABS, but the host was one of the most remarkable churchmen in England at that time; the Rt. Rev. G. K. A. Bell, Bishop of Chichester.

He was no stranger to the Bible Society. Only seven months before, on his first visit to Germany after the cessation of hostilities, he had met in the upper room of the Wüttermburg Bible Society in Stuttgart with the church leaders and representatives of the ecumenical movement, to hear the famous Confession of Guilt by the representatives of the German churches, for their failure to do more against the Nazi tyranny.

For more than a decade, Bell had spoken out first against National Socialism in Germany, then for the care of refugees from Germany, then for the internees, always for peace and just peace terms. He knew the people in Germany who had tried to overthrow Hitler, and he pleaded in vain for their support. As soon as Germany was occupied, he took a continuous interest in the way in which the British were behaving and the extent to which the occupying forces were helping to rebuild Germany.

When he returned from his visit to Germany in October 1945, Bell spoke and wrote. He would not keep silent until he had moved mountains. At Christmas, he broadcast to Germany insisting that while all that could be done should be done to relieve distress and rebuild the physical structures of Europe, the crucial need was for "the liberation of the soul of Europe," and he added "this can only be done by a spiritual power from outside, by something which military forces can never supply, nor our mechanized civilization provide from its own resources."[5]

A few months later, as the delegates met together in "Elfinsward," the Bishop was on the same theme and this time pinpointed the role of the Bible and the role the Bible Societies were playing already in the battle for the soul of Europe: "The Bible speaks today, once the conscience can be drawn to perceive it, with an extraordinary clearness—speaks not for warning only, but for comfort and inspiration. . . . There is something in the Bible which is immensely objective and massive in its simplicity."

With Bell's interest in the theater, it was not surprising that he took his illustration of this "massive simplicity" from a play written during the war, in which an Italian Fascist official ordered a peasant to do something which was contrary to his whole Christian upbringing. He refused by saying, "There is a law, long before Mussolini, which is superior to Fascist law, a very old law, a law as old as the world, six thousand years at the very least. You have said that I must obey superior orders and these I do." The official understood, or as Bell put it, "the reminder went home." It was clear from the first that this Bishop of Chichester, who had been such an inspiration for years to those in occupied countries and to resisters in Germany itself, was completely at home in this conference and at one with the objectives.[6]

Bishop Berggrav, himself a champion of the struggle against Nazism in his native Norway, expressed this clearly:

> There are representatives here from many countries in Europe, as well as from America, and we European nations who were under enemy occupation during all those years felt that you were the symbol or the representative of the heart of the Christians in Great Britain towards many of our churches. I really deeply wish to express how your name was a Christian symbol to us and how great was our gratitude towards you. You have been the bearer of something immensely valuable to us. I think you know how much we have thanked God for you, and I think we should be allowed to thank you too.[7]

Bishop Berggrav

For the greater part of this conference, the Bishop of Oslo, Primate of Norway, and therefore the senior churchman present, was in the chair. It was not his high rank alone which made him the obvious choice for the principal sessions when the substance of the conference was discussed. He had called Bell a "symbol," but Berggrav was also a symbol to many in Britain. He resisted the Nazi occupation of Norway with spiritual weapons. Thanks to the intervention of two distinguished German visitors to Norway, the aristocrat Count Helmuth von Moltke and the theologian Dietrict Bonhoeffer, he was not executed but put under house arrest. His influence became a legend, and it is said that because of his primary concern for their welfare his guards had to be frequently changed. Years later, in the very cabin where he had been under house arrest, he spoke of the young German guards of whom he grew quite fond. He invited them in out of the cold, and within a very short time he was looking at the photographs of their children. Human relations overtook the artificial hatreds of war. Such a man could bear witness to what the Bible had meant to him. He pointed out how much the Bible always means in times of stress: "In war time and especially in occupation time, the Bible explained itself to us. It is the usual experience all over the world that when a man is in need of God's Word, he gets it in the Bible, but when he is in no need, he finds the Bible a very difficult book."[8]

Berggrav was realistic in his estimate of the difficulties lying ahead. Like the others present he saw that their task concerned the remaking of Europe, which for him meant the remaking of individuals. The Bible could do it, but the task was enormous. The Bible Societies would have to work very closely with the churches and recognize that they had not fulfilled their responsibilities when they had produced and distributed the Bible. They may have to take a hand, as Kraemer had said in 1939, in teaching the *use* of the Bible. Berggrav never lost interest in that. It impressed him that the statesmen of the world were also moved by the message of the Bible, and he quoted the British Prime Minister Attlee going to his first conference with the U.S. President Truman on the atomic bomb. Before he left Attlee said: "I am going with hope, because I have seen how St. Paul's Cathedral is standing there above all the ruins of the center of London, as a symbol of the spiritual values standing above all the ruins of mankind. I am going, not frightened in my soul, but taking with me these three; faith, hope, and love, and the greatest of these is love."

Berggrav had his own stories of hope emerging from apparent hopelessness, as he told of the day of hope in Norway, which began in bitter despair, with everyone expecting civil war, and ended with a white plane flying over to say that peace was coming. He said, "It was like a revelation of how God can change a situation on this earth." He then added with reference to the frightening immensity of the task before the Bible Societies, "We, who had the experience of those things in the spring of 1945, should be the last ones to be frightened of an emergency like this."

Lilje could speak in similar terms from his experiences. "Elfinsward," from the beginning was to be no committee to remake structures, but more like a strategy for battle—a battle for the soul of Europe and for the world. When Lilje appealed for more printed Bibles for Germany, it was Berggrav who most clearly understood his appeal and responded at once:

> When such heavy burdens are laid upon the people as are laid on them in Germany, they will find the way better to the Bible. In the liberated countries, there is now a sort of relaxation which we all feel, and it is rather one of God's miracles that you, Dr. Lilje, come here and tell us of the new prospect and new hope for the Bible, and that you appeal to us to give you printed Bibles. I think this is one of the best appeals, and I know for my own country that it is of great value to us to be asked to get Bibles for you. I am quite sure that you will feel how deeply your appeal has been taken by all of us.

The Sessions

The first session on Monday, May 6, was chaired by Sir Graeme Tyrrell, the Chairman of the BFBS General Committee. It was personal and confined to introductions and welcomes with some description of what the purpose of the meeting was.

The second session that evening under the same chairman was an opportunity for Temple to outline the purpose of the conference. After reviewing what had been done in 1932 and 1939, he succinctly summed up the reasons for calling the "Elfinsward" Conference, now that the war was over: "For the purpose of getting information about the needs of the various countries in and beyond Europe, of pooling our knowledge, of thinking and taking counsel together, believing that in union is strength."[9]

More specifically he added that both the BFBS and the ABS hoped to set up a central office in Europe, which would be a clearinghouse for coordinating plans. The need had been seen in the 1939 Woudschoten Conference, and it was even greater now. Temple gave notice that, if the conference agreed, he would like to call a meeting of secretaries at the end of the conference to work out the details of the organization that needed to be set up for this. The Rev. William J. Platt of the BFBS and Dr. Eugene Nida of the ABS were appointed secretaries to the conference.

These preliminaries having been done, North presented the agenda and the conference proper began on the morning of Tuesday, May 7, with Berggrav in the chair. The themes were as follows:

1. The Bible in Europe—its significance in the remaking of Europe.
2. The immediate needs for the Bible.
3. Types of service rendered by Bible Societies.
4. The education of the home constituencies in Bible Society affairs.
5. Bible Society cooperation.

Of these five items the first four were dealt with during the day, on Tuesday, May 7. They constituted the main points made in John Temple's summary. However, item five was the vital issue of the whole conference, and it could not be dealt with summarily as one point at the end of a list. Discussions started on it Tuesday evening, but it took the whole of Wednesday to handle it fully. This was the deciding issue which was going to lead to the formation of the United Bible Societies.

Bible Society Cooperation

It was introduced by Temple who boldly stated that "one of the most important things the Conference had to face was how to plan and cooperate in facing this present position." The present position was a famine of Scriptures in Europe, which had been evident as early as 1940 and intensified during five years of war. He and North had talked this over in New York at the end of 1944. Temple had then gone to Norway, Sweden, and Finland. He was convinced that these three Societies were ready to join with the BFBS and the ABS in a cooperative effort. There must, however, be some Central Office in Europe. During the war, the Bible Department of the World Council of Churches (in process of formation) had helped them tremendously and shown the valuable work that could be done with such a Central Office. With tribute to his splendid work in this Department of the WCC, Olivier Béguin was introduced. This was an historic moment, beyond what anybody saw at the time.

It was Béguin's quite short address, factual in content, and unemotional, which did more than anything else to convince the conference that a Central Office in Europe was needed. The question, however, was where that office should be. The connection with the World Council of Churches led to the conclusion that both should be in the same city. Berggrav pointed out that meant London or Geneva, and he would prefer London.

A. L. Haig, whose work as the BFBS European Secretary brought him into closer contact with Béguin than any of the others, paid a tribute to his work and saw the value of this central office as avoiding overlapping as well as coordinating work done by various Societies in Europe. He went on to sketch out the way in which he saw the network of Bible Societies developing. In some countries, there were already national Bible Societies. In others, the churches were not ready for them; some would need to continue working as agents of the BFBS or ABS. All would need to be coordinated and developments carefully monitored. He emphasized that it was very difficult, if not impossible, to set up national Bible Societies before the full support of the churches in the country had been secured. He pointed to the specific problem of Germany, which would be one of the first to be taken up: "In recent years the BFBS had tried to leave the work in Germany to the various German Bible Societies (there were thirty-four in all), but it had not been possible to reach an agreement before the war, and the Nazi regime had made the position still more difficult."

Rutgers of the Netherlands Bible Society pointed out that, with the help of Béguin and the cooperation of BFBS, ABS, and the NBSS, the central question under discussion, as he saw it, was how to build upon the work which had already been done so effectively from Geneva during the war years.

Services to Be Rendered by a Central Office

North presented to the conference a summary of what the Central Office, if established and enlarged, could do for the Bible Societies:

1. Provide information for Societies able to contribute for the needs of others.
2. Coordinate contributions to avoid duplication of gifts.
3. Assist in exchange of experience in production, distribution, and promotion.

4. Interpret Bible Society work to church leaders in countries without Bible Societies.
5. Help the development of translation and publication for mission fields.
6. Administrative supervision of special areas.
7. Provide reports on editions available in various languages for the Societies which needed them.

On the basis of Béguin's experience, Haig's outline of the possibilities, Rutger's reactions, and this list by North, a resolution was passed under the chairmanship of Sir Gilbert Hogg of the NBSS:

> The Conference of Bible Societies assembled at Haywards Heath, England, on May 6 to 9, 1946, moved by the need of the world for the Word of God and by the deep Christian fellowship of those who work together for its spread: resolves to recommend to the National Bible Societies and National Committees representing Bible Society interests and work: That upon approval of six of the bodies eligible to membership, there shall be formed the United Bible Societies.

Draft Statutes of the United Bible Societies were attached. An Executive Committee, meeting annually, would be made up of one representative of each Society or Committee in membership. By July 11, 1946, six Societies had approved, and the Executive Committee was now empowered to appoint its officers.

But before the conference at "Elfinsward" adjourned, recommendations were made for the appointment of Temple as General Secretary, working from his own BFBS office.

CHAPTER THREE

The First Crisis

At "Elfinsward" Temple was invited to become the first General Secretary of the United Bible Societies, and this was confirmed by the Executive Committee in Amersfoort the following year. Thus, from June 1947 the UBS had its first General Secretary. He was not, however, expected to leave his office at the BFBS where arrangements were made to relieve him of some administrative duties, "that he might give the greater part of his time to the new assignment." This was a considerable sacrifice for the BFBS. Platt, another Methodist with missionary experience, was moved from the office of Home Secretary, where he had revolutionized the auxiliaries and youth work throughout the country, to become Assistant General Secretary to the Society from early 1947. Platt had been at the Woudschoten Conference in 1939 and was there appointed Minute Secretary. He was fully aware and supportive of the UBS. His assessment of Temple's contribution was impressive. Looking back he wrote:

> With the coming of Dr. Temple into this widening circle of Bible Society relationships and especially into the development and setting up of the United Bible Societies, his own particular gifts and spiritual insight were an added asset to what was a truly great conception. The impact upon world Christian leaders of the setting up of the United Bible Societies

has been such as could never have been achieved by a procedure which might have aimed only at increased efficiency or wider cooperation.[1]

Conditions of war had temporarily suspended defense claims to territory for Bible work in Europe. The American Bible Society had to take over some of the European work of the BFBS. It operated through Geneva and found exactly the right man in Béguin to direct the work. Once the UBS was formed, it was obvious that its first task was to adopt Béguin and the Geneva office. In Geneva, Béguin had established good links with the WCC and influenced its growing staff. He and Visser 't Hooft worked closely together, and they were both at "Elfinsward." Temple did not live long enough to administer an international organization. He travelled and built up contacts throughout the world, but the major administrative work was done in Geneva. The concentration of efforts in Europe, and especially Germany, made that inevitable. Geneva continued work started during the war. London had yet to discover its function.

Sharing the Vision: Germany

Béguin had worked enough with the Bible Societies of Europe to be able to speak with authority about them. He saw the need in Europe, a famine of Bibles, but also the limitations of the European Bible Societies. He saw the UBS as an instrument to alert the churches of Europe to the importance of Bible Society work. In a paper he wrote in April 1949 he was quite blunt about this:

> The annual collection (where there is one) is just regarded as a way of helping the local Bible Societies to provide wedding Bibles or Scriptures for catechumens. Church leaders as well as most of the members of the local Bible Societies are almost entirely ignorant of the world problem or even the European problems involved in Bible distribution.[2]

Although the UBS was not to be involved in fundraising for its own finances, Béguin saw the need to enlarge the vision and put upon the conscience of Bible Societies the cost of supplying the world with Bibles.

The Bible Societies are not free distributors of Scripture, but their prices are matched to the ability to pay. Thus, unlike other publishers, they could not calculate the costs of administration and production and fix the price to assure a profit. Subsidy meant raising money. This the Bible Societies had constantly to do, and each worked out its own method. Obviously the sharing of experience would improve the efficiency. The BFBS, for example, built up a network of "auxiliaries" throughout England and Wales, and encouraged its agencies overseas to do the same. The ABS developed ever more efficient methods of fundraising, publicity, encouragement of legacies, and skillful investment of funds. Béguin saw that these experiences and successful methods could be shared with those Societies who had been content to depend upon annual collections to meet their limited objectives.

He thus saw the work of the UBS as more than relief work for Bible Societies crippled by war. He saw beyond the immediate need of a war-shattered Europe to the possibility of a new vision for European Bible Societies. There could be visits by individuals who would stimulate work and give new ideas, but most of all he saw the need to bring representatives of the Bible Societies of the world together to "share the vision."

The natural first start was Germany, where the destruction had been greatest. Germany had many local Bible Societies which in 1948 formed themselves into a Union (Verband). On April 8, 1948, fourteen of the German Bible Societies met in "Bethel," Bielefeld, including the Von Canstein Bible Society, still working in Halle, the prestigious Wüttermburg Society based in Stuttgart, and several smaller societies which were little more than bookshops. The fourteen (and there were probably thirty-two Bible Societies in Germany at the time, some in the Russian Zone and unable to attend) unanimously agreed to the following resolution: "The above named Bible Societies hereby resolve to form the 'Verband der evangelischen Bibelgesellschaft in Deutschland' (Union of evangelical Bible Societies in Germany)."

The Verband needed the encouragement, the help, and the vision from the Bible Societies of the world, and the UBS could provide all three in the person of Béguin and his Geneva office.

In the autumn of 1948, Béguin called at the office of Edwin H. Robertson, the Religious Affairs Branch Officer of the British Control Commission in Occupied Germany, in the zonal headquarters of the branch in Bünde/Westfalen, to discuss what could be done to coordinate the many German Bible Societies in order that efficient help might be given to them. Their isolation was also the concern of the Religious Affairs Branch, and by the time of his visit, Robertson had been able to persuade the Control Commission that he could do his job better if his Officers Mess was converted into a base for Christian Reconstruction in Europe (the German section of "Christian Aid"). They decided upon a conference which was eventually held in April 1949. Permission was obtained to invite both Germans and foreigners to a British Officers Mess and to arrange accommodation (a permission rarely granted at the time). The conference was attended by representatives of the following Bible Societies: BFBS, NBS, NBSS, and the Swedish Bible Society, from outside Germany. Of the German Bible Societies, there were representatives from the Bergenland, Berlin, Hannover, Schleswig-Holstein, and Württemberg (Stuttgart). Béguin attended and helped to mold the informal conference. Both Christian Reconstruction in Europe and the Control Commission were represented.

The official relationship with the British Control Commission through the Religious Affairs Branch served Haig well. As European Secretary for the BFBS, he had sent substantial quantities of Bibles to Germany. He was able, while in Bünde, to arrange for the BFBS to have a blocked account in a German bank which could be used for travelling expenses for BFBS agents in Europe, for pensions for old employees, and for gifts to suitable charities. It was understood that the Verband would come under such a heading. This was a temporary measure, and it was hoped that by 1950 the German Bible Societies would be able to handle their own market.

But the Bünde Conference itself was of some significance, and that it was held at all in occupied Germany was an achievement.

The Significance of Bünde for Future Work of the UBS

Béguin saw Bünde as a model for the future. In his report, he wrote:

On several occasions in the past I have tried to interpret the value and importance of the UBS vision during private talks with the responsible people I had to see in order to get information about needs and national problems, or with church leaders in order to make them more conscious of the necessity for the churches to acknowledge their responsibility in Bible work and to take their share in supporting more strongly the work of the Bible Societies; but such meetings as at Bünde leave those who take part in them with a much stronger and more vivid impression of what this is all about. For the visitor as well as for the host they offer an occasion for the renewal of vision and the understanding of problems, for showing in a concrete way their interest in one another's problems.[3]

Those who came from outside Germany certainly expressed their enthusiasm for the meeting. Rutgers said that Holland would have sent four if they had been allowed that quota. He was strongly of the opinion that there was no better way of strengthening relations between Societies. He used the title United Bible Societies of the World, which Berggrav would have preferred at "Elfinsward." It was also clear to the Germans that while they were not able to make use of the UBS Council meetings in the way that the more established Societies could, regional meetings would give them a part, and this would also be true of many smaller Bible Societies throughout the world.

Béguin saw a future for such smaller meetings, where the language need not always be English and where regional problems could be discussed. Such meetings would have to be informal, but they would be valuable nonetheless. Béguin went further and questioned the need for a universal Council meeting every year with all the expenses that entailed and suggested that perhaps regional meetings would be more useful in helping the members of the UBS to grow together. Regional meetings, he wrote, "might extend to more people the vision of the necessity and urgency of worldwide and common action."

The German Societies immediately proposed a second conference similar to that in Bünde in about two years' time. Béguin found enthusiasm for regional conferences of this kind also in France and in Belgium. He had his criticism of the Bünde conference—not enough German representatives, no public meeting, a bad time of year—but these were guidelines for the future within the context of satisfaction with what had been done. "At any rate," he added, "this attempt has convinced me that some useful work could be done under the auspices of the UBS along the line tried out in Bünde."

A Change of General Secretary

When Béguin came to Bünde in April 1949, he was already the General Secretary of the United Bible Societies. Temple died suddenly while working in Hong Kong on November 30, 1948. From his appointment in 1932 to succeed Ritson at the BFBS he had been at the center of all the plans and dreams for the UBS. As its first General Secretary he had worked, combining his duties with those at the BFBS and then after one year, he was appointed full-time UBS General Secretary, leaving the BFBS.

The Council meeting in June 1948 in Dunblane was Temple's last, as it was also his first as full-time General Secretary. There he had stamped his mark on the UBS work. It was a relaxed conference, because the machinery for administering the work had already been set in motion, and it was functioning. The German Verband, together with the Federation of Swiss Bible Societies, were received into membership. Dr. Nida and Canon N. D. Coleman, who in 1944 left his academic post with the University of Durham to become Secretary for Translations and Librarian with the BFBS, had been to Africa and found a tremendous need for new translations and revisions. Sadly, Coleman died in an air crash on his return flight from Africa. His contribution to the translation work of the UBS was praised, and deep sorrow expressed at his loss. Nida, in particular, felt the loss of a colleague. The work was expanding, and the need to give Temple the full space of a General Secretary without BFBS work was evident. This was not to last long, but in those six months which remained he was able to work on the proposed *UBS Bulletin,* a quarterly publication designed to give a continuous record of what the UBS was doing and keep its members informed.

Temple began work on this at once, but a necessary visit to China held up the progress of the *Bulletin.* His sudden death brought the whole matter to a standstill, before all the preparatory work necessary for the launching of such a periodical was finished, and the publication of the *Bulletin* was postponed until after the 1949 Council meeting held in New York.

Olivier Béguin

Reports indicated that to the Standing Committee the choice of Béguin to succeed Temple was "obvious and unanimous." But there was some questioning. Temple and Béguin were different in many ways. Where Temple was conciliatory and confident with the massive BFBS behind him, Béguin was a man of ideas who was not a senior staff member of any of the major Bible Societies. Once appointed, it was obvious that Béguin was going to put a different stamp on the UBS. He was more than a successor to Temple, carrying on his work. He was dynamic and European in his thinking, although he quickly developed an international and worldwide attitude. He was a trained teacher with an excellent record in wartime. He worked for the Ecumenical Commission for Chaplaincy Aid to War Prisoners, which was part of the Prisoners' Aid Bureau of the Red Cross in Geneva. He was, in particular, responsible for the publication and supply of Christian literature for prisoners. The policy was, rightly, not to send books in bulk to camps without having received a definite request. It would have been easy to send books in quantity to some official of a camp which he might never have distributed. Béguin reports that:

> Each time a parcel of books is dispatched to a camp, a letter is also sent off at the same time to the prisoner who will receive the parcel, telling him how many books and the titles of the books that are underway. A card of acknowledgement is enclosed in each letter, and the card must be filled in, signed, and returned to this office by the prisoner as soon as he receives the parcel. There were a few cases in which we did not receive a card of acknowledgement. Sometimes the name of the prisoner had been given us by a friend or an acquaintance of the prisoner, and the address was often inaccurate. It did not occur to us to check up at the Red Cross each address given us by a friend of a prisoner, since we took it for granted that the address would be accurate. In other cases, the parcels did not reach their addresses because some prisoners (French)

had been released, and had left Germany when the parcels arrived. Other prisoners had been transferred to other camps. Usually, for prisoners transferred to other places, the parcels are forwarded to them without too much delay, and even sometimes the German commander of a camp advises us of the new address of the prisoner.

Most of the parcels, more exactly 95 percent, reached the prisoners to whom they were addressed. Béguin again insisted:

For the present time, the majority of our sendings are the result of a definite demand from a prisoner. The name and work of the Ecumenical Commission is spreading throughout the camp. And the number of Protestant prisoners who write us directly is increasing every month. As Y.M.C.A. secretaries are allowed to visit the camps, many prisoners turn over to them their requests, which in turn are transmitted to us through the Berlin Office of the Y.M.C.A., which advises their international office at Geneva.[4]

Béguin's Postwar Work

As soon as possible after the end of the war, Béguin went into Germany, on behalf of the American Bible Society, and surveyed the Scripture needs in 1946. His report to the ABS included the following:

I began my inquiries at Freiburg in the extreme southwest corner of Germany. I went to the home of the pastor who represents the Bishop of Baden for the French Zone, I asked him, "Have you received the Bibles for the parishes of the region which you administer?" "Oh, just a few," was his answer, and then he added, "Remember, for six years we have scarcely been able to secure any Bibles. All you sent were distributed in a flash." And then he used an expression I was to hear over and over again, which, literally translated, means, "it was like a drop of water on a hot stove."

"Have you enough Bibles for this year's confirmation candidates?" I asked. They had some but far from sufficient. And what would they do for the many refugees streaming in from the East? Then the pastor hastened to add, "Nevertheless, we are truly grateful to the donors who have thus enabled us to attend to the most urgent cases."

Dr. Krimm, himself once a prisoner of war of Austrian origin, put the urgent question: "When shall we receive the three hundred tons of pulp for the printing of Bibles? Fifty-five tons have come. What about the rest?" and then he added, "The quantities sent from America have been like a drop of water on a hot stove."

Dr. Krimm then described the process by which the books were distributed through the regional agencies to the parishes, evangelization centers, and home mission offices. He was grateful that there were some for each—enough to meet their thirst for a moment."

Béguin told finally of an experience which moved him deeply:

It was in the summer of 1945, shortly after the defeat. A German soldier who had been returned from Hungary—a prisoner of war and being cared for in a hospital—spoke to a fellow sufferer and prisoner, a German, and said that he had just received a magnificent gift. His comrade was curious to know what kind of a gift a prisoner, cut off completely from others, could receive. "The pastor has given me a Bible!"—"Well, he could have given you something better than that . . . a loaf of bread, for example!" The first soldier replied, "He had not got one himself." In passing on this conversation to the pastor he added, "But, pastor, the Bible is of more value to me than bread, even when I am gripped by hunger."[5]

Béguin was an ideal choice and did not need to be briefed about the hopes and plans that had come out of "Elfinsward."

The appointment was confirmed by the Council when they met in New York and Greenwich, Connecticut, in June 1949. The move to London took place in November of that year. When he was appointed, Béguin drew up his own plans for the UBS—a kind of job description.

This program provided the framework for his work from the start, and it expanded under his persistent hand. He remained General Secretary for twenty-two years, and those years saw a major expansion in Bible Society work. The year in which he took office, 1949, saw almost 20 million copies of Scripture circulated by the members of the United Bible Societies. In 1971 it was 171 million!

A Moment of Hesitation

After Temple's death there was a moment of hesitation about the future of the UBS. The succession did not pass all that easily to the next General Secretary. So long as Temple was in charge, there were few questions in London. But once he was gone, the issues so enthusiastically embraced were seen differently. Would it be enough, for example, to let Béguin continue his work in Geneva and not appoint a General Secretary in London? Fears were expressed that the UBS might become a super-Bible Society. The Council Meeting fixed for June 1949 in New York needed very careful preparation and not only by the American Bible Society. A General Purposes Sub-Committee meeting in the U.S. requested Platt to remain in New York for an extra four weeks after his visit to China, in order to attend the UBS meetings in June. After this request on February 18, Platt took the liberty of expressing his views about the future of the UBS in a memo dated February 22. The memo reveals a deep concern that the BFBS was going cold on any extension of the UBS—perhaps even considering cutting back costs. Platt pleaded that "there be no curtailment of budget or personnel and that no undue caution be exercised by the large Societies."

He was addressing himself primarily to the BFBS, and one of his arguments was that if there is a pulling back, "the smaller Societies, environed as they often are, either by a Christian community apathetic to bibling the world, or alien in outlook, will lose heart."

In defense of his concern, and of his plea, he quoted a private note to him from Berggrav:

> My only real concern would be if the BFBS <u>Committee</u> should be regretting that it invited us to start the UBS and to put in the "machinery." To my mind we have not at all too much machinery. A full-time General Secretary seems to me to be a condition which, if not realized, would show that we did not take ourselves or the UBS purpose seriously. On the other hand, I can quite well see that machinery as such is dangerous in the ante-chamber of the Kingdom of God, but we never had too much of it. A half-time General Secretary would not be master of his time and would always have to ask permission from his <u>real</u> master.

(the underlining is the Bishop's)

The "machinery" was minuscule—two Executives, one in London and one in Geneva.

Platt expressed his own hopes on three matters:

1. The continuation of a policy of UBS visitation and ambassadorship which Dr. Temple so splendidly initiated by the building up of world friendships in this work, though I realize, of course, that this could be done in one of several ways.
2. The appointment of a full-time General Secretary, working in London.
3. The continuation of the Geneva office with its "eye" on Europe and its very necessary contacts with the WCC, if we are to continue to share, and to get the Church to share, this world vision.[6]

Platt saw that the Council Meeting to be held in June 1949 in Seabury House, Greenwich, Connecticut, would be decisive for the future of the UBS. It was, and Platt's hopes were realized. He was in grand form participating in the Council and preaching in New York.

The Bible in the World

The Council meeting in New York and Greenwich confirmed the appointment of Béguin and left the issue of what to do with the Geneva office to a later decision of the Standing Committee. Berggrav, who resigned as Chairman because of ill health, was appointed honorary President, an office he held until 1957. North was appointed Chairman. Four new members were added. Twenty-four Bible Societies now made up the UBS. Berggrav was not present, but one resolution of the Council pleased him greatly: "In order to emphasize the nature of the UBS, a subtitle reading 'A World Fellowship of Bible Societies' be adopted for use on official documents and letters." He had always wanted the UBS to be called "The United Bible Societies of the World." Platt took up this theme in the public address he gave on the Sunday afternoon of the Council meetings. This public assembly was held in Fifth Avenue Presbyterian Church, and members of different nationalities processed into the Church. Around the pulpit were stands displaying Bibles, Testaments, and Portions, in a great variety of languages and scripts.

There were two addresses—one by the minister of the church and one by Platt.

Platt was good at quotations and illustrations, and this address was full of them. He began with a local reference to the thrill of an actor seeing his name blazoned in neon lights on Broadway and led on to the astounding achievement of the Bible Societies in the world: "Even the neon lights of Broadway pale before the fact that the United Bible Societies here today have collectively published over 1,000 million copies of Scripture."

He illustrated the need with the simplest of stories from West Africa:

A torn piece of paper has just been brought in from a distant village, written in crude English. It says, "A few months ago a clerk from the Coast came to our village and from his Bible he told us about God. And so we have built a small mud church. Now we meet there every Sunday. We sit, we stand, we kneel, but none of us speaks, because we don't know what to say!

Platt pressed home his point: "These are the dumb hands of the voiceless, voteless multitudes of our world crying out for some crumbs of spiritual food from off the rich man's table."

He illustrated his points from history and from contemporary situations. Platt's visits to China and Japan had deeply moved him. Much of the early work of the UBS was concentrated upon Europe. But Platt returned from Asia with a larger vision in mind:

The world is a very divided world—divided not only in ideologies, but in the ignorance and poverty and disease which hang over three quarters of it. I shall not forget for years the poverty of China which I have just visited; the man I saw dying on the roadside; the walking skeletons one met in the street. Nor is China alone!"

In Tokyo he had seen the industry and efficiency of the Japan Bible Society formed so recently, and he could not forget the farewell words from the aged secretary: "Well, Sir, you have seen us! You have seen what we are trying to do in difficult days. Please pray for us—do not go away and forget us."

All these stories, and there were many in that address, reinforced his final words:

> The Christian Gospel has been a lamp unto our feet and guided the footsteps of our forefathers during many generations. Shall we now withhold it from the door of mankind which can only begin to live when the Spirit of Christ comes in? "Inasmuch as ye do it unto one of the least of my little ones, ye do it unto me."[7]

The *UBS Bulletin*

The Council Meeting previously in Dunblane in 1948 had already, "laid a fine foundation of mutual confidence and trust and had produced many ideas and policies" which were to be developed further at subsequent meetings. Dunblane bore the imprint of Temple—"confidence and trust." Much more was needed. In his report of the Greenwich Conference, Somerville admits, "I for one felt that the results of our gathering in 1949 (Greenwich) were more definite and purposeful than the achievements of earlier conferences."

One example of this was the decision to publish two quarterlies instead of the one proposed earlier. It was seen that a specialized journal was needed for those engaged in translation. It was provided by *The Bible Translator*. The second was the original proposal for a *UBS Bulletin*, without the specialized translation material. This latter proved a success from the start. Temple had done much preliminary work, but the editor was Béguin, and his style was on it. The first issue was published early in 1950. It had about fifty pages, and contributors were drawn from various Bible Societies and international organizations.

It was in that very first issue that the Rev. W. C. Somerville, NBSS General Secretary, reported on the crucial Council Meeting in Seabury House, Greenwich. Among the new structures developed there was the setting up of "functional groups." This was an attempt to relieve the General Secretary of some of the growing details which the original vision had produced. Temple had to deal with everything while members of the Council could forget about the UBS in between meetings.

These functional groups at first included Translation Group and Audio and Visual Aids Group. Others would follow. While the General Secretary kept in touch, conveners of the groups would conduct their own correspondence on behalf of the UBS.

A Larger Task

Frank Laubach pioneered literacy campaigns throughout the world, with his "each one teach one" method. He spoke with experience and authority therefore when he said, "The answer to the world's problems is not a word, but a deed."

While Bible Societies deal with words, the act of giving the Bible was seen as a deed, which meant preparing the way for the entrance of the Word, which throws light upon the problems of the world. Somerville struck this note in his report:

> We heard afresh of the dearth of copies of the Scriptures in many different parts of the world. We heard of the new need caused by the spread of that same adult literacy in which Dr. Laubach had played so great a part. We have heard of the challenge of materialism. But we heard too of the steps being taken by the Bible Societies to meet the world's need, and we laid plans so that our resources will be utilized to the full. Information and technical skill will be counted as the common property of all. The larger Societies will help the smaller ones, and the younger Societies will be encouraged and strengthened in the various areas which they serve.

Somerville's report showed a widening of the vision. The recognition that literacy was expanding set new targets for distribution. The pooling of resources, information, and technical skill as the common property of all meant recognizing that some of the smaller Societies had contributions to make beyond that of being "encouraged and strengthened." In using its resources to the full, the UBS would deal not only with the dearth of Scriptures and the setting of new targets because of the growth of literacy, but also think through the way of assisting the church in its struggle against the growing forces of materialism. A task larger than many of the founders had realized was emerging. The

General Secretary was the first to see this, and he was stimulated and encouraged by North.

The Larger Context at Seabury House, Greenwich

The context was also enlarged by the presence at the conference of representatives of the WCC (Dr. Henry Smith Leiper, associate general secretary), the International Missionary Council (Dr. J. W. Decker, general secretary), and the World Council of Christian Education (Dr. Forrest Knap, General Secretary). Although each spoke of the work of his own Council, they all emphasized the important task of the UBS in what they were trying to do. This early initiative prepared the way for later cooperation with these bodies in joint study projects.

At Seabury House in Greenwich, North continued that practice of preparing a carefully worked-out paper which influenced powerfully the agenda of the conference. In future conferences a paper from North was always expected, sometimes to the consternation of those who had so carefully prepared the agenda. It came even when he was unable to attend. His voice was always heard, less by intervention than by prepared and thoughtful written statements.

There were others at Greenwich who had prepared papers on particular aspects of Bible Society work. Even from the titles of these papers it was evident that the problems besetting a Bible Society were more easily dealt with when it was possible to share them with others. Mutual help was the name of the game.

There was nothing arcane or theoretical about these papers. Each came out of real situations and sometimes nearly insoluble problems. The persistence of the view that Bible Societies should promote "use of the Bible" echoed Kraemer's challenge at the earlier conference. It was less controversial now.

Béguin went further in his report and selected specific work being done. He included a summary of the achievements of the various member Societies to give the full view of what was slowly emerging as a World Fellowship of Bible Societies. The interest was still very largely in Europe, although not entirely. Rutgers had much to say about cooperation of Bible Societies in Indonesia. Platt had a report to give on his

Far Eastern journey, February to May 1949. Béguin was naturally still between his two roles as European Secretary and General Secretary.

The Lessons of Hungary

Béguin made a significant visit to Hungary in 1949 and reported it fully in the *UBS Bulletin* the following year. It is no ordinary report but a description of what was being done in Hungary and a brilliant analysis of what this could mean for future relationships between churches and Bible Societies in countries under Communist rule. He was shrewd in recognizing that this was no temporary situation, like that of those countries which during the war had been occupied by Germany. Béguin assumed that the Church in Hungary could not be the Church if it identified itself with the West, any more than if it identified itself with Marxist ideology. The churches of Hungary had to learn how to witness to Jesus Christ in an atheist environment. The churches were being stripped, Béguin said, of their "rights" and their organizations, and he commented:

> What is important for them (the churches) is to fight against this human-
> ism whereby God is excluded, not with the blows of excommunication,
> but by faithful and persevering witness. Not by condemning it, but by
> molding it, if I may say so. Not with political weapons, but with the
> weapons of the Christian; not by means of theories on the rights of man,
> but by taking the Word of God into this world which knows it no longer
> and is suspicious of it. To be a witness *in* this world of revolution and
> not *against* it."

Béguin could even report that the "rediscovery of the Bible" was occurring in Hungary "as indeed it has in most of the churches behind the Iron Curtain." He was able to report a vigorous plan of Bible study set up by the churches in 1949—Bible courses lasting three weeks and grouping between forty and fifty participants. There were twenty-four such courses planned from autumn 1949 to spring 1950. One hundred laymen or pastors had been trained to conduct these courses. Béguin went into the details of their theological thoroughness. Naturally, beside this interest in the content of the Bible and its message for the world today, there was developing a concern for distribution. The Hungarian Bible Society planned a Bible Week in all the churches for May 1950. There was a new concept of the Church's responsibility with regard to Bible circulation. But it was still only a concept. Béguin concluded:

> The rediscovery of the Bible is, therefore, in this sense still theoretical; the day when it comes down to the arena where the messengers of the Good News are laboring, and when evangelization consists less of bringing back to *church* those who have strayed away, and more of leading to *Christ* those who do not know Him, on that day it will be impossible not to see—as those working in Hungary are now discovering—that the Bible alone can be the key which opens doors, the leaven which makes the dough rise, the light which reveals Jesus Christ, the cornerstone without which nothing can be built.[8]

That report on the visit to Hungary showed the kind of man who would now for more than two decades administer the United Bible Societies. He came from the center of the wartime struggle, not a participant even in that, but a servant of Jesus Christ, to all who needed him in the cause of Bible distribution and use.

CHAPTER FOUR

The Bible in Evangelism

———— ◇ ————

The Standing Committee meeting in Matlock, England, June 1949, decided upon the appointment of a research secretary who would undertake a study on the role of the Bible in evangelism and cooperate with the ecumenical organizations in Geneva. There was some vagueness about what was required. Some thought that it would be good to work directly with Dr. J. C. Hoekendijk, the secretary for evangelism of the WCC, from whom it was learned that the central theme of the next Assembly of the WCC would be *evangelism*. The details of that study were outlined by Norman Goodall in the "International Review of Missions."[1]

North, having in mind the negative attitude of powerful supporting churches in the U.S. to the ecumenical movement, was a little hesitant about the wisdom of tacking a UBS study onto a study already prepared for the International Missionary Council and the WCC, fearing it would compromise the UBS. He argued for an independent study with close links to the ecumenical organizations. He was also concerned about the appointment which had been suggested—Dr. A. M. Chirgwin—because he was a Missionary Society man and not a Bible Society man. He saw clearly the danger of losing the essential character of the UBS study in such cooperation, while recognizing the value of joint work. Most hesitations were overcome when Platt and Rev. Dr. Norman

Cockburn, both BFBS general secretaries, met Chirgwin on June 26, 1950. They were satisfied that he understood what they were after and that he was a suitable man to do the study. The next UBS Council Meeting approved the recommendation, and Chirgwin was appointed on October 10, 1950, agreeing to start work on the study January 1951. He spent the first month at Bible House, London, reading the documents and moved to Geneva in February 1951.

Quite apart from associations with the ecumenical movement and the suitability of Chirgwin, there was also a hesitation on the part of the major Bible Societies about any involvement in activities concerning the "use of the Bible." That was considered to be the work of the churches, which the Bible Societies served by producing Bibles. There had, in fact, been a long history of ambiguity on the part of many Bible Societies about their role in promoting "the use of the Bible." The ABS once had a department with this responsibility, but later decided to close it down because it decided that it should not be spending money in promoting Bible use in a country like the U.S. when there were so many people in the world who had no Bible to use. The BFBS had gone through similar swings of emphasis on this subject across the years.

Bible Colportage

The appointment of Chirgwin as research secretary, stationed in Geneva, had a multiple purpose. One was to retain a close link with the World Council of Churches. Bible Societies were primarily concerned with translating, printing, distributing, and subsidizing the sale of Bibles throughout the world. Their objective was to see that the Bible was available to anyone who could be persuaded to buy one at a price he or she could afford. Doctrinal comment had been resisted, but colporteurs, employed by the Bible Societies to sell Bibles and Portions in streets and at the doors of houses, had urged the Bible upon people in many lands and had not hesitated to commend it and even on occasion to explain its meaning to those who asked. But there was an uneasiness once the Bible Society stepped outside its allotted space and attempted to do what the churches should normally be doing.

Nonetheless, the enormous effort put into Bible distribution could not be expended without concern about Bible use.

There had been a history of colportage in the churches, but it had declined. When Bible Societies were formed in the 19th century, they took over the responsibilities which the churches seemed to have forgotten. That was a century or more ago, and the old methods were proving outdated. A new approach was needed, and the United Bible Societies took this up. Béguin used the occasion of the centenary celebrations of Bible Society work in Austria to arrange a conference of European Bible Societies in September 1950 in Vienna. This enabled European Bible Societies who had not been able to send representatives to New York for the UBS Council Meeting in 1949, nor likely to be able to afford representation at the Council in India in 1952, to have their own regional conference.

Three main questions were on the agenda for that meeting:

1. The Bible Societies and Bible distribution.
2. Bible colportage.
3. The rediscovery of the Bible in the Roman Catholic Church.

The second of these questions brought on the utmost concern in regard to the appointment of the study secretary. Béguin saw this when he compiled the *Bulletin* for the fourth quarter of 1950. Almost all the articles in that issue were concerned with colportage—in Austria, Italy, Argentina, Egypt, and Belgium. His comments in that issue included the paragraph: "More and more, the churches are becoming preoccupied with the problem of evangelism; it is impossible that along this line Bible Societies and churches should not meet and help one another to become more faithful and more ardent witnesses of the message of the Bible."

But how? Before any concrete steps could be taken, "a serious study of the situation and of the various aspects of colportage work and its relation to evangelism still needs to be carefully made."[2]

That explained Béguin's agenda for the Regional Conference in Vienna and the appointment of Chirgwin. But that appointment also provided a much-needed link with the recently formed World Council of Churches (Amsterdam 1948).

The Place of the Bible in Evangelism

All those who attended the Vienna conference were convinced that further study was needed. The UBS Standing Committee with the same concern had approached the World Council of Churches with an offer to second to that organization in Geneva a secretary whose special responsibility would be to introduce into the WCC Studies, then being prepared by one of its study departments, the particular problem of the effective promotion of the distribution and use of the Scriptures in evangelism. The offer was accepted, and the terms of reference for the secretary worked out. The Bible Societies knew that they had to maintain their independence and liberty of action, but they recognized their role as helpers to the churches, "who were particularly concerned with questions of evangelism."

They also felt that their presence in Geneva and the special activity of the research secretary would encourage an emphasis on the role of the Bible in the programs of the WCC.

Thus a burning issue for the UBS, namely Scripture colportage, and an urgent concern of the churches, evangelism, were brought together, and the initial purpose of the Geneva office to maintain links with the WCC were all contained in the multiple purpose of the appointment of the research secretary.

Arthur Mitchell Chirgwin

The man whom the UBS appointed as its first research secretary was experienced in missionary work. He was the first to hold the office of General Secretary of the London Missionary Society, which conducted the principal overseas work of the Congregational churches in Britain and which listed David Livingstone among its pioneer missionaries. Chirgwin had worked for the Society since 1920, and when the office of General Secretary was created in 1932, he was appointed to it. He came at a time of crisis to that office, when the finances of the Society were at a very low ebb, and he saw the support by the Congregational churches in Britain decline steadily to an all-time low in 1938. He conducted a vigorous campaign for higher contributions, inaugurated a special day of prayer throughout the denomination, canvassed every

Congregationalist in the country and sent letters of appeal to every Congregational minister and church secretary. His efforts halted the decline for a time. Then he guided the restricted efforts of the Society through the war years of 1939–1945. He was elected to the Chair of the Congregational Union for the year 1945–1946. Dr. R. Tudor Jones commented that the election to the Chair was "as much a tribute to his personal influence as it was to the esteem in which the London Missionary Society itself was held." Chirgwin retired from the L.M.S. in 1950.

Plans for Study and Action

Chirgwin began his UBS work in London at the beginning of 1951. In February he made contacts with ecumenical organizations in Geneva and consulted with Béguin about the details and pattern of his work. In June 1951 he was able to present to the Standing Committee meeting, in Sarpsborg in Norway, his proposed plan, and this was generally accepted. It was an incredible proposal because it looked more like a ten-year than a three-year plan. But quite clearly he had thought through what needed to be done, and he had worked it out with Béguin.

His paper was in five sections:

1. *The Place of the Bible in the History of the Church.*
   Some attempt will be made to describe the place that the Bible has had in the life of the Church, especially at the vital periods of its history.
2. *The Bible in the Daily Life of the Church.*
   The Protestant churches have generally claimed that the Bible holds a central place in their life and work; that it is their rule of faith and the standard by which their activities are to be judged. Can that claim be upheld today?
   It will also be necessary to inquire into the traditional attitude of the Roman Catholic Church towards the Bible, the translation of it into the vernacular, the use of it by lay folk, and its general wide distribution, together with the change that is taking place in these matters in Roman Catholic circles today. A somewhat

similar inquiry needs to be made in regard to the place of the Bible in the life of the Orthodox Church.

3. *The Bible in the Expansion of the Church.*
The Bible has been closely connected with the periods of growth and renewal in the life of the Church. In the case of the missionary movement the Bible has clearly a central place in the Church's evangelistic activity. Can the claim be made with equal validity in regard to the Church's other spheres and forms of evangelism? Is the Bible in fact an evangelizing agency? These questions need to be considered.

4. *The Bible in Our Time.*
It is claimed that the Bible has been coming into a more central place in the life of the Church during recent years; that during the war, and especially in the resistance of tyranny it played a crucial part. Men who were living under the most stressful and anxious conditions found that it spoke to their condition. Whether this revival of interest was permanent or passing calls for investigation.

The claim is also made that the Bible is the gateway to Christian unity and that through its study the churches are drawing together everywhere today. This is a subject which is worth investigation.

5. *The Bible for Everyman.*
The aim of the Bible Societies is primarily to produce Scriptures and put them into the hands of men and women everywhere. Does it follow from this that it is the business of the Bible Societies to see that the Bible, when produced, is read and studied? What should be said about the use of the Bible by the individual Christian? By the Christian family? By the Christian church (a) in its worship, liturgy, and ritual? (b) in its teaching? (c) in its evangelistic activity?[3]

Discovering the Power of the Bible

Chirgwin already had a considerable knowledge of the use of the Bible in the mission field, but inevitably it was restricted to the areas served by the London Missionary Society. During his three UBS years, he planned two extensive travels in order to collect material for his study. The first was to eight countries in Asia during 1952; the second, to eight countries in the Americas in 1953. The immense amount of material which he collected and some of which he included in subsequent publications changed his own views. In his previous work for the missionary society he knew in a general way that the Bible was important in evangelism, but now he confessed, "I had not realized what power the Scriptures had to change people and create churches."

He collected hundreds of authenticated examples of ways in which the Bible had played a dominant role in winning people and bringing churches into being. They ranged from a Confucian scholar to a Chicago gangster. He was persuaded that in the growth of the Christian cause nothing has played such an important part as the Bible. Many of his stories have since been used to appeal for support of the Bible Societies. His first conclusion from his travels, his reading, and his correspondence was expressed in a report to a UBS Council Meeting held in Eastbourne 1954 on the occasion of the Ter-Jubilee of the BFBS: "Again and again, and in country after country, the line of church expansion has been that there was first a Bible, then a convert, then a Church. In cases without number the Bible begins the process. It is the main factor first of all in winning the individual to Christ, and then in his hands, it becomes the main means of bringing a worshipping community into existence."

He documented this in countries as different as India and Brazil, Turkey and Thailand, Finland and the United States. Much of this material is included in a small book he published for colporteurs called, *A Book in the Hand*.

A second conclusion, which still lacked full confirmation with a year to go before he concluded his study, was that where the Bible is most eagerly distributed and studied, the Church grows most rapidly. He confessed that his main difficulty was in getting accurate information, but he was convinced by what he had seen that the thesis could be proved. Such a thesis was always difficult to prove because there were so many diverse elements involved in church growth, but Chirgwin was confident: "The evangelistic use of the Bible and the growth of the Christian cause go together too regularly and too closely to be dismissed as mere coincidence."

Much of this second argument was contained in his *The Bible in World Evangelism*. That book formed the basis for discussion at the Eastbourne Meeting in 1954. It was later distributed that year to all members of the Evangelism Section of the World Council of Churches Assembly in Evanston.

The third conclusion which he reached was that the Bible had always been used as a tool in evangelism, not simply as instruction for the believer or those already within the fold of the church. He went back to his study of the early church to show how this was so: "The Scriptures were used not merely for the instruction of Christians, as I had previously supposed, but for the evangelization of the non-Christians."

There were, of course, other means suited to the time and occasion, but the Bible had no limitations: "It is the only evangelistic tool that has been used always and everywhere with success."

His fourth conclusion was that the Bible is the tool of the pioneer. Almost every evangelist takes with him a Bible when he sets out to approach the non-Christian, whether in a South Indian village or a New York hotel. It was not enough to say that the Bible plays an important part in evangelism, something more positive than that was needed: "The Bible more than anything else, brings a man to a decision. It seems to be able to do what private conversation, preaching, and personal counseling often fail to do. It supplies something which pierces through a man's defense and gets right home to his heart and conscience."

Chirgwin saw the Bible as evangelism's cutting edge. "If that finding," he said, "can be got across to Church folk generally and to Church leaders in particular, at home and abroad, the inquiries of the last two or three years will have been worthwhile."[4]

An Ongoing Study

Chirgwin had done what he was asked to do, but his study was incomplete. His provisional conclusions were reported and amplified in the books he wrote. He left many examples of the power of the Bible and its role in evangelism. He also left the WCC and the IMC aware that they had a continuing interest in what the Bible Societies were doing.

In 1954, at the UBS Eastbourne Conference, April 28 to May 1, both Visser 't Hooft, general secretary of the WCC, and North indicated the need for such a work in close cooperation with the WCC.

Visser 't Hooft dealt with one aspect of the overall theme of that conference, which was "The Ministry of the Bible Society Today." He called his talk "Towards a Common Strategy on the Part of Churches and Bible Societies." He pointed out that although the ecumenical movement had drawn together many Christian movements and societies which had until now operated in isolation from the churches, no such close conversations had taken place with the Bible Societies. He added:

> It seems to me that the time has now come when such conversations ought to start in a serious and big way. I should like to think that the kind of relationship that has been established between the UBS and WCC is the beginning of that serious conversation.[5]

Chirgwin had opened the door, and it was much appreciated.

From the side of the Bible Societies, North spoke on "What the World of Today Requires of Us." Part of his talk dealt with the Bible Societies' relation to the churches and included the following:

> Our fundamental necessity in respect to the churches is that they support us. . . . A second matter in our relation to the churches and the people is our concern with their attitude to and use of the Bible. Our concern with this matter rests on so simple a basis as this: A church in which the use of the Bible is not a vital active part of the life of its members is not likely to support the distribution of the Scriptures to others.[6]

It was clear from these two presentations that Visser 't Hooft wanted a UBS presence in Geneva and that North wanted a study on the attitude and use of the Bible in the churches. That was later spelled out as "The Place and Use of the Bible in the Living Situation of the Churches!," and a second study secretary was appointed to begin work in Geneva, May 1956.

The Ten Year Old

In celebration of the tenth anniversary of the founding of the UBS, Béguin asked Berggrav to write a commemorative article for the *UBS*

Bulletin, a kind of presidential message. Berggrav replied that a presidential message was not his style, but he did write what he called "fireside remarks." The article carefully outlined success and failure but concentrated upon the great task ahead:

> A tenth birthday is no reason for great festivities, for these are only justified when one has the feeling of having accomplished something, or at least of having some sense of satisfaction with one's achievements. Yet the UBS feels anything but satisfied. After ten years of existence we do not look to past achievements but forward, knowing that very big tasks lie ahead.

Berggrav saw this as the reason for our jubilation: The tasks before us are so great that we feel them to be beyond our power. "Whenever God wants to bless men or a fellowship he makes overwhelming demands upon them, so that they shall realize how inadequate they themselves are."

With this introduction he outlined the way forward as far as he could see it. He did not hesitate to criticize what had been done, nor to underestimate the immensity of the task ahead, but it was a clarion call. Taking up Visser 't Hooft's call for closer links between the WCC and UBS, he outlined the need for a joint study. Although preaching and teaching people to read the Bible is a concern of the churches, the Bible Societies, he maintained, are also called upon to help and to find ways. He then continued:

> True, it has been proved in some parts of the world that the Bible may be its own best witness. But the European experience points the other way, as we were reminded at the conference near Zurich in 1955, in the question of the Ethiopian to Philip, "How can I understand, except someone should guide me?" (Acts 8:31).

From this point Berggrav developed the need for helps in addition to the "pure Bible text, without note or comment." "The Bible Societies," he insisted, "cannot be disinterested in what people do with their Bibles."

Then he outlined the reason why a second study secretary had been appointed:

Experiments are being made in various countries—Bible Weeks, Bible Campaigns—in which churches and Bible Societies cooperate. But further experiments, further study are needed in which Bible Societies and churches must cooperate, particularly in some areas where there is a tendency for the activity of the Bible Society to be taken too much for granted (by the churches) as something which "runs of its own accord," as it was expressed in 1949. It is not a question of the Bible Societies becoming something like churches or Home Missions, but that from the Bible Society side we should begin helping and perhaps enthusing the local churches, cooperating with them also in producing helpful literature and in colportage, which in many places has been proved to be excellent if well guided. This was our aim in appointing the UBS Study Secretary, as a link between the World Council of Churches, the International Missionary Council, and Bible Societies. The Rev. E. H. Robertson, who took up his work as study secretary in May 1956, will in the next few years be engaged in this work of path-finding.[7]

◇ CHAPTER FIVE ◇

First Steps in Translation Together

—— ◇ ——

Dr. Edwin W. Smith, secretary of the BFBS Translation Department (1932–1940) accomplished a great deal in the development of better methods of translation, but the large number of translations handled by the BFBS, particularly into African languages, prevented the progress he desired. James Roe, a BFBS staff member who was appointed to write the history of the BFBS from 1905, where William Canton had ended his "History" up to the Ter-Jubilee of 1954, reported the last Translation Conference arranged by Smith:

> The prospect of a great increase in African literacy, the need for even more thorough language surveys than those already available, the elimination of parallel translations or their synthesis in Union Versions, the intricate questions involved in the choice of orthography, and the provision of concordances—all these and many other matters were discussed at a time when the participants might reasonably have found excuses for nonattendance. The conference marked a further stage in the Society's attempt to obtain order and consistency in the field of world Bible translation, a field in which the vagaries of private judgement had for too long been vaguely identified with Divine guidance.[1]

One of the first signs of help after the UBS was formed came with the publication of *The Bible Translator* in January 1950. It kept those dealing with translation committees up to date on new insights about the science of translation, and it provided a forum for sharing concerns. Together with this publication came the dominant figure of Dr. Eugene Nida. For four decades he was the principal UBS spokesman on translation theory and practice. He wrote in the first issue of *The Bible Translator* that the quarterly was intended to deal with all kinds of translation problems faced by the "five or six hundred missionary translators throughout the world who are giving all or most of their time to the task of translating the Bible or Christian literature." He added: "The success of this quarterly will depend very largely upon the response of translators, as they contribute articles and submit to the editors their questions and comments about various problems."[2]

Dr. Eugene Nida

Nida brought a very broad interest to the Bible Society work in translation. In college, he had majored in Greek, but combined these studies with the science of linguistics. He received his doctorate in linguistics at the University of Michigan in 1943 while working with the Wycliffe Bible Translators. In addition to linguistics, he also studied cultural anthropology. North recognized his extraordinary gifts and invited him to join the staff of the ABS in November 1943. At "Elfinsward" he immediately found common ground with Rutgers. Both felt that the BFBS method was too dependent upon purely literal translation of the original text, a practice that sprang from the wholly worthy desire to be as faithful to the sacred text as possible.

Nida met Rutgers again, in New York, towards the end of 1946, and together they designed ways of improving Bible translation procedures. It was clear that their intention was not merely to modify or gently reform existing procedures, but to undertake a revolutionary change. The nature of this change could to some extent be illustrated by a conversation which Nida and Coleman had on their joint visit to Africa in 1948. One African language, Shilluk, for which the ABS had responsibility for translating the Bible, had a very definite way of talking about forgiveness, based upon the traditional custom of the tribal courts. When a case was settled and the accused declared innocent, the judge would spit on the ground. That meant that the case would never come into court again. The proper way to translate God's forgiveness into that language was to say that God spits on the ground. Coleman, with all his gentle devotion to the Scriptures, declared that he could never talk of God in those terms.

Nida saw the weakness of leaving the translators to ask for help only when they felt the need of it, with little assistance until the work was nearly completed. He was convinced that, in most cases, they did not know the problems they faced until someone who had special linguistic skills and training could point them out and offer help—from the beginning of the process. The principal task of translation consultants to this day is to be sensitive to the translators' problems. Nida changed the whole relationship with the translators in the field by his visits. But both he and Rutgers saw that more immediate and systematic help for the growing number of translators was desperately needed. It was for this reason that they proposed the publication of *The Bible Translator*. The BFBS was initially opposed to this, preferring as they said, the personal contact with the translators through correspondence that it had so carefully nurtured through the years. Despite BFBS reluctance, the ABS (Nida) and the NBS (Rutgers) won the day, and the UBS Council resolved to publish *The Bible Translator* which first appeared in January 1950.

A Long-Term Vision

Although not everything he wanted could be done at once, Nida kept a clear idea of the ultimate purposes of Bible Society work in translation before him and persistently pressed it upon the UBS. Looking back in 1995, he listed eight important factors in the development of a UBS policy for translation:

1. The growing cooperation in translation by the various Bible Societies.
2. Interconfessional cooperation involving both Roman Catholic and Orthodox constituencies.
3. The development of the Greek New Testament text published by the Bible Societies particularly for translators.
4. The Hebrew Old Testament Text Project.

5. The Versión Popular in Spanish and the TEV in English as models for popular language translations.
6. The development of translation consultants to assist in translation projects throughout the world.
7. The production of helps for translators: sample concordances, thematic indices, reference systems, and handbooks on separate books of the Scriptures.
8. The preparation of special helps for readers, including particularly the publication of study Bibles.

That was the agenda, but it took many years to accomplish and much work and travel on Nida's part. He was not alone. His wife, Althea, was a companion and collaborator, assisting in much of his training of translators, including teaching them to type! They averaged between seven and eight months in a year for fully forty years, travelling and helping translation committees. They were anxious to be there at the beginning of a translation and to go back again and again as the work progressed. What the UBS accomplished in the field of translation was enormous, but it took time. Only the single vision of one man over these forty years could have carried that through. When Nida left, the structure for such an agenda was in place and mostly accomplished.

"Without Note or Comment"

Dr. Paul Ellingworth, UBS translation consultant, addressing a conference in 1989, attempted to show how far the Bible Societies had come in fifty years from 1939, when the ABS, BFBS, and NBSS had their conference in Woudschoten.

At that conference, the BFBS laid on the table its rules for translators, which repeatedly insisted on the need to avoid "interpretation."

Those rules left unanswered the question of what is meant by "interpretation." In preparation for the 1939 Woudschoten Conference, the BFBS set up a subcommittee to look at the range of meaning in "without note or comment." The report of the subcommittee could not avoid the use of the word *interpretation*, nor could they clearly define it, but they added a new word which was to prove important in the future—

the word *doctrinal*. They concluded that the object of the Society would be carried out if the Bibles circulated by it, in whatever translation, contained no comment which could "be regarded as having a *doctrinal bias*."

Thus the BFBS formulation sought to deal with the fact that the various denominations of the Free Churches and the Church of England often held differing interpretations of key Bible passages. Any attempt to underscore one interpretation rather than another would be to invite controversy and possible loss of support. The NBSS strongly endorsed the "no note or comment" formula.

During this discussion, the major Bible Societies working in China published Scriptures with notes about cultural differences. Otherwise, many texts would be seriously misunderstood. This was also true of translations in other distinct cultures. Ellingworth had two other significant comments: "Agreement was bought at the cost of a reluctance to define certain key terms in the discussion, notably, *interpretation*, *explanation*, and *comment*. The delegates were unanimous that they were against them, but did not say exactly what they were."

His second comment was of a different kind. He pointed out the lukewarm attitude of the Bible Societies to the ecumenical movement which for a generation already in 1939 had been drawing churches closer together. At any rate, the time for interconfessional readers' helps which were acceptable, or interconfessional translations, was not yet. Even after World War II, when the UBS was in its infancy, North warned the UBS "not to step into the realm of what might easily become an interpretation of the Scriptures." In June 1949 in New York, at a UBS Council Meeting, he was again warning them that "a national society is not required, by its interest in effective distribution, to go beyond distribution into the process of interpretation or of training of the new possessor in the Christian faith."

Although, in principle, the work of the Bible Societies was to enable all the churches, regardless of doctrinal emphasis, to distribute the Bible and make its message known, it would be naive to think that its pioneers were indifferent to theological issues. The Bible had been for centuries before the Bible Societies were founded, the "Book" of the Reformation. John Wycliffe, William Tyndale, Martin Luther, Jonathan Edwards, and many others had made it their prime concern to snatch the Bible from the clerical secrecy of the Roman Catholic Church and make it available to the people, to the "boy who drives the plough" as much as to the priest.

Inevitably, therefore, the Bible Societies in their early days were seen as "Protestant." When the "Liberal" movement in theology seemed to question the authority of the Bible, it was those who resisted theological liberalism who upheld the reading of the Bible and the knowledge of its contents as paramount for the Christian faith. "No note or comment" seemed to place an absolute authority upon the Bible, read with the help of the Holy Spirit and unconfused by critics. These movements, variously called "evangelical," "fundamentalist," and "conservative," which were represented by British preachers like C. H. Spurgeon and American denominations like the Southern Baptists, Missouri Lutherans, various Pentecostal denominations, etc., had a prime interest in the work of the Bible Societies. Although the Bible Societies themselves tried to maintain a broad base of denomination support, it was evident that the evangelical movements would give the major support, in Britain and even more clearly in America.

The Unfinished Task of Translation

Although in 1939, the Bible Society could boast of "The Book of a Thousand Tongues" (edited by North), because the Bible or parts of it had been translated into more than a thousand languages, there was much more to be done. This was one reason why the second Woudschoten conference was called in 1947. At that Translation conference there were thirty delegates from nine countries, and twenty-six of them were involved in translation. It became very much a technical conference. Experiences were shared, including the problems faced in translating Hebrew and Greek words into languages where idioms and syntax were very different from those of Semitic or European languages. But there was also the question of priorities. The Bible Societies of the world had considerable, but not unlimited, resources in money and expertise. Translation procedures were also discussed at the conference, such as how more native speakers might be involved in translations into their own language. Up to that date, the greater part of translation work throughout the world had been done by missionaries who, with varying success, were required to learn the languages into which they sought to translate the Scriptures. When completed, these translations were submitted for checking and publication either to the BFBS or the ABS. It was natural therefore that the lead in all these discussions would be taken by the translation secretaries of these two societies: Nida of the ABS and to a lesser extent Coleman of the BFBS, although major contributions came also from the translators who had been sent out to Indonesia by the NBS. Thanks to a more cooperative and understanding spirit, which emerged from this conference, the translation of the Scriptures became a much more broadly based activity. A UBS Translation Sub-Committee was created to coordinate efforts, and later a system of regional translations coordinators was developed. The Woudschoten experience was so obviously valuable that it led to similar conferences being held in subsequent years, bringing together UBS translations personnel from around the world to discuss their mutual problems and share their experiences. It also led to a shift away from expatriate missionary translators to nationals for whom the language was their mother tongue.

Helps for Translators

Among the recommendations of the conference at Woudschoten in 1947 was that the UBS should publish helps for translators. The result of this was the publication in January 1950 of the quarterly journal, *The Bible Translator*, edited by Nida, who set the tone for the journal:

> This journal will attempt to deal with all kinds of problems, e.g. orthographies, Greek and Hebrew word studies, dialect difficulties, treatment of biblical idioms, cultural equivalences, and complications involving grammatical categories. In certain instances the discussion may seem somewhat remote from one's immediate translation problems, but often there are amazing similarities in quite unrelated languages.

Nida then went on to show how Greek passive constructions often had to be changed to active ones in languages as different and distant as Gundi in India and the Puebla dialect in Mexico. By contrast in Shilluk, a nilotic language of the Sudan, most active constructions in

Greek had to be recast as passive ones. Such diverse languages as Japanese, Korean, and Aztec had substantially the same problems in the use of honorific titles.

Until helps became joint efforts, the BFBS and the ABS published and supplied their own; for example, the BFBS "Rules for Translators" and the ABS "A Guide for Translators and Revisers of the Holy Scriptures." The ABS "Guide" provided a list of books of special interest to translators and eventually a list of helps for translators prepared under the auspices of the UBS. These included Bible references, Bible section headings, Old Testament quotations in the New Testament, and, after 1961, *A Translators Handbook on Mark* by Bratcher and Nida. The January 1960 issue of *The Bible Translator* was the first to list the various helps available to translators, some provided by the individual Societies and some the result of combined efforts under the UBS.

In order to accelerate the preparation of helps in the ABS Nida engaged two outstanding scholars. Dr. William A. Smalley, a missionary linguist with experience in French Indochina, joined the ABS translations team in 1955. He would later return to Thailand as a translations consultant and later as UBS regional translations coordinator for Asia and the Pacific.

The second was Dr. Robert G. Bratcher, who had been a professor of Greek and New Testament at the South Brazil Theological Seminary. Bratcher was later to become the translator of the Today's English Version New Testament (TEV) and chairman of the Old Testament committee for the Good News Bible. Bratcher, who was given the title of research associate, became the principal writer of a large number of ABS and UBS helps and, coauthored with Nida, the first translator's handbook.

Helps for Readers

It would seem that helps for translators would be a natural development within the UBS and that all concerned would be eager to move forward together. This was not always the case. The principal objection was the commitment of the various Societies to the principle "without note or comment." Surely, it was argued by some, marginal notes and translator's handbooks had no place if Societies were to remain faithful to their historic position.

Consequently, the Sub-Committee on Translations requested Nida to write an article which would set forth the principles and practices governing the use of marginal helps and explain what had been regarded by most Societies as a valid interpretation of "without note or comment."

His foundational article appeared in the January 1958 issue of *The Bible Translator*. There Nida pointed out that in practice the Bible Societies had normally regarded "without note or comment" as referring to doctrinal interpretations of the text and added that the various Societies had "published Scriptures with a certain number of marginal helps for readers." Among the allowable margin notes Nida distinguished two classes:

1. Identificational notes such as section headings and parallel references.
2. Explanatory notes which include such items as alternative readings of the Greek and Hebrew texts, alternative renderings of the original texts, and explanations of cultural differences.

In this same article Nida drew attention to four kinds of readers for whom different publications are appropriate:

1. Readers in new languages without a church and biblical tradition.
2. Average readers with a relatively long tradition of the Scriptures.
3. Special readers such as scholars and students.
4. Special audiences with a strong secular background.

Nida made it clear that a marginal note was not required just because a biblical custom is strange to the reader. More important was the comprehension of the average reader. However, if the text was so obscure it would be largely meaningless or misinterpreted by the average reader, some marginal help should be considered.

Such notes "should clarify and not complicate." They should have always taken into consideration the background of the reader, been as brief as possible, and "should have avoided all doctrinal interpretations or emotionally charged accusations and innuendos."

In 1954 the BFBS announced plans for a diglot edition of the Greek New Testament and simple English. This was to be a Greek/English New Testament in which the English translation would help make the meaning of the Greek clear to those who did not know Greek. The English was to be accessible to mother-tongue translators who did not have a grasp of literary English. The project did not receive support from the other members of the committee. Progress in the simple English translation faltered and eventually was overtaken by "A Translator's Translation."

The Text of the Greek New Testament

There was no question that the Societies and the committee wanted to make available to translators the best text of the Greek New Testament. The Nestlé text represented 19th century scholarship which was now out of date. Both the Revised Standard Version committee in the U.S. and the New English Bible committee in Britain had departed from the Nestlé text. Consequently it was thought possible at one point that a new edition of the Greek text could be produced which would take into account the changes made by these committees. This turned out not to be possible.

Another hope was that the International Critical Greek New Testament Committee, some of whose members began collating manuscripts in 1927, but were later interrupted by World War II, would provide the necessary textual basis for a new edition of the Greek New Testament. However, the slow pace of their work meant postponing the editing of a new edition indefinitely.

The BFBS, in consultation with the ABS, had decided to produce a second edition of its 1904 text, a text that was to contain "a thoroughly revised and improved critical apparatus" and had committed itself to a third edition of its text. In 1954 North proposed to the BFBS that the two Societies "should unite in sponsoring a fully re-edited text of the Greek New Testament to be prepared by a committee of three British and three American textual scholars, the new text to be accompanied by a suitable critical apparatus.[3]

North proposed to have a group of sixty or more consultants. The committee would prepare a series of volumes giving the reasons for the choice of special readings in the text and citing different opinions wherever important. The committee of six would meet for perhaps six weeks each summer for five years and have a full-time secretary. The costs were estimated at $50,000 to be divided equally between the two Societies.

The BFBS response was cordially negative: "Though we heartily endorse Dr. North's wish that our two Societies should always be closely allied in the support of biblical scholarship, especially as related to translation work, we feel that the present circumstances and the present proposal do not provide such an opportunity."[4]

The reasons given were that the Societies should wait for the results of the International Critical Greek New Testament committee. Perhaps more significant was the opinion of Professor G. D. Kilpatrick of Oxford, who was working on the preparation of the critical apparatus of the BFBS Greek New Testament. He held that it was impossible to do such work in a committee. He preferred to work individually and to consult the opinions of other scholars on selected issues. Nida met with Kilpatrick in an effort to change his mind, but had no success.

Since there was no possibility of the ABS and BFBS working together, Nida announced to the Sub-Committee on Translations in 1956 that the ABS had named an international editorial committee for the Greek New Testament project. These persons were Professors Bruce Metzger of Princeton Theological Seminary, Allen P. Wikgren of the University of Chicago, Arthur Voobus of the Chicago Lutheran Seminary, Kurt Aland of the University of Halle, and Matthew Black of St. Mary's College, St. Andrews, Scotland. Some twenty-five scholars had been asked to serve as consultants. Dr. Harold Greenlee had been appointed research associate to the editorial committee, and the first meeting was scheduled for August 1956 at Keuka Park in New York.

From its inception the NBSS and the Würtemburg Bible Societies joined this project. The NBS came in later and before the printing of the first edition the BFBS belatedly decided to join.

What made the UBS Greek New Testament unique was the critical apparatus which was designed principally for translators. It was restricted to variant readings that were significant for translators or necessary for the establishing of the text. By using ABCD ratings the translator could see at a glance the relative degree of certainty for each variant adopted as the text. Furthermore, a full citation of evidence was given for each variant selected. A further apparatus gave meaningful difference of punctuation.

Translation Advisers

From the early fifties there was a growing recognition of the need to provide translations advisers in the mission field. For this reason ABS had sent Mr. Henry Waterman to the Philippines. Dr. William L. Wonderly, formerly of the Wycliffe Bible Translators, joined the ABS team as a consultant in Mexico. Nida sent Dr. William D. Reyburn and his wife, Marie, a cultural anthropologist, on ethnolinguistic research assignments in Central America and to provide linguistic help for missionaries working among the Toba Indians in Argentina. In taking this initiative Nida was following a pattern established much earlier by the NBS in the Dutch East Indies.

By the end of the decade of the fifties the handful of translations advisers working under Nida's direction; Smalley, Wonderly, and Reyburn; was finding out how vast the job was and how few the workers were.

Translation at the UBS Council Meeting in Brazil 1957

Béguin reported in 1957, ten years after the Translations Conference in Woudschoten, that the main work of the functional group on translation had been the deepening of the fellowship and the discovery of possibilities of taking practical cooperative action. It was beginning to go beyond the field of consultation alone and had entered that of cooperative action.

The group could report progress in the field of language surveys. A pilot survey had been made on behalf of the ABS in the Miskito area (Nicaragua and Honduras). This survey had been thoroughly discussed and was to be checked by using the same method in three or four other areas.

Nida had also gathered material on the "use of explanatory notes in Bible Society editions":

Much progress had been achieved in the examination of accessories to the Bible text prepared by the ABS translation department, such as concordances, subject indexes, paragraph headings, lists of references and parallel passages, tables of weights and measures, etc. Some of these documents were now ready for publication and the suggestion of the sub-committee was that they should be produced jointly for publication within one or two years.

The translations departments of the BFBS, ABS, and NBS also had projects designed to help translators.

The BFBS was engaged on a Greek-English diglot.

The ABS was taking note of new information resulting from recent discoveries such as the Dead Sea Scrolls and preparing the Ancient Greek New Testament to be published possibly by ABS, NBSS, and the Würtemberg Bible Society in Stuttgart. The ABS was also preparing a list of Old Testament quotations in the New Testament which could be published under the auspices of the UBS. The NBS had completed its list of difficult Old Testament passages and asked permission to publish as an extra issue of *The Bible Translator*. In a Resolution that followed, the Council gave the authority to the functional group to proceed with all the translational helps. They were listed as Resolution 209. Nida persuaded the Council to agree to:

1. Ethno-linguistic Surveys
   A detailed treatment of ethno-linguistic surveys, employing the Reyburn Miskito Report as a basic document for elaboration and simplification, to be followed by a supplement giving the results of the application of the methodology in various strategic areas.
2. Reference System
   The development of an acceptable reference system especially for publications in the languages of the "Younger Churches," using as a basis the materials already prepared for the Spanish Revision, for example:

Section Headings: a system of section headings with parallel passage references for the entire Bible.

Subject Index: a short, approximately 30-page set of subject headings with carefully selected verses.

Old Testament quotations in the New Testament: a comprehensive list of all evident Old Testament quotations in the New Testament.

Table of Weights and Measures

Model Concordances of 45,000 and 25,000 line entries.[5]

Several Bible Societies cooperated in this work. A supplementary publishing fund, extraordinarily modest of £1,000, was set up. A new structure of translation work was in process of formation. What was at first a functional group had become a subcommittee of the UBS Council.

Note: The UBS functional group on translation from the beginning had to work with the limitations so clearly expressed by North: "effective distribution," but *not* "beyond distribution into the process of interpretation."

◇ CHAPTER SIX ◇

The Place and Use
of the Bible

——— ◇ ———

The BBC showed a special interest in the proceedings of the Second Assembly of the WCC at Evanston in 1954. Its theme had already been taken up in 1953 in a unique broadcast from the meeting of the twenty-five theologians who prepared for it at Rolle in Switzerland, exploring "The Christian Hope." As assistant head of religious broadcasting, Robertson had been responsible for that program, and, although he was not able to go to Evanston, he had recordings of the proceedings flown over to him every night. It was when he was trying to develop programs from this mass of recordings that an unexpected telephone call came from Evanston by the Rev. Eric Fenn, BFBS literature secretary, and Robertson's predecessor at the BBC. He asked if Robertson would consider an invitation to work for the UBS as study secretary for a limited period. Later Olivier Béguin called, and they discussed the whole project. There was no way in which Robertson could free himself before May 1956, but the proposal was attractive and challenging. He accepted. It was a major study to be undertaken by the UBS in cooperation with the WCC and the IMC, and it needed to be accomplished roughly in the period between the Evanston Assembly (1954) and the Third Assembly of the World Council of Churches in New Delhi planned for the end of 1961. Those two Assemblies had the very relevant themes of "The Christian Hope" and "The Light of the World" respectively.

The UBS could not fail to have an interest in both these themes, but its particular concern was the attitude of the churches to the Bible and the use they made of it, not only in evangelism but also in the building up of the spiritual health of the churches themselves. The title chosen for the new study was, therefore, "The Place and Use of the Bible in the Living Situation of the Churches." From the beginning it had a threefold objective: first, to find out the real situation in the churches with regard to Bible use. This meant the gathering of facts and figures from many different countries, the asking of pertinent questions, and the use of various means to discover the role played by the Bible and the use made of it in the everyday life of the congregations. It was clear that although questionnaires could be used and were, they needed supplementing by visits to congregations and denominational head-quarters to get behind the answers given to questions in written form. Statistics compiled by denominations, by councils of churches and by statistical bureaus were necessary, but they provided only a con-text within which Bible use could be studied in the "living situation."

Having gathered considerable information, the second objective was to assess it. It was one thing to word a question carefully, quite another to discover how to interpret the answers. The assessment of this material yielded evidence of particular examples of Bible use, some more effec-tive than others. This promising material was further investigated, often by specific visits and involvement in the processes, until principles could be worked out for methods and attitudes of mind necessary for faithful Bible study. At an early stage, it became clear that certain methods of depth Bible study, certain forms of group meetings, and the rapidly developing house churches in many countries showed evi-dence of effective use. On the other hand, some negative results emerged. For example, despite many experiments, especially in the U.S., no satisfactory method had yet been worked out for presenting the Biblical truths in terms of the issues of an industrial society. Both the discovery of effective methods and particular deficiencies and needs led to the writing of a large number of exploratory papers for comment.

These papers were circulated widely, and the comments often clarified the material accumulating in Geneva.

The third objective was to put the results of these investigations into practice through certain projects. The churches who received the first questionnaire and who answered it carefully were waiting for a response. They were often seeking advice. Any living study called forth questions and demanded answers in terms of activity. This study was not to be a theoretical or stratospheric study; it was to help and enthuse effective use of the Bible in the "living situation." The experience of one country was offered as an example to another. Thus, lessons learned in Holland and other countries which developed their industries late were used in Norway as the Church there faced the baffling problems of industrial growth. This was not initially planned but arose as the result of studying the place and use of the Bible in Norway. As soon as one began to study a church, one began to become involved in its problems. The experience of Bible Weeks in Germany, which was still using methods worked out during the grim days of National Socialism, led to experimental Bible Weeks in England. The successful Kirchentag in Germany, following the war, provided a basis for a Kirk Week in Scotland. Later this developed into Church and Bible Week in Syracuse, New York. Such undertaking of specific projects put the results of research to the test and spread the influence of what was thought to be fruitful ideas.

These three objectives—to study, to assess, and to act—were in the study from the beginning and grew together feeding each other. It was clear that there could be no final blueprint presented to the churches as the ideal method of Bible use or Bible study. Instead, there were descriptions of methods which had proved fruitful in specific cases and then tested under different conditions and offered to the churches as a possible way forward. Reports were prepared from different parts of the world, telling of rediscovery and renewal, circulated to the churches that they might be stirred to examine for themselves how the indispensable resources of the Bible may be made truly fruitful in their life. This was, of course, no disinterested study. Behind the experimenting with methods and analysis of practices there was a conviction that the Bible is the World of God. Here, if one knew how, one could meet with God. Here, if one were serious-minded enough, one could hear God speak.

Relations with the World Council of Churches

The WCC provided an office and facilities for the UBS study secretary in their central premises then at 17 Route de Malagnou, Geneva. He was invited to all WCC Central Committee meetings as a staff member and worked continuously with the Study Department. This made it possible to introduce the study of Bible use and influence into other studies than his own. This was particularly true of studies of "Areas of Rapid Social Change," the "Nature of Human Values in Industrial Life," etc. In order to guide his own particular study a committee was formed drawn from UBS, WCC, and IMC. The committee met at regular intervals and received for comment all the documents circulated, the books as they appeared, and reports of activities and travel of the study secretary. The chairman of that committee was Bishop Eelis G. Gulin of Finland.

As the WCC and the IMC "integrated" during the course of the study, it was, in fact, the Joint Division of Studies and the UBS who appointed the members of the committee. They were Béguin (UBS), Dr. Robert S. Bilheimer (WCC, staff), Dr. Fridtjov Birkeli (IMC and Lutheran World Federation, Norway), Bishop Eelis G. Gulin (WCC, Finland), North (ABS), Platt (BFBS), Baron van Tuyll (NBS), Dr. Heinz Renkewitz (WCC, Germany), and Dr. Walter Zimmermann (German Bible Society). In the course of the years, two other Bible Society men took part in the work of the committee: Dr. Laton E. Holmgren and the Rev. Paul Collyer (both ABS). There were others who occasionally joined the committee, notably Victor Hayward of the WCC. It was a formidable committee and never hesitated to send a document back for rewriting. In addition to the committee, a long list of readers of manuscripts insured a careful scrutiny.

Throughout the five years of the study the UBS had a working relationship with the WCC, even though at times issues were viewed differently. The study secretary attended the last Assembly of the International Missionary Council in Accra, Ghana, at the end of 1957, and together with the UBS president, Archbishop Donald Coggan and the secretary of the Bible Society of India, Dr. A. E. Inbanathan, he reported to the Third Assembly of the World Council of Churches in New Delhi in 1961.

The Questionnaire

The basis of the study was a questionnaire, which was carefully edited by the committee and sent out to one thousand local churches throughout the world. The areas for study had to be limited, and inadequate work was done in Africa and the Pacific Region. An extensive visit to Latin America laid the foundation of the study there, and it was decided to concentrate the questionnaire on Brazil. At the end of the study, the Rev. J. W. Linkemann (ABS) was appointed study secretary for Latin America (1962-1963).

After an extended visit to Asia, the Study Secretary concentrated on India, Burma, the Philippines, and Indonesia. At the end of the study, the Rev. S. J. De s Weerasinghe of Ceylon (later Sri Lanka) was appointed UBS Study Secretary for Asia (1962–1965). Europe was easier from the point of view of travel, and throughout the study it was possible to make repeated visits to projects and churches. The study secretary concentrated on West Germany, Norway, and the German Democratic Republic. In the U.S., the study secretary was greatly helped by the use of the ABS Office in New York and by its regional secretary in Minnesota, the Rev. Carl Larson. Although the U.S. provided a considerable amount of material from many different states, the concentration was on Ohio, Missouri, Texas, and New York. The questionnaire was divided into five major sections:

1. The Place and Use of the Bible in the Revitalizing of Worship
2. The Place and Use of the Bible in the Restoration of a Sense of Close Christian Fellowship
3. The Place and Use of the Bible in Determining Ethical Attitudes
4. The Place and Use of the Bible in the Social and Evangelistic Witness of the Church
5. The Place and the Use of the Bible to Determine What Are the Central Convictions of the Christian Faith.[1]

Once replies came in—and they did in vast quantities—the classifying of the answers became a major task. Many of the answers required follow-up and involvement. This led to visits to selected churches and the devising of programs. One result was the development of Bible weeks on the basis of the German method which proved enlivening and effective in many parts of the world. Long after the study was finished it continued to grow in areas such as Australia (1966 Church and Life Week), which had not been included in the study.

Publications

From the earliest months of the study, the religious press in Britain, Germany, and Norway, as well as ecumenical journals, opened their columns to descriptions of the experiments. Equally important was the generosity of the BBC World Service which enabled the study secretary to report weekly on the progress of the study in many parts of the world. There were thus broadcasts, articles, documents with limited circulation, and church conferences to make known what had been learned from the questionnaire and involvement in some of the experiments in Bible use. There were, of course, reports to the committee and articles in Bible Society publications. But there was also a series of six short books, published from 1960 to 1963, which contained the essence of what the study had achieved. The series was called, "The Bible in Our Time":

1. *The Recovery of Confidence*
2. *Bible Weeks*
3. *The Bible in the British Scene*
4. *The Bible in East Germany*
5. *Methods of Bible Study*
6. *The Bible in the Local Church*

The New Delhi Assembly

The Third Assembly of the World Council of Churches was held in New Delhi, Nov. 18 to Dec. 5, 1961. It was remarkable for many reasons: the first WCC Assembly in Asia, the entry of the Orthodox churches into the WCC, and the strongest appeal so far from the WCC to halt the growth of armaments and devote resources to development. That last appeal was to all governments and peoples, made under the constraint of obedience to "the Lord of history, who demands righteousness and mercy and is a light unto the nations and hearts of men." The appeal was also to the churches to support "the unremitting efforts" for justice and peace.

"The Bible and the Churches' Task"

The UBS was asked to cooperate in the evening session of Dec. 1 and played the major part. There were three presentations under the heading, "The Bible and the Churches' Task." The Archbishop of York, Dr. F. D. Coggan, took as his theme, "Facing the World's Need." After a brief historical introduction, he illustrated the achievements of the Bible Societies dramatically. "Before the Bible Society movement began, the number of languages in which Scriptures had been published was seventy-one. It is now 1,165." At once he moved from the glorious achievement to the unfinished task. He made good use of charts as he outlined three things to be remembered:

1. In many of those 1,165 languages only *parts* of the Bible have been translated.
2. There are still over a thousand languages, mutually unintelligible, in which some parts of the Bible at least should be translated.
3. Many of these translations desperately need radical attention and revision, in the interests of accuracy and "meaningfulness." Many were made by men whose zeal and devotion were unrivaled, but whose knowledge of the relevant languages was severely limited.

After showing how the times were propitious for new efforts in translation and distribution of the Bible, Coggan went on to illustrate the renewed interest in the Bible, both in the emergence of a Biblical theology and the vast sales of modern translations of the Bible—the New English Bible sold two and a half million copies in the first few months; J. B. Phillips found three and a half million buyers and Ronald

A. Knox, over two million buyers. But from that rosy picture he turned to emphasize "two other facts of immense importance":

1. *The population explosion*
   In less than an average white man's lifetime, the population tripled, and the percentage of Christians declined steadily.
2. *The growth of literacy*
   There was a passion for reading in Asia and Africa. What should they read? That was one of the greatest challenges of the day.

Coggan's charts were to help his audience see that what he said was statistically established and trends understood. His final chart was to show that Bible circulation during the decades of this century failed to keep pace with the increase in population. He ended with two direct questions to the churches:

1. In the strategy of the Church, is enough stress being laid on Christian literature, in view of the rise of literacy and the menace of anti-Christian literacy propaganda?
2. In the strategy of the Church, are those handmaids of the church—the Bible Societies—enjoying the support which they deserve, support in skilled manpower and in finance?

The president of the UBS used all his skills as a teacher to make those questions disturb the minds of all present.

The study secretary took as his theme, "The Use of the Bible" and moved from Coggan's question, "*What* shall they read?" to his main interest, "*How* shall they read?" He selected from the study of the past few years three issues which had constantly recurred:

1. The effect of new translations of the Bible among the nations newly awakening to independence.
2. The new confidence in the Bible in Europe.
3. The reasons why renewed interest has not led to greater results.

The Bible was recognized as a book for times of crisis. Berggrav had long ago said that the Bible was powerful in wartime, but tended to become a difficult book when the war was over. So often the Bible said things people did not want to hear. Even when its meaning is crystal clear, people often did not want to understand. "This unwillingness to hear some new thing, except in times of great disturbance, plays a bigger part in weakening the voice of God through the Bible than we are prepared to admit."

The study secretary ended on a note of hope, based upon a new openness to the Bible, a renewed confidence and a renewed openness: "When both are fully grown, we may see Bible use as effective in time of peace and prosperity as it can be in time of crisis. But that time is not yet."

The third presentation was given by Dr. A. E. Inbanathan, general secretary of the Bible Society of India and Ceylon, on the theme, "The Bible in Evangelism." He paid tribute to the work of missionaries who had come to India and translated the Bible into the local languages. Then he turned to two parts of a study being prepared in Asia: the problems of using the Bible in evangelism and the biblical understanding of evangelism. He then outlined how the study would attempt a better understanding of the use of the Bible in evangelism. Building upon the studies of Chirgwin and Robertson he outlined the steps of the new study:

1. How is the Bible used in evangelism? As the cutting edge of evangelism? As a collection of words for today? As a source of rules for ethical behavior? As a book with which one merely proves some truths?
2. Are special parts of the Bible particularly used? And which parts?
3. Is it true that so-called revivalism only one particular stream of Biblical teaching is used?
4. What examples and data can be gathered to answer these questions?[2]

The study was also to look at the relevance of the Bible in modern society. Much of this was similar to the two previous studies, but now it was to be seen from an Asian point of view. The study secretary appointed for Asia, Weerasinghe, spent some time with Robertson and other study secretaries in Geneva, London, and the U.S. He eventually produced parallel books in Asia to the original Bible in Our Time series.

Final Report to the Standing Committee

Although he left Geneva after the New Delhi Assembly, the study secretary continued on a part-time basis through 1962. This enabled him to complete work on a conference in Jerusalem at which the various churches in the Middle East reported on their use of the Bible within their different traditions. This conference, held in 1961, brought valuable information about the use of the Bible in the Orthodox churches and the development of Bible use in the Roman Catholic Church, stimulated by the *École Biblique* in Jerusalem. During 1962, the report of this conference with edited texts of the papers read was written up, and the series "The Bible in Our Time" completed. Thus, the final report to the UBS Standing Committee was not made until the Stuttgart meeting in November 1962. The report dealt with seven major issues which had been raised during the study and left these as material for his successor:

1. The new kind of small group which is becoming a characteristic of church life, almost universally.
2. The growing interest in "living" translation, rather than a concentration upon accuracy.
3. The new emphasis in Bible reading which stresses relevance to daily life, less what the Jews did with their pots and pans and more, "What does this reading mean to me in my life?"
4. The acceptance of the Biblical message, in whatever terms, as essential for communication with those who until now have not been reached;
5. The changing concept of the Church caused partly by the ecumenical movement, the Second Vatican Council, and those radical Christians who are finding the Bible more relevant to secular structures than traditional church teaching.
6. The growth of real concern for a renewal of Bible reading in the Roman Catholic and Orthodox churches.
7. The spread of Bible Weeks with a great variety of structures,

bringing the churches face-to-face with what the Bible is really saying to them in this generation about themselves, their witness, and their future.

The full text was in the Appendix to the Minutes of the Standing Committee. It read like an interim report. It *was* an interim report. That same meeting of the Standing Committee in Stuttgart heard Béguin say that the work of the UBS had greatly increased, and in this field of study a new subcommittee had been appointed on "The Effective use of the Bible," as well as further study on the Roman Catholic Church and the Bible. He was also able to report the appointment of a new study secretary, the Rev. G. H. Wolfensberger, a Board member of the NBS. Wolfensberger served from 1962 to 1967.[3]

The Involvement with the World Council of Churches

The Study on the Place and Use of the Bible was fully integrated into the Division of Studies of the WCC. Structurally, this was assured by the composition of the Advisory Committee which supported and directed the work.

Within two months of his appointment the study secretary was a participant in the WCC Regional Conference on the Responsible Society in National and International Affairs. He was expected to help draft that section of the report which dealt with "The Bible and Social Decisions." A few quotes from that section showed how seriously the WCC took the contribution of the Bible Societies to their thinking:

> The Bible decisively illumines the minds and hearts of Christians as they face the problems of the social order. It does this because God through His revelation in the Bible frees man from fear and narrow loyalties which distort judgment. It does this because it reveals the true nature of the world under God as known in Christ and the true nature of man. When choices are most limited, and when a man needs above all courage and hope and the realization of forgiveness, God's Word in the Bible may lead directly to the most important political decisions; for example, the decision to hold fast to the conviction that Christ is Lord above every government or other earthly power. In other situations, when more

possibilities are open, when men may plan for the future and work for long-term constructive solutions, the Bible provides an ultimate source of judgment upon society, the general direction in which man should move, and the basis for self-criticism and repentance.

It provides concrete judgments upon specific wrongs against humanity. It enables us to see all persons as loved of God and in the light of His purpose for them.

The Bible speaks to us through the revelation of God in Christ and not through specific texts taken out of context. . . .

And so it continued, both accepting the authority of the Bible and asking for a careful and serious use of its message in the secular issues of the time. Approaching the specific problems of men today, the report listed ways in which the Bible clarifies our vision:

It provides the basis for the understanding of the dignity of man as created in God's image. It reminds us that man was not made to be a slave of things or of institutions or of collectivities or of other men, but to be a free and responsible creature of God. . . .

In the light of biblical revelation we can understand the many ways in which men become the victims of the pride and the greed of other men, often good men who are self-deceived, and that there is no pattern of institutions, no economic system which is secure against such injustice.[4]

Throughout the next five years, the study secretary was a member of the staff of the WCC Division of Studies and his study an integral part of the work of the Division.

At that time, the UBS was closely involved with the WCC. At Evanston in 1954, delegates at the WCC Assembly received a copy of Chirgwin's book on his study; at New Delhi in 1961, the UBS had part of the Assembly program; at Uppsala in 1968, the UBS was represented through the General Secretary as a Fraternal Delegate, but no specific part of the WCC Assembly program was UBS responsibility. The preparatory statement in the booklet, "New Delhi to Uppsala" reads, "Contacts with the United Bible Societies have remained close, particularly through the presence in Geneva of one of its study secretary and through mutual representation at meetings."

After that, there was a recognition of UBS presence at Nairobi in 1975 but no reference at Vancouver in 1984. Undoubtedly, the involvement of the WCC with UBS has considerably weakened over the years. On the UBS side, no appointment of a successor to Wolfensberger was made, but the UBS retained an office in Geneva at the WCC Centre. Dr. Hans Rudi Weber continued a presence of one person specifically concerned with Bible, and he was partly financed by the UBS. He admitted that he was not greatly involved in the statements or the thinking of the WCC.

Reasons for Decline

There was no doubt that the General Secretary of the WCC influenced the attitude to UBS and the role of the Bible. Visser 't Hooft was completely supportive. He was present with Olivier Béguin at "Elfinsward" and followed the development of UBS Studies with personal interest and enthusiasm. A decisive conference on Church and Society in Geneva in 1966 arranged by the WCC seems to have directed attention more towards political issues. This was followed by the appointment of Dr. Eugene Carson Blake as General Secretary. Blake was a courageous protester in his own country, the U.S., against the unjust treatment of black people. He came to Geneva with that reputation, and it was under his leadership that the special fund was set up to combat racism. His successor, Dr. Philip Potter, a West Indian, continued the political emphasis in the WCC. So it continued with some estrangement from the Biblical emphasis of the UBS and of Visser 't Hooft. There was nothing in the Report of the World Conference on Church and Society in 1966 that could lead to the UBS moving away from the WCC, but there was throughout a movement of the WCC away from its prime interest in unity towards its political significance in witnessing to the social injustice of the society and the plight of the oppressed.

Among the "observers" who represented some twenty-three international organizations, there was no representative from the UBS.

The Faith and Order section of the WCC, which was usually less concerned with secular and political issues, was less affected by the Church and Society conference or by the change of General Secretary, but even there the Bible Societies found problems. The authority of the Bible was stated, but every report came out with complicated qualifications which often annulled the clear statement of confidence.

The Faith and Order conference held in Louvain in 1971 was a good example. Under the heading of "Interpreting the Sources of Our Faith" there were two sections—"The Authority of the Bible" and "The Council of Chalcedon." At once, the report on "The Authority of the Bible" had a section on "The Problem," outlining confessional differences and the influence of historical criticism and historical remoteness. This was followed by an attempt to find some kind of authority; then a discussion on revelation and diversity of interpretation. After taking refuge in "Holy Spirit, Church, and Inspiration" there was need for a fifth part on "The Use of the Bible." This was disappointing and would have been better if the UBS had been involved. It was not without value, but a few quotes showed its weaknesses:

> We are not to regard the Bible primarily as a standard to which we must conform in all the questions arising in our life.

> At the same time, the Bible must be read with the expectation that it can disclose the truth to us.

> The Bible is a critical book. It is impossible to fit it into the generally prevailing thought of the day.

> The forms in which the biblical message is expressed are inseparably bound up with the historical situation of the people of Israel and of the primitive Church.

Then after pointing out that the biblical writers spoke in terms of the issues of their time and we must in a "two-way relationship" bring it into our time and the questions of our time, it salvaged quite a lot in the closing paragraph:

> The contemporary interpretative process enables the one message to remain living Spirit and not dead letter. This sheds new light on the problem of a right relationship between unity and diversity, and between norm and change. How can the Bible prove its authority in face of the changes of our time which lead to so radical a criticism of traditional

claims to authority? How can we interpret the message of the Bible in such a way that, at one and the same time, its authority is respected and it sets us free to understand the demands and opportunities of our present time?

Despite a concluding expression of confidence that the Bible will ultimately demonstrate its power afresh, the questions remain questions.[5]

Bible Society Support and the WCC

The traditional supporters of the Bible Societies were obviously Bible-loving Christians. They were also, particularly in America, liable to be very anticommunist. From the beginning the staff of the WCC aroused suspicions on the second attitude. At Amsterdam in 1948 the delegates had refused to condemn communism until they could agree to a similar condemnation of capitalism. The staff were also suspect of being liberal and holding a less than exalted view of the Word of God. Once the generation of biblical scholars—Visser 't Hooft, Karl Barth, Emil Brunner, Edmund Schlink, Reinhold Niebhur, and others who were prominent at the Evanston Assembly in 1954—had passed, there was a strong suspicion that their successors were liberals and of an extreme kind. This was confirmed when they were seen to be politically left wing.

The crisis came with the setting up of a special fund to combat racism, which was used to support black people in South Africa, some of whom were known to use violence in their struggle for equality with white people. Not all accusations against the WCC could be substantiated, but there was enough to worry more conservative churches, who were the main supporters of Bible Societies everywhere. The Germans were the first to react and withdraw their financial support for the WCC temporarily. But the issue was serious in most countries and perhaps most serious in the U.S. where the greatest support for Bible work was raised. If churches like the Southern Baptists, the Missouri Lutherans, and others withdrew their support from the ABS, it would be serious for the whole work of the Bible Societies throughout the world. This did not happen, but it might have had there not been skillful negotiating by the ABS.

Thus, while the WCC withdrew from a central concern with Bible work, which had been evident in the time of Visser't Hooft, the Bible Societies themselves were uneasy with a relationship which might lose them their major support, as the WCC became more politically conscious and more radical in biblical theology.

CHAPTER SEVEN

A Renewed Vision

———— ◇ ————

North, Wilkinson, and Temple all played their part in the making of the United Bible Societies, but the principal architect was North, who remained longer as a moving force than either of the other two. With his extraordinary gift for precise analysis and his capacity to see the far-flung ramifications of any proposal, he guaranteed the realization of those dreams of 1932.

On his retirement in 1956 as the ABS senior executive it was said of him that, "He sometimes wondered why his colleagues brought in experts to aid them in their work, for he himself, in the highest sense and long before the present-day craze, was an eminently successful do-it-yourself executive."

North was born on June 22, 1888. His father, Frank Mason North, was a mission society executive and the author of the hymn which sung to this day in many churches, an expression of his and his son's deep concern for the need of the multitudes:

> Where cross the crowded ways of life,
> Where sound the cries of race and clan,
>   Above the noise of selfish strife,
>   We hear Thy voice, O Son of Man!

Every verse of that hymn resonated the longing that those in need and despair, in "shadowed thresholds dark with fears," "those hearts

of pain," "these restless throngs," must hear the voice of the Son of
Man.

From such a household, North brought more than competent administrative skills to the service of the Bible Society. He never lost the vision
of the children of men, "learning the Savior's love" and "following
where his feet had trod." North was brought up as a Methodist and
remained one all his life. He studied in three universities, did graduate
work at Union Theological Seminary in New York, taught History of
Christianity and in 1918, was ordained into the ministry of the Methodist Episcopal Church. He was a military chaplain in World War I
and held various editorial and educational offices, afterwards in his
denomination, and lectured at Drew Theological Seminary, New Jersey,
from 1919 to 1924. He married the daughter of the then ABS General
Secretary, the Rev. Dr. William I. Haven, and after three years as
executive secretary of the China Union Universities, he was appointed
first associate, then ABS General Secretary in 1928. His father's hymn
must have been in his mind when he coined the phrase that gave
spiritual context to all his Bible Society work: "The Bible is 'The Positive
Answer to the World's Despair.'"

The minutes of the meeting of the Board of Managers in January
1957, which noted his retirement as General Secretary, summed up
the character of the man and his achievements succinctly:

> Dr. North's thinking is always Christ-centered. He seldom writes or
> speaks publicly of the Bible without a reference to Him whom the great
> Book reveals and commends. This has been the secret of Dr. North's
> vision of his work as a worldwide work embracing not only that of the
> American Bible Society but of all the national Bible Societies. It has been
> during his three decades of service with the Society that all semblance
> of overlapping and competition between various Societies engaged in
> international work has been gradually eliminated and he shared largely
> in the creation of the United Bible Societies in 1946.

The Turning Point

The principal characters who had created the UBS and guided its
infant steps were passing from its leadership, but the General Secretary,
who continued, did not let the occasion pass without drawing strength

from their memory. Some major changes came between the Council meeting held in Brazil in 1957 and that in Grenoble in 1960. Berggrav, although quite ill, went to Brazil to preside over the Council for the last time. North made his last appearance as vice-chairman. Both were unanimously elected honorary life members. After the meeting in Brazil, Prem Mahanty, General Secretary of the Bible Society in India, died in 1958. During that period Darlington of the ABS, who as associate treasurer had handled most of the finances of the UBS since its formation, and Platt, who had persuaded the BFBS to continue its support of the UBS after the death of Temple, reached retirement age, and both were elected honorary life members. These stalwarts were replaced by a new generation: Berggrav by the Rt. Rev. Donald Coggan, at that time Bishop of Bradford; Mahanty by the Rev. H. M. Arrowsmith, General Secretary of the BFBS in Australia, as Chairman of the Council; Darlington by ABS's Charles W. Baas; Platt, as Chairman of the UBS Council, first by Mahanty and then Arrowsmith. These new men stood upon the shoulders of their predecessors.

Béguin made special reference to Berggrav when he paid tribute to these pioneer leaders at the Council Meeting in Grenoble in 1960. With him, North, Platt, and Mahanty, they formed a great team. Béguin's tribute was warm and appreciative:

> These were men of vision. For them, the world fellowship of Bible Societies was something real. Remember Bishop Berggrav's plea, year after year, in the early years of the UBS, that our very name should embody that vision of the worldwide nature of our task. Remember Prem Mahanty, at our last Council meeting, stressing the oneness and the global nature of the worldwide task of the Bible Societies. For these men this world vision was an intrinsic part of Bible Society ethics; its expression by a closely knit fellowship of Bible Societies, embracing the whole world in their concern and their work, was, in their eyes, a necessity inherent in the vocation of the Societies and an essential part of their nature. A world fellowship, they taught us, was the normal expression of Bible Society spirit at its best. These were men of vision.

Béguin also said these were modest men, and he began to show that the Bible Societies had good reason to be modest. Yes, they were circulating 25 million to 26 million copies of the Scriptures each year:

Bibles, New Testaments, Portions, Sermons on the Mount, Christmas Stories, etc. In 1959, they had even topped 29 million. This was no cause for pride or complacency, he insisted. The world population increased by 50 million a year. Each week, the schools and literacy campaigns of the world produce a million new literates. Against this demand, the world output of the Bible Societies, fifteen years after the end of the war, "still seems to halt at the level of twenty-five years ago."

In his report for the year 1961–1962, Béguin spoke of a turning point in 1961:

> After fifteen years of modest existence and gentle progress, the UBS last year was given a New Look. This, indeed did not alter any of the basic tenets of our organization. But new emphasis was laid on service and on the fact that the UBS is not a Bible Society, though being wholly and deeply involved in Bible Societies' concerns. And this within the New Look, meant more services and increased cooperation among the Bible Societies.[1]

UBS Headquarters

The New Look appeared most obviously in the new headquarters— new in three ways: new personnel, new location, and new work. At first Béguin and Miss Margaret Sullivan were the only UBS staff, joined later by Dorothy Nears and Lynn Bates. These four people had faithfully serviced the headquarters office for ten years. Then after considerable persuasive pleading by Béguin, authorization was given to double the staff with the appointment of an assistant secretary, Mr. Tom Hawthorn, and his secretary, Miss W. B. Harvey, together with a junior typist. It still did not represent overstaffing for a headquarters office of an international organization with work on six continents. Neither had the new appointments relieved the strain very much, because they had in fact brought extra work with them. Sullivan had been more than ten years with Béguin and eventually her working span as Administrative Secretary to the General Secretary would be listed as 1949 to 1972. It was that kind of long and faithful service which gave solidity to the work of the UBS.

Hawthorn joined the staff in 1962, and he had as his specific task the Public Presentation of the Bible Cause. This had been his main occupation when he was organizing secretary of the Johannesburg agency of the Bible Society of South Africa. This side of UBS work had been undeveloped and needed someone with his experience to show how fruitful it could be. He later took up the task of following UBS concerns in the field of production, again an area previously "in abeyance." Béguin saw the possibility of extending the work rather than relieving pressures. With his usual confidence, he could say, with this new staff, that "assistant and general secretaries and their staff look forward to a fruitful period of teamwork."

In Geneva, Robertson and his secretary, Miss Lesley Walmsley, constituted the rest of the staff, and for a time the new study secretary, Wolfensberger, had the benefit of the same secretary to carry on the work.

New staff meant the need for more office space than the BFBS could provide in Bible House, on Queen Victoria Street. Fortunately, splendid new space was found across the road and up the street in the Salvation Army building (International Headquarters) at 101 Queen Victoria Street. The move, of course, meant increased budget. Béguin added with his usual wry humor, "We in no way want to indulge in lavishness and luxury." The move from the BFBS was good for the sense of independence that it gave, but there were losses as well. Former BFBS facilities and staff services had now to be provided for. Moreover, visitors to the BFBS might not always walk up the street to meet and confer with the UBS staff.

But much more was growing in the UBS program. Béguin summed it up concisely when he wrote,

> Indonesian emergency program and printing plant program; conference on distribution; new subcommittee on the effective use of the Bible; further study on the Roman Catholic Church and the Bible; working out of project lists; preparing and launching a prayer sheet.[2]

This, of course, came on top of the routine work and the need to keep in close touch with the study secretaries. Béguin freely admitted that not all this was done by headquarters staff. He could draw upon the help of UBS officers and individual Bible Society personnel. But in the long run, he was responsible for it to be done. And often he moved as in a mine field. The UBS was fortunate to have such a man at this time.

The Effect of the New Look on Member Bible Societies

Fifteen years under the charming influence but firm direction of its General Secretary had led to a different kind of UBS from that envisaged at "Elfinsward." Growth and change were inevitable, and by 1961 it was very considerable. In that year the UBS formulated a redefinition of its original terms of reference. It began now to see its function:

- As an agency of all the Bible Societies, in the service of all, discharging certain tasks for the benefit of all.
- As a meeting place for the exchange of ideas and experiences and for the confrontation and subsequent harmonizing of divergent points of view.
- As a platform from which the Societies together could look at the worldwide task and devise how best together to go about it.
- As an expression, towards the outside world, and particularly the other world Christian agencies, of the basic aims and tenets of the Bible Society movement as a whole.

That was how Béguin saw it, as he wrote his report for 1961–1962. The motivation was also clearly seen, "in relation to the Bible Societies, the UBS as a reaffirmation of the oneness of their purpose and divine charter and a fresh recognition of the necessary interdependence under the leadership of Jesus Christ, the head, and with the help of the Holy Spirit, the spirit of guidance."[3]

The implications of this new spirit meant that all member Societies needed to look at their own cooperation. The UBS was, after all, as Béguin often insisted, more than a pattern of councils, committees and subcommittees, and general and regional secretaries, it is also and primarily "the amount of true cooperative spirit and regard for one another which its member Societies put into their own work. For them too, the age of individualism has come to an end, to be replaced by consultation and cooperation."

Buck Hill Falls, 1962

The UBS was now becoming a forum of creative thought about how the world task could best be carried out. Béguin persistently stressed the need to change the old way of thinking of national Bible Societies undertaking separate activities with separate goals from the UBS. Each Bible Society was a part of the UBS, and the UBS was part of each Bible Society. His Swiss experience of cantons, all Swiss, helped him explain that one cannot think of the American Bible Society, for example, as being distinct from the UBS. This new structure of thinking, of course, no more deprived, the Bible Societies of their autonomy than Geneva was deprived of its autonomy by being Swiss. Each Society needed to train its committees to think in UBS terms. And as a supreme example of this Béguin quoted the consultation in April 1962 in Buck Hill Falls, Pennsylvania, an ad hoc consultation by the ABS and BFBS general secretaries (the Rev. Norman Cockburn, the Rev. John Watson, Dr. Charles Baas, Dr. Robert Taylor, and Dr. Laton Holmgren). The representatives of these two Societies came together to review all aspects of Bible Society work, especially translation, and agreed to share all responsibilities and costs in the context of an overall UBS global strategy. In view of their combined size, they could have divided up much of the world according to areas of influence, but that was not the structure of their thinking. In ordering their own affairs, these two Societies agreed to work with all others and so prepare the way for wider and more intensive cooperation in the worldwide task.

One of the first to respond to this appeal for others to join in this wider cooperation was Prälat Schlatter of the Union of Evangelical Bible Societies in Germany. He asked for some satisfactory arrangement whereby Societies not at that time supporting work overseas could be enabled to take part in the worldwide task. Others followed, and the spirit of that first Buck Hill Falls consultation became the vision of a new form of cooperation in which there would be closer cooperation between supporting and supported Societies in the planning of work and the allocation and use of funds. The Societies were not yet ready for a "World Service Budget," although that was the logical next step. They were content in 1962 to express deep appreciation of the spirit of fellowship shown by the ABS and the BFBS in the ad hoc Buck Hills Falls arrangement and to encourage other societies to join in the worldwide task.

The Magnitude of the World's Needs

The challenge of the General Secretary's remarks at Grenoble in 1960 had given to the new leaders a new task. Coggan, Arrowsmith, and Baas were moved to take on that task with vigor. They heard, as did all members of the Council, the call for greater production and also for a truly worldwide service. For the sake of those who did not hear it at first, Béguin reiterated the facts: "We circulate nearly 29 million copies, almost 40 percent of them in the U.S. alone, more than 60 percent in the 'Christian west.'"

That there had been no significant rise in circulation over the past twenty-five years was a shock to many. This further fact that the Bible Societies had predominantly served the "Christian west" added to the sense of inadequacy. Béguin pointed out the dangers of complacency:

> There is no escaping the fact that unless we radically transform our policies and speed up our action, very soon, in India, in Muslim countries, in Buddhist areas, not to speak of the Communist countries, even the few of the older generations who have been under Christian influence or at least have had some contacts with Christianity, will be replaced by a younger generation where Scripture teaching is forbidden, will be completely ignorant of the Gospel of Salvation.[4]

It was a powerful appeal and set the Bible Societies on a new course. As usual Béguin was reflecting something already in the air and giving substance to it. A partially successful "Three Million Gospels Campaign" had been carried through in Africa. When the UBS Standing Committee met in Eastbourne, December 1961, it proposed a five-year thrust, tentatively called, "New Testaments for New Nations." Platt had often said that as the new nations of Africa come to independence, one of the most significant facts about them would be that the new leaders were mission-trained and came to power with a Gospel in their hand. Words like that inspired the UBS to press on. It was a "renaissance" period for Africa and Asia as colonialism died. In this renaissance, as in the time of the Reformation, the Bible had a vital part to play. The facts which Béguin had referred to were plain enough: "In sixteen years since the close of the second world war:

- Half the population of the world has come into independence.
- The number of new literates is estimated to be 50 million annually.
- The increase of membership of the Christian churches is only 2 million per year.
- The increase in world population is 50 million per year.
- The present volume of Scriptures is not sufficient to provide one portion of Scripture for each new reader.
- The central task of the Bible Societies is to encourage and promote the wider circulation of the Scriptures.[5]

Apart from these basic facts which brook no delay, there were three other points made at Eastbourne:

1. The study by Chirgwin had made clear that the distribution of the Scriptures was an effective method of taking the Gospel to the unevangelized.
2. There was evidence that there existed organizations and political parties who were distributing printed literature in many languages with the express purpose of alienating people from Christianity.
3. There is much still to be done by Bible Societies to improve the presentation of Scriptures; both types of Scripture and techniques of circulation are urgently in need of investigation.

The tentative title, "New Testaments for New Nations," which Holmgren had proposed at Eastbourne, because he wanted the first ever UBS global distribution campaign to put its special emphasis on the "new nations" being created in those days as colonialism came to an end, was not retained. His proposal was adopted, but the title was changed to "God's Word for a New Age." Holmgren's title, of which only the word "new" was kept, was shot down by Inbanathan, who asked if he had intended to include India as one of the "new nations." When Holmgren said yes, Inbanathan smiled and reminded the committee that India had a history before America had a geography! As they worked on a new title, the concept enlarged to include all types of Scripture—not only New Testaments—and all countries. "God's Word for a New Age" had a universal ring and a contemporary vision. It caught the imagination of the churches.

In that same month, December 1961, the new President of the UBS, Bishop Coggan, was presenting the need to the Third Assembly of the World Council of Churches in New Delhi, with charts and statistics.

In the following year, October 1962, a UBS Conference on Distribution was held in Stuttgart, attended by twenty-six delegates from seventeen Societies and three Agencies. The Standing Committee's proposal for a three-year global Scripture distribution campaign was soon accepted and renamed "God's Word for a New Age." It became the focus of the Council meeting held in Hakone, Japan, at the end of May 1963. There the Council accepted, for the first time, responsibility for a united global distribution effort, involving all member Societies.

God's Word for a New Age: Hakone, Japan, May 1963

The President was in the chair for the morning and afternoon sessions on May 29, 1963, and the retiring Chairman of the Council, Canon Arrowsmith, introduced the proposed campaign. In doing so, he expressed his belief that "the Bible Societies had arrived at a moment of extraordinary significance and opportunity."

The discussion covered the ground necessary to face the financing of the program and the methods to be used, and reference was made to the Latin American Penzotti Institute method for training of colportage leaders. A committee was formed to oversee the campaign: the Rev. E. G. Alves, general secretary of the Brazilian Bible Society; Canon H. H. Arrowsmith (Australia); Dr. Laton E. Holmgren, the newly appointed Chairman of the Council and Standing Committee and ABS secretary; Dr. A. E. Inbanathan, general secretary of the Bible Society of India, the successor to Mahanty; and the Rev. J. T. Watson, a BFBS secretary. The convener was to be the UBS General Secretary.

The first task of this committee was to draft a detailed resolution, which eventually ran into thirteen paragraphs, and was accepted after further discussion by the UBS Council. The first paragraph put the campaign into memorable form:

A Bible for every Christian home;
At least a New Testament for every Christian;
At least a Portion for all who can read and for every new literate;
An opportunity for every church member to share in local Scripture distribution.

The "Hakone formula," as it was called, remained memorable in the life of the United Bible Societies. Very often in Council meetings and conferences great statements were made and plans outlined which have stimulated discussion but were often forgotten. This particular formula was never forgotten, and it remained a constant challenge to the work of the Bible Societies throughout the world. This was the objective; not so much the numbers but rather the targets for the Bible—the Christian home, the individual Christian, the new literate, and the sharing of church members in Scripture distribution. It was a kind of benchmark to see whether the Bible Societies were doing their work. It was not, of course, achieved all at once.

This was a three-year plan, 1964, 1965, and 1966. The target for the end of 1966 was an annual world circulation of Scriptures of 150 million. The resolution also included "endeavor to stimulate churches, councils of churches, and also educational and other appropriate bodies to share in the planning of the campaign, in the distribution of Scriptures and in financial support for the project."[6]

The whole campaign was launched on Whit Sunday 1963, in Rikkyo University, Tokyo, by the President, who was by now the Archbishop of York.

Coggan took as his text, "We hear them telling in our own tongues the great things God has done" (Acts 2:11).

He dealt at once with three kinds of hunger—of the body, of the mind, and of the heart for love. Unless these three hungers were satisfied, life was "poor and weak and anemic." The Church of Jesus Christ, he claimed, was deeply concerned with these three hungers. The Church faced three difficulties in seeking to offer food for mind and heart as it proclaims the love of God: the sheer size of the world, illiteracy, and the babel of tongues which separate peoples.

Coggan committed the Bible Societies to take up the challenge, but it was in the face of much competition. There were many alternatives available, but the goal was to see that the teeming millions hear in their own language the good news of God's love. The Bible Societies committed themselves, but they could not have accomplished their task without the dedicated support of the churches:

> To this task, then, I call you in this great assembly in Tokyo tonight; and far beyond the confines of this hall; I call you for the sake of those millions who have the right to share in the experience of the grace of our Lord Jesus Christ and the love of God and the fellowship of the Holy Spirit. In the name of that triune God I call you, whose is the kingdom and the power and the glory for ever.[7]

It was a great sermon and a great project.

Béguin, in his usual practical way commented, "'God's Word for a New Age' must not be made a gimmick. Doubling or trebling our statistics is no aim in itself. Figures are a thermometer of the missionary temperatures of our supporting constituency. Let us not succumb to the illusion that by rubbing the thermometer we increase the temperature!"[8]

The Bible Societies and the Churches

At the beginning of 1962, Coggan had proposed that a church leaders' world conference—with an emphasis on the young leaders—be called as part of the Third Jubilee of the Netherlands Bible Society in 1964. Béguin gave his support to this as part of what he called "the UBS task and concern to develop constructive and live contacts with the churches at a world level." The adoption of the "God's Word for a New Age" campaign made such a church leaders' conference almost mandatory.

Coggan was willing to call the conference, and he had already sounded out a number of church leaders. The Standing Committee suggested a conference of about eighty—fifty church leaders and thirty Bible Society representatives.

The Study on the Place and Use of the Bible in the living situation of the churches had been conducted under the guidance of the UBS and the Division of Studies of the World Council of Churches and the International Missionary Council (1956–1962). It was a logical step to call together church leaders on a worldwide basis to consult with the UBS. Effective Bible study work required effective relations between the specialists in the Bible Society world and leaders of the churches they serve. Of course, the Bible Societies had a specialized job for which, as Béguin said, "we have slowly and painfully equipped ourselves." But the very fact that the Bible Societies discharged a specialized task within the Church did not exempt them from listening to what the church leaders had to say about their work, particularly when they had critical remarks to make.

The Church Leaders' Conference

The conference was held in Driebergen, Holland, in 1964. The NBS made this a highlight of the ter-jubilee celebrations and hosted seventy leading churchmen from forty-five countries. Coggan, who issued the invitation, made clear that what he sought was a frank and practical discussion of the relationship between the Bible Societies and the churches, especially in the light of the "God's Word for a New Age" campaign. He opened the conference with a forthright challenge to the churches to seize upon rather than neglect the critical issues of the day. His address was titled "God's challenge to his Churches in this Age."

About three quarters of the conference were church leaders and one quarter officers of Bible Societies, all of which belonged to the UBS. Coggan began by outlining the steps that had led to the calling of the conference. He gave three reasons for calling the conference:

1. Many church leaders had not asked themselves the double question; what do the churches expect from the Bibles Societies, and the Bible Societies from the churches?

2. The population explosion and the rapid rise in world literacy have together faced the Christian Church with the critical question, "What shall they read?"

3. The particular crisis which the Church faces today and which it will be judged upon what it does with it, is "to seize the opportunity presented by print and radio and television in a world which is rapidly becoming literate."

When he spoke of the decision taken in Hakone in 1963, he said:

We in Tokyo hardly dared to look beyond the end of 1966, but in Driebergen we must do so. We must think in world terms. We must look at least to the end of this century. We must plot how to kill that attitude in our own churches which views the work of the Bible Society as an optional extra, and we must plan how to make our people see that this is of the very *essence* of the church's mission. Let our thinking be statesmanlike. Let us refuse to get sidetracked onto minor issues. Let us hold on to the big things—the love for the world which He made and for which Christ died—the need of man who cannot live by bread alone—the crisis and the opportunities facing the Church—the joy, the strenuous fun of facing it.[9]

The conference dealt with many issues, concentrating upon those relationships between the churches and the Bible Societies which bear directly upon the distribution and use of the Bible. Apart from many practical proposals, there emerged a general desire to involve the Roman Catholic Church in this enterprise. A message was sent from the conference to the churches, and it contained suggestions for ways of involving the churches in the work of the Bible Societies.

There was no doubt that the conference at Driebergen proved a watershed in Bible work worldwide. It committed the churches to this work, which had often been thought of as a speciality of the Bible Societies. Coggan was delighted with its results and saw the need for continuing such joint "Bible Society-Church" consultations. Unless the results of Driebergen were taken seriously and acted upon, "God's Word for a New Age" would be little more than a slogan. This campaign was to be a campaign of the Churches, in cooperation with the UBS.

Among the points listed from the Driebergen Message to the Churches, three could be acted upon at once:

1. Editions of Bibles, New Testaments, and Portions to be published with aids for readers in close cooperation with the churches of the area.
2. Closer cooperation with the Orthodox and Ancient Eastern Churches on the question of modern translations and aids to readers, including illustrations.
3. The Second Vatican Council had opened up the way for cooperation with the Roman Catholic Church to a greater extent and with greater boldness than ever before.

The conference expressed its conviction that "if we have the courage to use the Scriptures today, to listen to the Holy Spirit speaking to us in our tongues about our own times, we shall find them to be, in truth, God's Word for a New Age."[10]

CHAPTER EIGHT

The Bible Societies and the Roman Catholic Church

—— ◇ ——

The Bible Societies, through most of their history, have been largely managed and staffed by members of Protestant churches. The Evangelical Revival which swept the BFBS into existence in Britain was a Protestant movement, and all the Societies which followed throughout the world served primarily Protestant communities. Approaches were made to the Roman Catholic Church in the early years, but the time was not ripe. The Bible Societies became and remained Protestant.

The Roman Catholic Church and the Bible

The attitude of the Catholic Church to the distribution of translations of the Bible was puzzling to Protestants. On the one hand, it affirmed that "the Church has always venerated the divine Scriptures, just as she venerates the body of the Lord," but on the other, the history of the Roman Catholic Church appeared to be one of prohibition and great reluctance to put the Bible into the hands of the laity without adequate safeguards. To continue the quotation above, her reason for restriction was partly indicated in the words that follow: "Since from the table of both the Word of God and the body of Christ she unceasingly receives and offers to the faithful the bread of life, especially in the sacred liturgy."

This quotation from the Document on Revelation (Dei Verbum) from the Second Vatican Council contained the unchanging attitude to the Bible of the Roman Catholic Church.[1] Why then the restrictions? Why the need for safeguards? The first answer must have been the nature of authority in the Church. The "magisterium" specifies the teaching and the communication of the Sacred Scriptures. It did this in such a way that easy access to the Scriptures for the laity became very difficult. But why? And what made this state of affairs arise? The most satisfactory answer to those questions that have been found were in the writings of Cardinal C. M. Martini. Martini admitted that in recent centuries there had been a distancing of the Church from the Scriptures, particularly so far as the laity were concerned. But it was not always so. For the early Christians, in the period of the Church Fathers and well into the Middle Ages, the Scripture was the basic book for the formation of the Faith. No catechism existed nor substantial theological works. The education of the catechumen, the regular instruction of believers, and the preparation of students for the priesthood was all done from the Bible. The first indication of concern came in the twelfth century. In a letter to Pope Innocent III of 1199, the Bishop of Metz wrote of his concern about some of his faithful lay people, both men and women, who had translated parts of the Bible into French. They were enthusiastic about what they discerned in the Gospels and the Epistles and were meeting secretly, preaching as though they were priests. They seemed also to be showing themselves very arrogant towards their parish priests. The Pope replied without taking any drastic action, but asked the bishop to investigate the nature of the translation and to keep an eye on the movement. This was the beginning of those movements for reform which grew in the later Middle Ages.

Increasing Restrictions

The Church reacted with more and more rigidity as it saw such movements threatening both the unity of the Church and the purity of its doctrine. By 1229, at the Council of Tolosa, the Church assumed a position regarding biblical translations and direct access to the Scriptures by the laity which was strongly negative. In subsequent centuries similar prohibitions occurred, such as the Council of Oxford in 1408, which prohibited any translation of the Bible which did not have official approval. Prohibitions were often enforced by the civil authorities, but they were never total or universal. While in the sixteenth century under Ferdinand and Isabella in Spain, it was established by law that no one should possess for himself any biblical version, Bibles circulated nonetheless. In Germany, between 1450 and 1500, twenty-five editions of the Latin Bible and fifteen in the vernacular were printed. In Basel, eighteen editions of the Bible were printed during that time, and in Italy, twenty-seven Bibles, mostly in Venice, although some in Rome, Naples, Brescia, Piacenza, and Vicenza. Of these twenty-seven, ten were in the vernacular. In the last year of the fifteenth century, 5,400 copies of the Bible were printed in Italy. The Bible, despite the restrictions, was available in the vernacular as well as Latin. (Jerome's Latin Bible, which formed the basis of the *Vulgate*, was an attempt to give a wide readership, including laymen and women, to the Bible in a language they could understand.) The growth of Martin Luther's Reformation led to prohibitions under Paul IV in 1559 and Pius IV in 1564 which show the purpose of these restrictions: "Being clear from experience that if it is permitted to have Bibles in the vernacular *without discrimination*, more harm than good is done."

From this point on, translation and publication of an entire Bible in the vernacular by Catholics ceased. All the Italian complete Bibles published after the mid-1500s were of Protestant or Jewish origin. There is one exception—a reprint of Malermi's translation, but in fact there is nothing more for about two centuries. Not until 1757 was general permission given for vernacular editions of the Bible and then "on condition that they were approved by a competent authority and furnished with notes."

Selections Available: A Slow Change

This does not mean that for two centuries the laity was deprived of all contact with the Scriptures. The Gospels, the books of the New Testament, and various selections were published by "competent authorities." In addition, books of the Bible (Old Testament and New Testament) were explained in public readings and preaching. However, direct contact of the laity with the Bible was not frequent. This led to a laxity on the part of the clergy, who were not stimulated to study the Scriptures deeply. In theory, the Bible remained the "food and rule of preaching and religion," but until recent times, the individual faithful were not exhorted to read or study the Scriptures in any depth. (Even during the discussion of *Dei Verbum*, the document of the Second Vatican Council on "Revelation," there were those who made requests that there be safeguards in making the Bible freely available to the laity.) Slowly, the situation began to change. As early as 1893, Leo XIII in his encyclical, *Providentissiumus Deus* gave a new stimulus to biblical studies. Pius X at the beginning of the new century encouraged the circulation of the Gospels for families. In 1914, the Codex, *Diritto Canonico* gave approval for translations into modern languages, and Benedict XV in his encyclical, *Spiritus Paracletus*, emphasized the admonitions of St. Jerome, that there should be an assiduous study of the Scriptures by the faithful—especially the New Testament. On August 22, 1943, the Pontifical Biblical Commission declared that versions of the Sacred Scriptures, made according to proper authority, can be lawfully used by the faithful for the development of their spiritual life—for private use. Finally, the climax to this development came on September 30, 1943 with the encyclical of Pius XII, *Divine Afflunte Spiritu*, which recommended that all means be used to stimulate among Catholics the love and knowledge, the distribution, and the daily reading of the sacred books.

A Step Too Far

An encyclical in an "open letter" from the Pope and *Divine Affluente Spiritu* surprised those who were not too preoccupied with war at the time. But there had been other encyclicals before which had roundly condemned the work of the Bible Societies. Those who assembled at "Elfinsward" after the war did not give too much attention to the encyclical that marked a climax in the biblical movement in the Roman Catholic Church. They waited. Then in 1950, the same Pope Pius XII issued his most controversial encyclical: *Humani Generis*. It was controversial for many reasons, and it seemed to Protestant observers, at least, that the Pope was putting the clock back. Those who had hoped for a biblical renewal in the Catholic Church read with disap-

pointment the warnings in this encyclical of 1950 "against some dangerous aspects of the new enthusiasm for Bible reading." The dangers, the
encyclical explained, lay in "interpreting Scripture in a purely human
way" or at least not "according to the spirit of the Church which our
Lord Jesus Christ has made guardian and interpreter of the divine
truth as revealed by God." The Pope indicated that Bible study without
very careful guidance by the Church would endanger "the truth of the
faith and Catholic doctrine." When the brief historical survey by Martini is considered, these words seem reasonable enough and part of the
perennial concern of the Catholic Church. But for those who hoped
for more openness and perhaps cooperation with the Bible Societies, it
was a disappointment. The Pope did not stop with one cautionary
encyclical. In 1955, an instruction was sent out with his authorization
and approval that any Bible study circle or group of a public or permanent nature must be subject to very careful supervision and guidance,
always under episcopal authorization. Bible Weeks or Bible Days were
also required to have episcopal authorization. This tightening of control
seemed repressive to Protestants. The Bishops were asked to follow this
biblical movement carefully and to check "related books or articles
published or in preparation."

Béguin, who followed the movement carefully, was less surprised,
and in his article for the *UBS Bulletin,* he tried to explain the purpose
of this supervision:

> One should not read more into such instructions than they really contain.
> They do not ring the death knell of the biblical movement—they are a
> call to order. In a Roman Catholic perspective, nothing could be more
> legitimate. For the need of the Church authorities today is less to encour-
> age a new movement than to make sure that it does not get out of control.
> For the biblical movement in the Roman Catholic Church is not an
> artificial movement imposed from above. Its very success is a sign of the
> intense pressure which has developed from below. In sociological terms,
> one could say that we witness a democratic upsurge of the *laos*—the
> people of the Church who want to get hold of the riches which so far
> were only the privileges of the clergy: an immediate relation to the Truth
> instead of mediated contacts. The declarations made by the hierarchy
> have encouraged the movement and have at the same time helped to
> channel it in the right direction.[2]

Béguin was shrewd in his assessment of the democratic upsurge, which he witnessed himself in the prisoner-of-war camps he served during and after the war, and in his work among students.

Reasons for Change

Cardinal Martini pointed out that the affirmations of the Second Vatican Council in *Dei Verbum* were not new, but after the prohibitions and restrictions and cautious attitudes of previous centuries, the free access of all to the Scriptures which they promoted was different from earlier statements. There were two reasons for this change:

> The first is the growing liturgical sense of our time. In contrast to a situation which Rosmini characterized last century as, "The Five Wounds of the Church," the separation of the faithful from the priest at the altar, we are now united (clergy and laity), after a half century of liturgical renewal, in a consciousness of a more profound unity of the worshipping community. The liturgy is heard more profoundly than at one time by the faithful. The active participation of the worshippers in the Celebration daily improves in quality. It is natural that in this context, the liturgy encourages the reading of the Bible. It can be said that the liturgical and the biblical movements grow together. It is possible today to recommend the reading of the Bible to the faithful with confidence that they will give it pride of place, with their reading directed towards and in union with the Church, which has given it a privileged position within the liturgical celebration.
>
> The second reason is the growth of the sense that the Church is the Body of Christ and a community of believers, a community in which all receive the same Spirit and, whatever their office, share the same faith. The Church, therefore, nurtures frequent and spontaneous communication between its members.[3]

After further discourse on this, Cardinal Martini concluded with a quote from *Dei Verbum:* "Just as the life of the Church grows through persistent participation in the Eucharistic mystery, so we may hope for a new surge of vitality from intensified veneration for God's Word, which lasts forever."

The Second Vatican Council

On January 25, 1959, Pope John XXIII, after a mere ninety days in office, made the completely unexpected announcement of his plan to convoke the Church's Twenty-first Ecumenical Council, the first since Vatican I of 1869–1970. After nearly four years of exhaustive preparation, in which many scholars who had recently been in much disfavor were involved, the Council opened on October 11, 1962. The gentle Pope John chided the prophets of doom and called for the healing of the world by the medicine of mercy. Within less than nine months he was dead and a new Pope, Paul VI, opened the second session on September 29, 1963. He made it a major program of his pontificate to complete the Council which his predecessor had summoned.

For UBS purposes, the document of greatest relevance to emerge was the one on "Divine Revelation" and in particular the chapter on The Divine Inspiration and the Interpretation of Sacred Scripture. That chapter opened with a firm statement on the divine inspiration, indeed divine authorship of the books of the Bible: "Those divinely revealed realities which are contained in Sacred Scriptures have been committed to writing under the inspiration of the Holy Spirit." More precisely, "the books of both the Old and New Testament in their entirety, with all their parts, are sacred and canonical because, having been written under the inspiration of the Holy Spirit they have God as their author." The Greek text of II Timothy 3:16–17 was used to support this conviction. There were sections following which illustrate this from the Old and New Testament separately and then the all-important section for the Bible Societies on Sacred Scripture in the Life of the Church. In this section the divine Scriptures were linked with the Eucharist as equally venerated and equally received and offered to the faithful by the priest. Then came the crucial part: "Easy access to Sacred Scripture should be provided *for all the Christian faithful*. But since the Word of God should be available at all times, the Church with maternal concern sees to it that suitable and correct translations are made into different languages, *especially from the original texts* of the sacred books." Most important of all for the Bible Societies was the concession that "if, given the opportunity and the approval of the Church authority, these translations are *produced in cooperation with the separated brethren* as well; all Christians will be able to use them."[4]

Professor F. C. Grant, emeritus professor of biblical theology at Union Theological Seminary, New York, an official observer at the Second Vatican Council, commented on the "Divine Revelation" statement: "A beginning has been made, a wonderful reawakening has taken place, which will reach out to the utmost bounds of earth and human history. Thank God, a brighter path is opening up before us than any our fathers were compelled to tread."[5]

UBS Initiatives

Before the Vatican Council, Béguin had perceived the movement in the Roman Catholic Church and recognized its importance for Bible Society work. In 1958, he published in the *UBS Bulletin* for the second quarter of that year a long article on "The Biblical Movement in the Roman Catholic Church." This article was circulated to all member Societies and amended or completed according to suggestions received. The Lutterworth Press then agreed to publish 3,000 copies of this 25,000-word book. All this was written before the Second Vatican Council, although before publication a new section had to be added relevant to the deliberations of the Council while it was still in session. The UBS Council Meeting in Hakone, Japan at the end of May 1963 received this information and also a report from Béguin which showed his continuing contacts. He stated that in all his conversations with Roman Catholic leaders "there was clear evidence that the (biblical) movement was likely to gain momentum and that Roman Catholic authorities would increasingly concern themselves with the Bible in their efforts towards unity." He advised that so far these efforts were uncoordinated, but that joint action in translation might soon be possible, and later joint distribution.

Not all the hesitations were on the Catholic side, and they soon appeared at the UBS Hakone Council Meeting following Béguin's report. The Rev. Wilfred J. Bradnock, translation secretary of the BFBS, pointed out that the question of cooperation with Roman Catholics was, in several ways and certainly in the minds of many, closely related to the problem of the production of the Apocrypha and of notes and comments. He warned, "Unless we were extremely discreet, we would be in danger of precipitating a divisive movement in the Church, which was the opposite of what the Bible Societies wanted to achieve."

It was Nida of the ABS who took the positive line and endorsed Béguin's suggestion that translation was the most likely field for cooperation. Nida reported on discussions which had just taken place at the meeting of the UBS subcommittee on translation in Manila, suggesting that the Bible Societies should take the initiative in arranging for conversations with those leading the Biblical movement in the Roman Catholic Church. Some Bible Societies and Agencies had already taken early steps toward possible cooperation. Brazil and France, however, thought it not wise to pursue the matter further for the moment. The BFBS, on the other hand, had given permission to the Roman Catholic Church to use the Bible Society text of the Swahili Bible in Tanganyika. Watson of the BFBS argued for "a liberal attitude in the Bible Societies' relations with Roman Catholics," in the interest of a wider circulation of God's Word.

Another indication of warmer relations between Bible Societies and the Roman Catholic Church happened without much fuss at the Driebergen Conference in 1964. Cardinal Alfrink attended the conference by invitation. It was a courtesy, because he was the highest ranking Catholic of the host country, the Netherlands, but there was some significance in the fact that he was also a Catholic biblical scholar. This was probably the first time ever that a Roman Catholic Cardinal was present at an officially sponsored Bible Society meeting. In that same year, a conference of the translation committee meeting in Crê t Bérard, which produced the first draft of "Guiding Principles for Cooperation in Bible Translation" agreeable to Roman Catholics and the Bible Societies, was attended, albeit unofficially, by Roman Catholic scholars.

Cardinal Bea

Throughout the process which led to cooperation between Bible Societies and the Roman Catholic Church, the one who carefully guided it through the official channels was Cardinal Agostino Bea. Stjepan Schmidt, in his definitive biography called Bea "the cardinal of unity." Bea first proposed to John XXIII the formation of the Secretariat for Christian Unity, to which the Pope agreed with enthusiasm. Bea was a German, born in 1881, a biblical scholar and rector of the Pontifical Biblical Institute in Rome for nineteen years. He was a Jesuit and one of those referred to as a "Bible Bishop"—a scholar who had taught biblical studies before he was appointed bishop.

In January 1967, when he was opening a meeting at which representatives of the UBS met with members of the Secretariat in Rome, he emphasized the importance of what they were doing:

> It would not be an exaggeration to say that the possibility of our cooperation is one of the most important developments in contemporary Christian history. It defies decades, even generations of suspicion, and in some cases even hostility. It compels us to examine more thoroughly and evaluate more honestly our different attitudes. We find ourselves on the threshold of a great enterprise.

Earlier in February 1963, when the UBS approached Bea suggesting a meeting, he advised waiting until the Council published its "Dogmatic Constitution on Divine Revelation," but he agreed to the small, informal meeting at Crêt Bérard in November 1964. After the publication of the document on Divine Revelation, which contained the crucial section on "Sacred Scripture in the Life of the Church" (usually referred to by its opening words, *Dei Verbum*), he proposed a plan for collaboration with the Bible Societies to Paul VI, who responded favorably at once. The Pope then conferred upon the Secretariat the task of working for the realization of the project in the spirit of *Dei Verbum*.

Throughout these proceedings, Bea was seriously ill, and died in November 1968. He was succeeded by Cardinal Willebrands, who had assisted him and continued the work in the same spirit as Bea. The biography of Agostino Bea was dedicated to Cardinal Willebrands, "who in every way has assisted Cardinal Bea in his construction of the Secretariat for Christian Unity and now gathers up and develops the inheritance."

A Jesuit Addresses the UBS Council

The most public step happened, like so much else in the sixties, at Buck Hill Falls. The minutes of the UBS Council Meeting in Buck Hill

Falls, Penn., read, for the second part of the morning session May 19, 1966, "The Rev. Walter M. Abbott, S.J. was invited to address the Council." In this prosaic way the minutes recorded a mammoth step in relations between the UBS and the Roman Catholic Church. The concluding ceremony of the Second Vatican Council was on December 8, 1965. By February 1966, Abbott, an American Roman Catholic editor, had received the "Imprimatur" for his book *The Message and Meaning of the Ecumenical Council*, which contained the texts of the documents of the Council, with notes and comments by Catholic, Protestant, and Orthodox authorities. The book was fresh off the press and in a paperback, English translation, selling at 95 cents in the bookstores of America. Abbott spoke with knowledge and authority. On April 4, Pope Paul VI approved Cardinal Bea's request that Abbot be appointed a personal assistant to Cardinal Bea for implementing Vatican II on the Bible with a special focus on study of the Bible Societies with a view to possible collaboration in more than translation. Within one year of this UBS Council meeting, he was appointed director of the Office for Common Bible Work at the Vatican, which he remained until 1978. If there was to be cooperative work with the Roman Catholic Church, the UBS would have to deal with this Jesuit priest, and it did over many years. But on May 19, 1966, he was new to most of the Council members and probably a little suspect by some.

He came straight to the point: "In the Second Vatican Council's Decree on Ecumenism, the Roman Catholic Church had finally, fully, and formally joined the ecumenical movement." He said this with approval, because for eight years prior to the Second Vatican Council, as editor of *America* magazine, he had tried to encourage the idea of a common Bible. His reasons were forthright: "Without agreement on the Bible and common use of it, the movement for Christian unity has no future."

Abbott was able to describe the evolution of Roman Catholic thought since Pope John XXIII called together the Catholic bishops of the world for the Ecumenical Council. He emphasized that the rediscovery of the theology of baptism as given in the New Testament had formed the basis of membership, "in the Church and of Christian brotherhood beyond Dogmatic limitations." He continued in this vein:

The Decree on Ecumenism taught that, for the Roman Catholic Church, Protestants and Orthodox were fellow Christians and that the approach to them should be one of "understanding, respect, esteem and even affection." In the process of clarifying its understanding of the Church as the People of God and of "our brethren in this People of God," the Roman Catholic Church had recovered a primary focus on the Bible.

Father Abbott pointed out that there was great ferment in the Roman Catholic Church about the precise role of the Bible, and in dealing with this ferment they had discovered the Bible Societies. Then he concluded, "In discovering what you are and what you do, and in coming to discuss the possibility of cooperating with you, we come with an attitude of respect for a prophetic function of the People of God."[6]

Interconfessional Cooperation in Translating the Bible

This forthright speech gave impetus and urgency to the discussion of a topic which had been raised frequently at UBS Council and other meetings almost from the beginning of UBS history. The UBS Committee on Translation, in particular, had had lengthy discussions with Roman Catholic Biblical scholars and had drawn up a preliminary "Outline of Proposed Guiding Principles for Possible Cooperation by Roman Catholic and Protestant Translators of the Bible" at Crét Bérard, November 10–13, 1964. The document, largely from the pen of Nida, was not ready for presentation to the Council in Buck Hill Falls because more time was needed to get full agreement from Roman Catholic and Bible Society secretariats. The Rev. W. J. Culshaw, secretary of UBS Committee on Translation, was able to report that this document outlining proposed guidelines had been sent to the Secretariat for Christian Unity at the Vatican, and word was received that it would be accepted without change. Since then the document had been sent to all Bible Societies and Agencies. It was not until 1968 that it became a jointly agreed policy. The "Guiding Principles" as adopted by the UBS and the Roman Catholic Church remained in force until 1987. In summary they were listed as "Interconfessional translations will continue to be based on a Hebrew text of the Old Testament and a Greek text of the New Testament which have been agreed by scholars from various church traditions. Drafting and reviewing the translations is to be carried out in close cooperation with the aim that the new text will be acceptable to, and be used by, all Christians and Christian communities who speak the language into which the translation is being made." The clear goal was to provide all speakers of any given language with a common text. That would mean a common witness to the Word of God in the world of today.

Rapid Progress in Cooperation

The mammoth step taken by inviting Father Abbott, S.J. to address the UBS Council in Buck Hill Falls in 1966 might have been a token gesture, but two things made it more than that. The Secretariat for the Promotion of Christian Unity at Rome was determined to implement the decisions of the Vatican Council as soon as possible; and the UBS, represented by Béguin, its General Secretary, by Holmgren, the chairman of the Council and Executive Committee, and by the highly creative Nida, was eager to meet the challenge after long years of preparation and hope.

Within a year of the UBS Council meeting at Buck Hill Falls, the Executive Committee met in Geneva, September 1967, under the chairmanship of Holmgren. After dealing with the "Guiding Principles" and congratulating Abbott on his initiative, the committee heard from the General Secretary that a suggestion had been received from the Secretariat for the Promotion of Christian Unity that the UBS Executive Committee should designate three of its members to attend a conference in Rome during Easter Week, 1968. The three who attended this meeting with representatives of Roman Catholic Bible Societies and publishers were Holmgren, Watson, and the UBS General Secretary. Before that conference took place, however, representatives of the Vatican Secretariat for Promoting Christian Unity were invited to the meeting of the UBS Executive Committee in London, January 10, 1968, and a whole day was devoted to discussions on cooperation with Roman Catholics in Scripture translation, production, and distribution. The Roman Catholic delegation included Bishop Jan Willebrands, Executive Secretary of the Vatican Secretariat for Promoting Christian Unity; the Rev.

R. J. Murray, of Heythrop College; Mr. T. H. Rittner, General Secretary of the Catholic Truth Society; and, of course, Abbott. Their reception was a warm and friendly one since Abbott and other Roman Catholic observers had by this time attended several UBS Regional Conferences and in this way the network of fraternal relations had been strengthened and enriched. In 1967, Béguin had produced another issue of the *UBS Bulletin* devoted to the Bible Societies and the Roman Catholic Church. This issue went much further than that of 1958, which had detected a biblical renewal, but also saw the restraints being placed upon it. This time he could report advance not only in statements from the Vatican II documents, but also in real signs of cooperation. Willebrands welcomed the fact that copies of this issue had been sent to the presidents of the Roman Catholic Episcopal Conferences worldwide, adding, "and this has renewed in them the insights they were given more than a year ago when we sent them information about the Bible Societies and a questionnaire about Scripture needs and the possibilities of meeting those needs."

This working through the Episcopal Conferences was of particular interest to the UBS, because at about this time the structure of the UBS itself was being regionalized with the appointment of Regional Secretaries and the holding of Regional Conferences so that decisions which formerly were taken outside the region concerned, were now taken by regional committees. The UBS was, therefore, able effectively to cooperate with Roman Catholics both at the world and regional levels. What was emerging was cooperation—at first on a small scale but with scope for development—in translation, definition of the accepted text, production, distribution, and finance.

Explaining the Reasons for this Cooperation

Once the "Guiding Principles for Interconfessional Cooperation in Translating the Bible" was agreed, the world had to be told. At the Executive Committee meeting in London, January 1968, a press communiqué was discussed and amended. It was eventually agreed to leave Father Abbott and the UBS General Secretary to fix the date of the release of the communiqué and to take the necessary steps for its distribution. The communiqué issued which announced this agreement also explained how it had been possible. There were three reasons given: first, the Second Vatican Council; second, the decision by many Bible Societies within the organization of the UBS to make available editions of the Bible to meet the various requirements of the churches in respect of the canon of Holy Scripture; and third, that many Bible Societies were now providing new substantial helps for readers and non-doctrinal annotations in their Scripture editions, which many Roman Catholics found acceptable and useful. The two anxieties that some had expressed were thus addressed, not without subsequent difficulty and protest; the extra canonical books (Apocrypha) and the question of notes and comments.

These two thorny questions were not easily or quickly settled. After Abbott's address to the Council in 1966, there was need for consultation in which the UBS was involved, largely through Holmgren. He moved with care and always assured that he had the authority of the UBS Executive behind him. The progress of these negotiations can be followed through 1967 and 1968 in three principal meetings:

- **1967**—Béguin, Watson, and Holmgren attended by invitation the meeting of Roman Catholic Bible Societies and Publishers in Rome, to explore ways in which they could effectively implement the mandate of Vatican II regarding "easy access" to the Bible. That meeting was chaired by Cardinal Bea and Holmgren. Both chairmen made considerable concessions to their traditional stance. The UBS delegation had been authorized by the Executive Committee in Berlin, September 1966.
- **1968**—A Roman Catholic delegation headed by Bishop Jan Willebrands attended the UBS Executive Committee meeting for the purpose of discussing many aspects of UBS-Roman Catholic relationships. The most explicit issue was the "Guiding Principles."
- **1968**—Béguin, Watson, Nida, and Holmgren attended by invitation a second consultation at the Secretariat for Promoting Christian Unity, in Rome. At that meeting, the Roman Catholic Federation for the Biblical Apostolate was organized under Cardinal Willebrands, now president of the Secretariat. Pope Paul VI received the conference participants at noon on Wednesday, April 24.

Every one of these meetings shattered previous traditions and established new precedents for both the Bible Societies and the Roman Catholic Church.

As Abbott had been the key figure on the Roman Catholic side, Holmgren steered the agreement through the UBS. For three decades he served as an officer of the American Bible Society and at the same time played a major role in the UBS. He was chairman of the Council, 1963–1966, and of the Standing Executive Committee, 1963–1972. In close cooperation with Béguin he guided the UBS through difficult waters. He had helped develop cooperation with Roman Catholics in America and in his retirement summarized the history of these relations:

> It was the intention of the ABS founding fathers that Roman Catholics should be included in their fellowship, but the invitation they sent out went unheeded. But following the pronouncements of Vatican II regarding the importance of Scripture in the life of the believer, the ABS offered to be of service to Roman Catholics as it had been to Protestants for a century and a half. This time the invitation was accepted and the first Roman Catholic attended an ABS Advisory Council meeting; another addressed the Annual meeting; still another became the first Roman Catholic member of the Board of Managers; and still others became members of our staff and Officers Council. Also, in this connection, the ABS during this period reversed a decision made in the early days of the Nineteenth Century regarding the publication of the Apocrypha/Deuterocanonicals and for the first time in its history published an English text of its own making, which bore the imprimatur of a Roman Catholic Archbishop.[7]

This attitude and the concessions that had been made had to be explained and defended both to Protestants and Roman Catholics. Holmgren was asked to make personal visits to Bible Societies and Roman Catholic offices in Latin America which required all his negotiating skills. That assignment meant two extended visits to almost all the countries of South America. He found little open hostility, but considerable anxiety, especially among conservative evangelicals. He also called on the principal Roman Catholic prelates in each country and was warmly welcomed, but most of them said that he was the first Bible Society person they had ever met!

The World Catholic Federation for the Biblical Apostolate

In 1968 Cardinal Bea invited leaders of Catholic biblical organizations to a meeting in Rome for discussion about possible coordination of their work with the work of the UBS around the world.

The idea of the federation of these Bible movements was first put forward in 1951 by a Catholic monk, Pius Parsch of Klosterneuberg, a monastery near Vienna. He had worked for years encouraging Catholics to read and study their Bible, not only in Austria, but throughout the German-speaking world, and he was fully aware of the existence of the Bible Societies. His plea in 1951, *Bibel und Liturgie*, was, "Now we must set to work and get in touch with the Bible movements of other countries to create some form of federation. This would lead to a Catholic world organization for the biblical apostolate which would gradually win over the entire Church."

Considerably later, October 6, 1964, during the third assembly of the Second Vatican Council, Bishop Emil Cekada of Skopje, Yugoslavia recommended the setting up, under the auspices of the Holy See, of an international Bible society *according to the model of the United Bible Societies*, for the translation and production of the Bible in all languages.

During Vatican Council II, the eightieth Deutsche Katholikentag (a German Catholic Congress held every two years, alternating with the Evangelische Kirchentag) was held in 1964 in Stuttgart. On the recommendation of Bishop Dr. Carl Joseph Leiprecht, patron of the Catholic Bible Work, the Katholikentag was given a biblical and ecumenical orientation. At the opening "ecumenical" service, 50,000 copies of the New Testament with a prologue by Cardinal Bea were distributed. Cardinal Bea took part in the Katholikentag in Stuttgart. Dr. Otto Knoch, the Director of the Catholic Bible Work, met Bea and recommended a meeting of the German Bibelwerk with similar work in other countries. Austria and Switzerland were already affiliated to the German *Bibelwerk*. Bea, as Director of the Secretariat for Promoting Christian Unity (SPCU), was more than sympathetic to the idea.

Knoch was already in contact with the Württemberg Bible Society, and Bea also visited the Bible Society. The Wüttemberg Bible Society encouraged cooperation with the Catholic Bible Work and agreed to include the text of the Vulgate in its list of scientific texts for publication. Knoch pressed for close collaboration with the UBS, but not membership.

The General Committee of the UBS

The UBS had worked through triennial meetings of the international Council, but the cost of convening the Council had prompted the formation of the smaller General Committee, whose first meeting was held in Edinburgh, September 14–18, 1969. This General Committee was under the chairmanship of Rev. Dr. A. E. Inbanathan of India, and its members were elected on a regional basis, with three from Africa, four from the Americas, four from Asia-South Pacific region, and five from Europe.

The report of the meeting in the *UBS Bulletin* covered four columns and dealt with an award for distinguished services (the first to be made, to the Rt. Rev. D. Kurt Scharf, Bishop of Berlin), membership of the UBS (four new members and fourteen new associate members), and a message from the meeting concerning the third phase of the "God's Word for a New Age" campaign, which was called "Serving the Seventies." No mention was made of the decisions about including the Apocrypha. It was still a very controversial issue. However, a careful statement was made from that General Committee: "In view of much recent discussion, and considerable misunderstanding, about the policy of the United Bible Societies in relation to the deutero-canonical books commonly called the Apocrypha, the United Bible Societies' General Committee meeting in Edinburgh in September 1969 wishes to make the position clear, as follows:

1. When the Authorized Version of the English Bible was published in 1611, all copies contained the Apocrypha. The same is true of most of the early translations such as Luther and Valera. Subsequently, however, editions without the Apocrypha appeared from

time to time. From its formation in 1804 down to about 1826, the British and Foreign Bible Society's circulation of Scriptures included editions with the Apocrypha: but in view of the controversy at that time, regulations were then adopted excluding such circulation. Most, but by no means all, Bible Societies have since operated under a similar limitation until recent years.

2. In June 1964, a world conference of Church leaders and Bible Society representatives, meeting at Driebergen in Holland, urged that the Bible Societies should undertake their task of worldwide circulation of the Scriptures with renewed vigor, and recommended that "where the churches desire and specifically request it the Bible Societies should consider the translation and publication of the books commonly called the Apocrypha."

3. It should be noted that the churches desiring to have the Apocrypha are not only (as sometimes supposed) the Orthodox and Roman Catholic; but also (for example) Angelicans and Lutherans, who value the Apocrypha as supplementary to the Old and New Testaments, though they do not regard its books as part of the canon.

4. It needs to be stressed that each member Society remains an autonomous body within the UBS family. Subject, therefore, to the basic aims and conditions of the partnership, each Bible Society makes its own decisions as to the texts which it will or will not publish or distribute. This freedom applies, of course, in relation to editions with the Apocrypha.

5. It continues to be the normal policy and practice of the Bible Societies as a whole to publish the Holy Scriptures without the Apocrypha. When editions with the Apocrypha are published, this is often subject to the following arrangements:

   a. That there should be a specific request from the responsible body of the church community desiring such an edition.

   b. That the deutero-canonical books should be included as a separate section, between the Old and New Testaments.

   c. That the full additional cost of providing this separate section should be carried by the requesting church or in some separate way, so that in any case there is no subsidy for the Apocrypha from general UBS funds.

6. The Committee feels it desirable that when Bible Society editions of the Bible include the Apocrypha, it should be preceded by a clear explanatory note which indicates the difference of value attributed to these books by the different churches.

7. A categorical assurance can be given that no group which has *not* requested an Apocrypha edition will receive one, and that no one will be involved in translation or distribution of the Apocrypha against his wish or conscience.[8]

CHAPTER NINE

"All Things in Common"

———— ◇ ————

The Financial Crisis of the BFBS

In 1957, following the Suez crisis of 1956, the BFBS, like every organization in Britain, suffered severe financial problems. It became so extreme that the BFBS treasurer, Ivor Crouch, ordered the printing to stop until finances could be guaranteed. The Americans had large reserves, and it was natural for the BFBS to turn to them for a loan. The first request was for £80,000. Later it became obvious that more than a quarter of a million pounds would be needed. The ABS was ready to help, but with conditions. As Dr. Robert Taylor, at the time General Secretary of the ABS, said, "We can raise millions of dollars for work in Europe and India, but we cannot raise a cent for the BFBS!"

At that time, a UBS-sponsored conference was planned for European and American Bible Societies to meet in Amsterdam, May 1957, to discuss the problems of translation. The ABS authorized the attendance of two members of the Board and four members of staff. Platt asked if the staff representation at this Amsterdam conference could return via London and consult. The four staff members were Taylor, Holmgren, Baas, and, because this was a translation conference, also Nida. The first three were involved in the London discussions about finance. The

ABS minutes describe the purpose as "discussions . . . regarding greater cooperative effort in Europe, Africa, the Middle East and Southern Asia." Britain was *persona non grata* in the Middle East, but the other three areas were BFBS territory, particularly if we read India for Southern Asia. Holmgren and Baas remembered this visit as an extremely difficult one. Platt felt that he was losing his empire—particularly in Africa. Holmgren had been in the ABS only five years, but his fine negotiating skills were already evident. It was not exactly a friendly Platt who received him with his map of Africa filling the wall behind his desk. The object, however, was achieved, and the ABS provided the necessary finance, while the work in India and Europe was shared. The importance of Baas at this meeting between ABS and BFBS was also both essential and prophetic of the part that he would play in the future administration and finances of the UBS.

The agreement reached was that the BFBS and the ABS share equally in their annual contributions to the Bible Society of India and Ceylon, remitted to London for the publication of Scriptures for India and because of "present shortages, the ABS at once will make full payment to London of its contributions for the complete current year." It was also agreed to extend the Joint Agency concept to include parts of Africa, France, and elsewhere on the usual basis of fifty-fifty payments. Again to assist the present crisis, the ABS agreed to pay the full amount for the current year. The third element in the agreement showed the extent of the crisis which the BFBS was at that time facing: "The ABS . . . will make payments to the BFBS for all bills for paper, presswork, binding, and transportation as they fall due on Scriptures published for the ABS and the BFBS." This arrangement was extended to other Joint Agencies.

The three ABS men—Taylor, Holmgren, and Baas—had traveled to Europe by ship to give them time to work out such an agreement, which turned a present crisis into a permanent cooperation. All three should have taken credit for it, and Platt was statesman enough to see its necessity. The hand of Holmgren could certainly be seen in the overall strategy and the hand of Baas in the financial details.

The meeting of the ABS Foreign Agencies committee which received their report was on June 24, 1957, within eight months after the disastrous invasion of Egypt by British, French, and Israeli armies. Looking back, Holmgren saw his role at that time as consistent with what he did all through his long service to the Bible Societies:

> What I set about doing was to try at every opportunity that presented itself, in every private conversation, in every meeting, in the Bible House in New York, and in meetings with others across the world, to promote the idea that we can do the work better, more effectively, more efficiently, touch and reach more people, more places, if we do it cooperatively, in partnership.

The missionary strategy of the Church was changing in the sixties, as the younger churches of Asia and Africa called in question the way in which they were being represented in the West. Béguin put this succinctly in 1963:

> The true Africa, the true Asia, have to be given as the background for fundraising and no longer the folkloric picture, the tear-drawing descriptions, the hair-raising challenge or success story; above all, no longer that spirit of complacency by which the good West is upheld against the background of the underdeveloped (spiritually speaking) rest of the world![1]

Gradually missionary societies who had been sending and giving began to recognize a partnership with the indigenous churches which had come into being largely as the result of their efforts. Béguin talked of the "the oneness of the task of one Church in one world." He recalled the words of Premanand Mahanty at the meetings in Rio de Janeiro in 1957: "The work is His, the money is His; the work is one, let the money be one!" It was one thing to agree with Mahanty that "the work is one; let the money be one." It was quite another to put it into practice.

Premanand Mahanty

Mahanty, who had been general secretary of the Bible Society of India and Ceylon since 1949, died unexpectedly in 1958. He was an outstanding Indian Christian who gave his talents, which were many, to the work of the Bible Society during the last nine creative years of his life. He was able to inspire large support for the Bible cause among the churches in India and recruited from them many active workers, both salaried and voluntary. He brought drive and energy to the furtherance of work in India, and once elected to the UBS Standing Committee he gave guidance with his consecrated purpose to its work. He was chairman of the Council when he died.

His last report to the Executive Committee of his own Society in 1958 illustrated the vigor of his leadership right to the end: "nine new auxiliary branches, bringing the total to seventy-seven, with 900 voluntary workers—more than twice as many as in 1954."

For 1957 he reported an increase in women's groups, which he had organized, of more than one hundred, making a total of 541, with five full-time women secretaries located throughout India. The number of members (donors) too had increased during the year from 12,000 to 15,000 which was three times more than the last triennial report. It was typical of his vision that in 1958, he could say, "If this Society could enlist 100,000 members, the problem of the annual deficit would be solved."

To reach this target, he called upon every member to enlist at least one new member each during the coming year. In ten years of independence from 1947 to 1957 India had changed much. The upsurge of political interest that had led to the independence movements, before 1947, was given over to constructing a political system which would be secular rather than dominated either by an outside power or by its religion. Christians did not have a very happy time in those first few years of independence because they were often thought of as associated with the British Raj. However, they managed to win through and persuade fellow Indians that they were independent churches. It was at this point that it became important that the churches should be indigenous. What emerged was the decision that India should be a secular state. This meant no privileges for religion and very considerable problems of organization. It meant disputes between political parties, even assassination and a growth of secularism. These years were troublesome years and years of rapid change. India was becoming aware of herself, and she was aware of her powers. Even her military powers were exercised occasionally. She was able to see that what she had to do was to build a nation which was basically an Indian nation and not dependent any more than necessary upon the rest of the world. It was, after all, the largest democracy in the world and was able to hold elections. Not everything was perfect, but there was an idealism in those years. This presented enormous opportunities—there was an openness to new ideas, provided they were not too closely tied to old ones. The Bible Society shared in the difficulties as well as the opportunities. There was a movement towards greater literacy, an openness in broadcasting, and a chance now for the Bible Society to take hold of the new age, the new India, and become part of it, even taking some part in fashioning it in a way that would be good for the people and for the country.

It was thus from a position of growth, with a clear vision of the task in India and Ceylon and an awareness of the growing demands for Scriptures, that Mahanty spoke at his last meeting of the UBS Council: "The work is one, let the money be one."

And he was not only thinking of his own country. He had in mind the needs of all Asia and pleaded for global acceptance of the challenge. His death was a great loss to the Bible Society movement throughout Asia. When the Standing Committee met in Singapore in June 1959, they appointed the chairman of his Society to take his place on the committee: Mr. J. S. S. Malelu, another powerful voice from India.

Malelu's Initiative

At that first meeting in Singapore, Malelu gave expression to Mahanty's plea for pooling the funds. Until the London conference of 1932 support of Bible Society work around the world was largely a matter of an affluent society in the West, sending funds, books, and personnel to countries in what was then known as "the Mission Field": countries in Asia, Africa, and Latin America. Relationships were strictly unilateral between the sending Society and the receiving agencies. The London conference, however, introduced a completely new revolutionary idea that support for the total world work would be greatly increased if two or more supporting Societies would pool their resources in meeting the needs of certain agreed designated countries; with one of the supporting Societies assigned administrative duties in each case, the other being a kind of silent partner. The idea of pooling resources in support of joint work was born in London in 1932, not in Singapore in 1959. If it had not been for the joint agency idea and the intervening years of working out the practical procedures involved in administration, the Malelu proposal would not have been possible. The Malelu proposal was not entirely new, since some on both sides of the North Atlantic had been discussing the idea well in advance of the Singapore conference. However, those from the ABS, BFBS, and the other Societies of the West were pleased that someone from Asia became an articulate spokesman for the concept.

When he spoke at the UBS All-Asia Regional Conference in Singapore, May and June 1959, he took as his topic, "Asia and Our Global Obligation." Malelu and Mahanty, the man of business and the scholar, had worked together both to recognize the need and to raise the necessary money for subsidizing the Bibles they sold. It was obvious that India and Ceylon, or for that matter, "All-Asia," could not buy the Bibles at cost price. They had to be subsidized, and the long connection with the BFBS meant that most of the subsidy came from London. But wherever it came from, the direct subsidy of one Bible Society by another meant dependence. Both Mahanty and Malelu knew that the only way to retain the independence of Bible Societies was sharing rather than subsidizing.

Malelu did not begin his paper with this issue. He first of all spoke of the great advances that had already been made in the UBS. He spoke with authority and knowledge of Bible Society work in Asia. He soon came to the subject of how the Bible Society work in Asia was to be financed. He commended the changes so far. For example, his own Society, which once received aid only from the BFBS, now received also from the ABS and the NBSS. Then he argued that such collaboration should be taken further. Why not let the UBS function as the channel through which the Bible Societies of the world pool their resources and administer aid, not from one rich Society to a poorer one, but from the central pool in a truly cooperative manner? Malelu was wise enough not to tell the UBS how to do this, but contented himself with saying that "the constituent Societies of the UBS should decide—through such machinery as may be devised—how much can be given to each needy Society from a pool to which *all* the constituent Bible Societies would have contributed."

That little word, *all,* held the key to his proposal, which was not for a fund provided by the larger and richer Societies for the benefit of the smaller and poorer ones to cover their deficits, but a fund to which all would contribute and from which all may draw as needed. He spelled this out in a significant paragraph, the heart of which was as follows:

> Some of the constituent Societies would contribute to the pool more than what they received from it (if they need to receive anything at all), while others would receive more than they give. But the point is that every constituent Society of the UBS would become a giving Society, and be expected to give also—not merely to receive as so many of us are doing at present. The distribution and allocation of inter-Society aid would moreover not be the sole prerogative of the giving Society but would be a function cooperatively performed by all the constituent Societies of the UBS. . . .[2]

This paper, and particularly the concluding proposal, was recognized at once as making important points for the future operations of the UBS. It was submitted to various committees and much discussed. It formed the basis of Resolution 227, a significant resolution at the UBS Council Meeting in Grenoble in 1960. That resolution thanked Malelu for his paper, recognized its significance for other parts of the world as well as Asia, and asked the Standing Committee to collate information, sound out the various Societies, and recommend appropriate action.

A Slow Response

The next meeting of the Standing Committee to which Malelu's paper had been referred was held in Arnoldshain, Germany, in November 1960. By then no comment had been received by the UBS General Office from any Society, although it was known that the boards and staff of several Societies had considered it and approved of the suggestions made. It had therefore to be referred to the next Standing Committee, but with a strong resolution "that the Bible Societies be requested to give full consideration to the suggestions put forward in Mr. Malelu's paper and to report their views on the subject to the UBS General Secretary before May 1, 1961."

The General Secretary sent out a circular letter as requested in December 1960, and only two Societies replied—the NBSS and the NBS.

The subject was not retained on subsequent agendas, but Watson (BFBS) suggested that the Bible Society of India and Ceylon review the paper at its triennial Council meeting in 1962 and bring any conclusions they might reach to the next UBS Standing Committee. The UBS General Secretary attended that BSIC Council meeting in Bangkok and commented:

> I was deeply impressed by the high quality of the deliberations, at many points, and by the most valuable contributions of several of the top-ranking Church leaders, Indians, during the meeting. This showed me how important it is for a Bible Society to work out the closest possible type of relationship with Church leadership in every land. In saying this, I have not primarily in mind the possibility of raising more money for our work—although this is certainly an important element in less affluent areas just as much as in the wealthy West. But I am thinking of our ultimate responsibilities for the circulation of God's Word.

But no conclusions from a consideration of Malelu's paper were brought to the Standing Committee. India and Ceylon, like other countries in Asia at that time, had their minds set on the forthcoming All-Asia Bible Societies Conference to be held in Manila, May 17-23, 1963. It was this conference that concerned Dr. A. E. Inbanathan, Mahanty's successor as General Secretary, when he reported to the Council of the UBS in Japan in 1963. With the glow of the experience still on him, he presented the report of the Manila Conference. It dealt largely with Asia's part in the "God's Word for a New Age" campaign and heartily welcomed "the proposal of the Standing Committee of the UBS to make special efforts to increase the circulation of Scriptures in order to meet the growing and urgent needs of this new era throughout the world."

He welcomed also the proposal that each National Bible Society should "participate in financing the campaign." There were details of plans for publication and distribution, singling out particular areas of need, using other organizations and channels, developing Bible Society channels of distribution, using mass media, etc. There were decisions about the "use of the Bible" and proposals for the "indigenization of Bible Society work in Asia and closer cooperation with the churches." A significant recommendation was that "the Bible Societies in Asia do everything possible to increase self-reliance in finance, beginning in the sphere of distribution."

"World Budget"

Things really began to move in 1964, when for the first time the UBS Standing Committee spoke of a "world budget" and asked for contributions from all Societies, encouraging them to support the work, "in areas in which they had no direct (or indirect) responsibility or commitments," principally through "God's Word for a New Age," the campaign that had been launched the previous year in Japan. There was no global budget operating at that point. All Societies were, therefore, asked to contribute to the combined overseas budget of the ABS and BFBS. Almost all Societies were at that time supported financially by at least one of the two major Societies, and some were agencies or "joint agencies." In 1964, a procedure known as "equalization" came into operation. It was a way of sharing the deficits of the world service budget among the net-contributing Societies, after all the other Societies had made their contribution.

The General Secretary suggested that consideration might also be given to the advisability of Societies working together towards goals attainable over a period of several years, as well as continuing the year by year budget pattern. Experience had shown that new programs and imaginative developments could be stimulated in many areas if Secretaries were invited to work out a four- or five-year plan of advance as a background to their annual budgets. Such a procedure would have seemed almost essential where a program of increased distribution would have required a prior building up of distribution machinery, such as the appointment of distribution promoters. Publicity given to such medium- or long-range policies would have probably provided an incentive for increased contribution all over the world. The Standing Committee might have considered the setting up of a four-year, world-wide program of advance, combining the plans of all the individual Societies, ready for the Council in 1966 to commend.

The stimulus of this way of thinking about finance globally led to other Societies joining in as supporting Societies. The most startling change came in West Germany, where the Bible Societies a year or two earlier had been net-receiving Societies. At one leap, in response to a challenge from Béguin, Germany offered to finance virtually the whole of the translation program of the Bible Societies.

The Regional Structure

The idea of a regional structure did not develop overnight. It had for many years been in process of formation. It began with the appointment by the ABS and BFBS years earlier of "fraternal secretaries" who took up residence in various overseas locations; for example, Robertson in Japan, Morris and Nelson in Brazil, Mortenson in Japan and South-East Asia, etc. These men served as conduits transmitting information, requests, and advice from the home base to the overseas location—sometimes a joint agency, sometimes an autonomous Bible Society. At first, the appointment of these "fraternal secretaries" was made unilaterally, but later jointly. (But for the success of these experiments in regional assignments, the notion of establishing regional offices would have been much harder to accept later.) However, it became clear that some kind of regional structure had to be worked out in detail.

The UBS Council meeting at Buck Hill Falls in 1966 undoubtedly was the indication that the UBS had really come of age. The establishment of regional structures meant that the coordination of the administration of the work hitherto handled out of London and New York was now devolving upon regional centers. There were already a number of autonomous Bible Societies in existence which, although receiving significant financial help from ABS, BFBS and others, were in practice self-governing. The new regional structure was to accelerate this trend to the point where the work would essentially be the work of national Bible Societies, served by the UBS.

At Buck Hill Falls the UBS moved away forever from being primarily a forum for consultation between Societies, a kind of clearinghouse for ideas, and took on delegated major administrative responsibilities through its regional and global committees and staff. The prime architects of this profound change were Béguin and Holmgren.

A World Service Budget could not work efficiently from one central point. The UBS required a regional structure. Four UBS regions were designated to administer certain aspects of Bible Society work in Africa, the Americas, Asia-Pacific, and Europe-Middle East. Each was to have a UBS office, but there was some discussion about where it should be. If any of the regional offices had been set up permanently in London or New York, it would be impossible to avoid feeling that they were regional offices of the ABS or of the BFBS. Eventually it was decided that they must each be in the region and called regional centers. Some of the specific functions of these regional centers were not evident at first, but eventually they included consultancy services to national Bible Societies in their region, administering the region's share of the World Service Budget, setting regional priorities, and conducting training programs. The regions also provided an efficient link between national Bible Societies and the UBS at the global level. The growth of the UBS made a regional structure necessary. It was doubtful whether a World Service Budget could have operated without it. Once formed on paper, the regions had to be staffed and a committee structure established. This took some time.

The regional centers were very slow, in fact, to develop; perhaps deliberately so. They were regarded with considerable suspicion at the beginning by many larger Societies in each region, and the regional secretaries had to move with extreme caution. The addition of staff, especially technical consultants, was undertaken only after considerable rapport had been established between the regional centers and the member Bible Societies in the region. At the early stages, despite their UBS label, the regional staff were regarded by most as the handmaidens of the traditional colonial giving societies, primarily the ABS and the BFBS.

The first regional conferences were held in 1967—Africa, Europe, and Asia-Pacific, and in the following year, the Americas. Regional committees were soon formed with eight to ten members, who met once a year to review, supervise, and stimulate the work in the regions, develop regional policies, and encourage the development of new Bible Societies. To each region, a regional secretary was appointed, who was assisted by a number of regional consultants, some of whom lived in different parts of the region. These consultants were appointed for specific functional responsibilities, such as translation, production, fundraising, etc. The question of who appointed the regional secretary and to whom reports should be made remained a matter of controversy for some time.

Winds of Change—Twenty Years After

Bishop Berggrav accepted the task of looking back at the growth of the UBS after ten years of existence; Béguin took up the same task ten years later and gave his article the title "Winds of Change,"[3] which was current at the time. (Harold MacMillan, the British Prime Minister, had first used it about the changes in Africa as nation after nation in that continent achieved independence from colonial rule.) Comparing the two tasks and the two ten-year periods, Béguin accepted Berggrav's judgment, borne out by experience, that the UBS had to show its viability in its first ten years and its identity in the next. The UBS was viable, and it had just about discovered and made clear its identity as a world organization, with a world fellowship, a world translation program, a world budget, a world service with worldwide information, and a world relationship between the churches and the Bible Societies. Béguin made his case in characteristic style: "The UBS was meant to be a world body. It is now becoming truly world representative."

At the beginning of the life of the UBS, three Bible Societies had a Translation Department (BFBS, ABS, NBS). Now there was a complete integration of the translation program throughout the world and within two years, he could report, "a world budget for translation work, to which half a dozen Societies contribute."

Writing on the eve of the Council Meeting in Buck Hill Falls, 1966, he could say of a world budget that for years the takeoff failed, but 1963 gave the start. He saw a natural development from the challenge presented at New Delhi to the World Council of Churches in 1961 by the UBS President to the launching of the "God's Word for a New Age" campaign in 1963 in Japan. This led on inevitably to a world budget:

> For the first time all UBS members have joined in a worldwide undertaking; for the first time there has been a joint program on a world scale; for the first time the possibility of a worldwide planning of efforts, of financial resources, and of men has left the realm of wishful thinking and appeared practical and practicable.

Structures, of course, were not enough. In the sixties, a remarkable change had taken place in the financing of Bible Society work. For some time, the UBS had "been filled with the desire to see the continental European Societies take their full share in the world cause." Apart from the NBS and to a certain extent the Norwegian Bible Society, these continental Societies had taken no responsibility for the cost of overseas work. That was now changing. Béguin set the target for the coming year: "Europe has been called upon to contribute one quarter of the total amount to help those Societies unable alone to meet the cost of the work." The U.S. would contribute half and Britain and the Commonwealth, one quarter.

Of course, money was not the only element to be shared. Béguin pressed for a more international staff and reported some progress already in this. The first regional center had been set up in Mexico for Latin America. A service center was already emerging in Africa. "Service in the cause is no longer the privilege of a few from the West; increasingly it has become the task and responsibility of nationals working for their own country and serving in one worldwide task." The UBS was beginning to find its true identity as the UBS of the world, for the world, and with a world vision and constituency.

This article by the General Secretary appeared in the *UBS Bulletin* for the second quarter, 1966. It was the eve of the celebrations of the 150th Anniversary of the American Bible Society held in New York to be followed by the UBS Council Meeting in Buck Hill Falls. There Béguin, in his annual report, developed this article into a "state of the union" message which showed the strength and confidence of his leadership, not only reporting on what had been done, but pressing forward to a more definite pattern of work.

Towards a Truly International Fellowship

Referring to his "Winds of Change" article and acknowledging the progress made in the past few years, Béguin looked to the future:

Having taken stock of the situation, the task of our present Council consists now in determining the main course of action which should be followed in the forthcoming years in order to make of the Bible Society movement an organism fully and effectively adjusted to the conditions of the world it has to serve.[4]

During an interview in New York some years after this, Béguin looked back over the 25 years of the UBS and defined the period after Buck Hill Falls as the third period of growth. Viability and identity led to maturity. The statement by Béguin to the Council in Buck Hill Falls in 1966 pointed forward to the maturity or adulthood of the UBS. At the Council they were in the process of forming worldwide structures, and he set before them the vision, using the word "truly" repeatedly to show that he saw the danger that committee decisions and even proposed structures could not alone guarantee an international spirit. With detail and with encouragement based upon what had already been achieved in the adolescent years of the UBS, he pressed forward to:

- A truly international structure and outlook
- A truly international service center
- A truly international pattern of planning and administration
- A truly international fellowship

Under each heading, he shrewdly outlined the achievements and hinted at the limitations, but he did not stop there. He described the next step. Under a pattern of planning and administration, for example, he outlined four steps so far taken and added:

Linked with the evolution, I see a fifth step! If some form of regional grouping becomes acceptable for our fellowship, I would submit that regional secretaries should also become responsible to such groups, reporting to them, consulting with them, requesting their suggestions.

They would not need to remain, as they have to be at present, the conveners of the groups; they would rather function as their consultants and advisers, their servants, their deputy spokesmen in the running of current affairs.

He was aware that there were many practical implications of such a view. He also saw as did his audience that he was calling in question the prevailing ideas of authority. It would mean reviewing traditional assumptions governing various phases of the work, such as the relative authority of the general boards and committees of the older Societies. One thing emerged from this part of his report, that more than the structure of the UBS was evolving and gradually changing. A satisfactory pattern of planning and administration was necessary if the new structures were to work for the good of all—the parts as well as the whole.

He was impressive and inspiring in his vision of the future. After almost two decades in the leadership of the UBS, which had achieved more than its founders had dreamed, he spoke with confidence and deliberateness of the point of no return which the Bible Society movement had reached:

The Bible Society movement has reached the point when no one can plan alone on behalf of others and decide on their behalf; when no one either can plan and decide for himself without regard for the opinion and problems of the other. It is together that the work in its indissoluble unity has to be planned, organized and discharged, each one assuming its responsibility and its task within the framework of the collective, reasoned, considered consensus of the whole fellowship. Pluralism offers today the best guarantee for the collective exercise of liberty. In our new age the individualistic freedom of initiative has to be replaced by a collective freedom of decision, which involves the largest possible number of individuals in the discussion and in the decision-making process, and invites the voluntary support of everyone for the collectible choice of the community.[5]

$\diamond$ CHAPTER TEN $\diamond$

The Jewel in the Crown

—— $\diamond$ ——

The history of the UBS showed remarkable growth in organization, skillful structuring, enthusiasm, and world vision. Statistics were impressive. Béguin's phrase, "collective freedom of decision" was becoming a reality. With all this progress, it was necessary to remember that the "product" was of central importance. The whole Bible Society work, nationally and internationally, depended upon the Bible. In one form or another, the Bible was accepted by all the churches of the world as authoritative, uniquely so. There were many different theories of inspiration, but these were not the concern of the Bible Societies. The heart of the matter was to circulate Bibles in a form that truly represented the original Scriptures, accurately translated into languages which were accessible. That was the "jewel in the crown": translation.

If this supreme task of the UBS was to be accomplished, it would be necessary for the various national Bible Societies to cooperate. After much tact and understanding, this had been accomplished. There were still differences of attitude to the deuterocanonical books, but these differences were accommodated. The long separation of the Roman Catholic Church was overcome, although some prejudices remained. At the end of Vatican II, Roman Catholic priests and bishops sought help in translation.

The UBS Committee on Translation

The growing role of the previously named functional group on trans-lations, the Bible Societies throughout the world taking a share in translation more widely than before, the growing need for the UBS to concern itself with this activity and to participate in it as the UBS, and the value perceived in cultivating the churches in this translation work all led to the formation of the UBS committee on translation.

The committee was proposed at the meeting of the UBS Standing Committee in Stuttgart in 1962, commended to member Bible Societies and adopted at the next UBS Council meeting in Hakone in 1963. It was agreed that the following Bible Societies would be permanent members of the committee: ABS, BFBS, NBS, the Bible Societies of India and Ceylon, Norway, and the Philippines.

Nida was at that time Executive Secretary of the Translations De-partment of the ABS and was already playing the major role in UBS stimulated translation work. In 1971, he was appointed UBS World Translations Research Coordinator, a post he held until 1980. The Committee had its functions defined in 1962 as "to arrange for consulta-tions on translation matters between member Societies of the UBS and concerning all types of helps for translators and readers."[1]

The Greek New Testament

Translation began with getting the original text right. A text which could be used by translators all over the world and of all denominations was the objective. In 1955, when the ABS, NBS, and the Württemberg Bible Society set up an international and interdenominational commit-tee of textual scholars to prepare such an edition of the Greek New Testament, it was not possible to involve Roman Catholic scholars. The first edition was published on August 26, 1965 under the imprint of the UBS and the German Bible Society. By that time relations were quite different with the Roman Catholic Church. The second edition appeared in 1968, and Carlo Maria Martini was involved in its prepara-tion. There were only a few textual changes, although significant, but the main difference from the first edition laid in the evaluation of evidence for the variant readings. The third edition, however, was a more thorough revision. These changes were not only due to new developments in New Testament study, but also in numerous recommendations resulting from members of the Committee as they worked with the text of the first edition. Although the Committee now included Roman Catholic scholars, and such were also consulted outside the Committee, it was soon found that there was no difficulty between scholars. When there were differences in the Committee, they hardly ever followed denominational lines. The recommendations coming from experience of working with the first edition came primarily from Kurt Aland, who had been working separately on the twenty-sixth edition of the Nestlé-Aland text. As a result of the Committee discussions, more than 500 changes were made in the third edition of the UBS text. The result was a common text for Nestlé-Aland and UBS. It was published in January 1975, but before that Metzger, on behalf of the Committee, edited A *Textual Commentary on the Greek New Testament* (1971). Subsequent editions of the Greek text appeared in 1982 (a corrected third edition) and October 1992 (fourth edition). Throughout these changes Carlo Maria Martini (now Cardinal Archbishop of Milan) remained on the Committee and gave it his careful attention and the value of his considerable scholarship. Although not on the Committee, Orthodox scholars (Syriac, Coptic, Armenian, Ethiopian, and Georgian) were consulted.

This common text, the most accurate that modern scholarship and church use could prepare, corrected by the prestigious Nestlé-Aland text, was the essential basis for confidence in the translation work of the UBS. Unlike other scholarly texts it was especially constructed for translators, giving variants and assessing their relative merits.[2]

The Translation Consultants and Advisors

After full discussion with the Committee, a pattern of teamwork was agreed. A very pertinent paper which Nida prepared in September 1968 for the translation department of the ABS showed the kind of people he wanted to recruit, and it defined very clearly the role of the translation consultant:

> He or she has two functions: educational and advisory.
> In his educational function he assists translators with their particular

problems; in his advisory function he helps Bible Society administrators to understand some of the complex problems of translation as they are related to other phases of Bible Society programs.

The consultant is a member of a team, because while some are essential linguistic specialists, others may be specialists in biblical languages. No consultant is competent on his own. He works always in a team even if it has only two members! His educational function will involve selecting and training translators, setting up committees, guiding translation committees as they develop principles of procedure, helping to resolve technical problems and to arbitrate between significant differences. He or she will give expert opinion, test the acceptability of translations, prepare the manuscript for the printers, and even arrange for proofreading. His advisory function is in two directions, enabling information and understanding to flow between Bible Societies and translators. Apart from his expertise, the consultant must have a keen intellect, a capacity to communicate, a willingness and a desire to work with all types of Christian people, and a warm personal touch, and a sense of humor, so that he can be empathic with others, but not take himself too seriously.[3]

In addition to translation consultants there were also translation advisors, who exercised a similar function, but who usually were not so highly qualified or had fewer responsibilities. The international character of these consultants and advisors was of importance in the translation work. In every team there were a number of people speaking different languages as their mother tongue and always when the translation was being made into a particular language there was at least one person whose mother tongue was that into which the Bible was being translated. In this way, the team was made fully aware of the cultural factors that play such a large part in arriving at a satisfactory understanding of, and appreciation for, the biblical text.

Translators

The UBS did not impose a translation upon any church or local Bible Society. The translation consultants, however, discovered the need and suggested a translation. Usually the initiative was with the churches or with the Bible Societies in the particular region.

Translation consultants became familiar with their area and they traveled a great deal. During that travel they learned the needs of the area and consulted with Bible Societies and church leaders. Although the translations were done to meet the needs of the churches, the translation itself always belonged to the Bible Society. Whenever possible, the translation was done by translators into their own native language. It was, however, important to select competent translators and in this the translation consultant or advisor had an important role to play. Usually a translation consultant held workshops to discover who was competent to do translation in a particular area.

The number of translators varied enormously in practice. The UBS usually recommended a small group, of three or, at most, five translators, especially in areas where they were set apart to work virtually full-time on the translation. They worked together possibly with a missionary who was an exegete or a local professor at the university who was qualified to explain exegetical terms and the translation of peculiarly difficult Hebrew or Greek phrases.

The team met, and the consultant met with them, visiting from time to time, not only to answer questions and to deal with difficulties, but also to suggest problems that they may not have seen. It was the consultant's task to make clear the issues and see that they are dealt with. But ultimately, the translation was done by the translators. They had to be accepted by the churches to which they belonged.

Institutes for the Training of Translators

Until the early seventies the UBS conducted a number of large institutes for translators lasting a month or even more. Dr. Philip Stine, who later succeeded Heber Peacock in 1984 as translation research coordinator and inter-regional coordinator (title changed in 1988 to translation services coordinator), had a vivid memory of the first of these workshops which he attended. The year was 1968, and the purpose was to see if he was the right man for Nida and if he liked what the UBS was doing. The training institute was held in the Philippines and lasted for four weeks. More than 100 translators came from the Philippines, Thailand, South Pacific, Papua New Guinea, all over Southeast Asia, and the Pacific area. Almost all were engaged in translation—missionaries and indigenous workers. They were at various levels of education and proficiency. Wonderly came from Mexico, and there were others who, like Stine, were being considered for UBS staff: Dr. Barclay Newman and Dr. Daniel Arichea. All eventually joined the staff. These large workshops were scheduled from 1963 until 1973, when the last was held in India.

As the number of consultants grew from thirteen to seventy, a shift to smaller workshops meant that several worked only with four or five languages in the one country. Eventually, frequent workshops were held with no more than one or two languages, and these lasted two or three weeks initially, followed by a period of work in their own translation area and then back again for a further week. These shorter and more frequent workshops had some disadvantages. The larger workshops had been used not only to train translators, but also to train new consultants. Later, triennial consultations were held, and these became opportunities for consultants to broaden their experience.[4]

Version Popular: *God Comes to Man*

Like the King James Version in English and the Luther Bible in German, the Spanish-speaking peoples of the world had their classic translation: the Reina-Valera Bible. A revised version of it was prepared by a committee appointed in 1950. The Spanish language had changed greatly, and some corrections had to be made, but as few as possible. The main changes were additional useful features which made the reading easier—cross references, historical events, and sources of quotations, all at the bottom of the page instead of the customary center column. A concordance was added. Nida told about this revision with evident approval, according to the American Bible Society Record, December 1960: "The intention of the revisers was to produce a revision which will bring a blessing to countless thousands as they discover the power—the Living Christ while reading the pages of the Book of books." For all this, Nida saw the need for a popular version of the Bible in Spanish, not to replace this accepted revision of the classic, but to be used by those who had little schooling.

He noted the way in which the ground had been prepared for this in the work of the revisers: They had made contact with hundreds of groups in Latin America and Spain; pastors and laymen had been involved, marking up their Bibles to show where revision was needed; the committee which organized the revision included four presidents of seminaries and one poet. All knew that, if the Spanish Bible were to reach a wide readership, it would need to be further revised. That could not be done with the classic translation, but there was room for a "common language version." It was produced with the title *Dios Llega al Hombre (God Comes to Man)*. In two years it sold more than two million copies.

It was not long before speakers of other languages in Latin America were asking for a similar version in their own tongue. The first to achieve that were the Aymara of Bolivia. They already had a New Testament in their language, but they wanted one that would "speak as plainly as the Spanish *Version Popular*. Dr. Jacob Loewen, a UBS translations consultant, explained that many Aymara Christians wanted this popular version to share the good news of God with their fellow Aymaras living in Bolivia and Peru. The Bible Societies responded, and the book of Mark was soon produced in popular Aymara. Then they could say in Bolivia, "Now God talks the way we speak." Loewen wrote a lively article for the American Bible Society Record with that title, in which he explained how the Bible Society responded:

> The Bible Society in cooperation with the Commission on Aymara Literacy and Literature at once organized a training program to meet this felt need. At the first meeting in La Paz in September 1967, some thirty representatives of the various evangelical groups in Bolivia met to study the principles of "Common Language" translations. At the second session held in January 1968, translated portions prepared as "home work" by the translators in training were studied and revised.

There were further sessions and many problems, but in the studying and resolving of them they eventually reached their objective: "to make their own New Testament speak to the thousands of Indians on the shores of Lake Titicaca."

The New Testament in Today's English Version

The need for such a version in English was recognized about the same time, although a little later than the Spanish *Version Popular*. It was expressed by the Rev. M. Wendell Below, on the staff of the Home Mission Board of the Southern Baptist Convention. Nida handed the task over to Dr. Robert Bratcher, a Southern Baptist, who was on his translation team at the ABS.

Bratcher began work at once, and early in 1962 he sent a memo to Nida, with the heading, "Random Thoughts on the Nature of a Simple English Version of the New Testament." In it he set out the guiding principles for the translation. A further encouragement came when the ABS published in March 1962, Miss Cressman's simple English version of John with the title, *He Gave His Only Son*, illustrated by John Lear. Both translations by Miss Cressman, Mark and John, were proving popular in Liberia—and elsewhere.

Bratcher completed his tentative version of Mark in September 1963, "in a form of English designated as 'Popular English.'" The ABS Advisory Council was favorably impressed with the samples which they studied and overwhelmingly approved.

On October 16, 1964, Bratcher's Mark was published as *The Right Time* with line drawings by Miss Annie Vallotton, a Swiss artist living in Paris, whom Nida was able to contact. This version was circulated mostly in the U.S., but also abroad, and 600,000 copies were printed.

Even before the publication of *The Right Time* the ABS Translations Committee had enough confidence in the translation to set up a task force to work with Bratcher and complete the whole New Testament.

The New Testament was nonetheless essentially a one-man translation by Bratcher, who completed the last verse of Revelation at 9 A.M. on July 23, 1965. A few weeks later, Nida and Holmgren were in London talking with the BFBS, who were less than enthusiastic about the new translation. Nida and Holmgren had no hesitations about it. Meeting in St. Ermin's Hotel, in London, they agreed to recommend to the translations committee and the Board of Managers that the text should be known as Today's English Version and that the title of the New Testament should be *Good News for Modern Man*. Holmgren personally designed a cover which would have mastheads of English language newspapers throughout the world. There was no disguising their enthusiasm, despite the British hesitation. Back in New York, they found the ABS translations committee also a little cautious. They recommended the publication of the New Testament in Today's English Version, but "on a provisional basis, subject to revision based on comments from scholars and suggestions from those who use it on the field." With this proviso, the ABS Board of Managers approved the publication.

On September 15, 1966, it was published with an initial edition of 150,000 copies. The growth in circulation was prodigious, and within six years from publication, the ABS reported a circulation of 35 million copies.

Helps for Translators

The BFBS was meanwhile following a different line in translation. Its translation department saw the task of the Bible Society to be that of helping translators, not to translate a competitive version. Instead of giving its support to the TEV New Testament, they supported efforts to provide helps for translators and published in a limited edition a series of books dealing with the books of the Bible one by one with a model translation side by side with the Greek text. For its purpose it was valuable, but when the translator's translation of the New Testament was issued for a wider public, it lacked the life of a good version in English. As a Greek-English diglot it was published between 1958 and 1964. When in 1973 it appeared as a Translation on the market it had the UBS Greek New Testament as its base text. *The Bible Translator* at this time carried a section called "Helps for Translators," and it summarized what had been done by 1972:

Helps for Translators

Since 1969 we have published *The Bible Index, The UBS Greek New Testament with Lexicon, A Textual Commentary on the Greek New Testament,* and *A Translator's Handbook on Luke.* The following items are in press: *A Translator's Handbook on Acts, A Translator's Handbook on the Johannine Epistles,* and *A Translator's Handbook on Romans.*

In 1972 *The Bible Translator* was converted into two new series—a technical series (issues 1 and 3, January and July) intended primarily for the publication of articles of a technical nature; and a practical series (issues 2 and 4, April and October), appearing in a new red cover, for the publication of articles of a more practical nature.

In 1970 a new position was created: UBS translations research coordinator. Dr. Eugene A. Nida was appointed to this task. His responsibility as translations research coordinator is to coordinate the overall preparation of Helps for Translators, and in this capacity he works in cooperation with the Subcommittee on Helps.

A very extensive range of Helps for Translators is in course of preparation or is being planned. The growing series of Translators' Handbooks will soon include *Ruth, John, Philippians, Galatians,* and other books. Of particular interest to Old Testament translators is the preparation of a special Help on problematical passages, in which some 3,000 passages are being evaluated in order to assist translators in making choices toward the best possible renderings. The Old Testament Textual Committee has met for three consecutive summers, and it is hoped that they will be able to complete their work in about three more years. The result of their work will not be to produce a new edition of the Hebrew text, but rather to provide several books of both a practical and technical nature.

Of significant interest is the preparation of a *Greek New Testament Wordbook* for translators under the direction of the UBS Sub-Committee on Helps. Professor Johannes P. Louw, Dr. Eugene A. Nida, and Professor Rondal B. Smith have succeeded in classifying approximately 15,000 different meanings in 700 basic semantic domains. The purpose of this Wordbook is to provide translators with a more usable tool based upon lexicographical principles and procedures which will produce more accurate information concerning the meanings of Greek terms and their relations to each other than has ever been done in any other Greek dictionary. It is estimated that it will take approximately five years to complete this project.[5]

In fact, the project was completed in five years, and many of the things which were suggested in the 1973 report were fulfilled. For example, the translators' handbook for each book in the Bible was completed.

Writing in 1995, Nida listed the steps by which the UBS had accomplished so much in the field of translation. Those accomplishments are enormous and continue to grow. Looking into the future, he said,

Elfinsward Conference House in Haywards Heath, England, where the United Bible Societies was founded on May 9, 1946.

The decisive meeting in New York, 1949, with Rev. Dr. William Platt (middle row, far left) and Rev. Dr. Olivier Béguin (last row, second from the right).

Rev. Dr. Eric M. North, General Secretary of the American Bible Society, (1927–1957) and Chairman of the UBS Council (1949–1954).

Bishop Eivind Berggrav, first President of the United Bible Societies, (1949–1957).

Rev. Dr. Olivier Béguin (left) the longest serving General Secretary of the United Bible Societies (1949–1972) speaking with Rev. Canon Arrowsmith, General Secretary in Australia (1951–1967), and Chairman of the UBS Council (1959–1963).

Two eager students from Thailand reading the special Student's Edition of the Good News Bible.

Dr. Eugene Nida, architect of the UBS translation policy.

Mr. Bernard Tattersall, General Secretary for Administration of the BFBS (1966–1978), and joint Treasurer of the UBS (London office).

Translation Consultants at the important Winneba Conference in 1963.

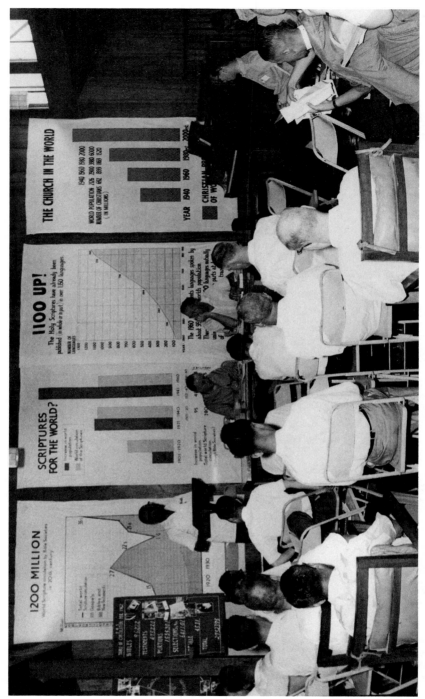

Asia General Secretaries at a conference in Manila, Philippines, May 1963.

The UBS President, the Rt. Rev. Donald Coggan, later Archbishop of Canterbury, with Dr. Billy Graham, at the 150th Anniversary of the American Bible Society, May 1966.

Rev. Dr. Laton E. Holmgren, General Secretary of the American Bible Society (1955–1978), Chairman of the UBS Council and Executive Committee, and a main architect of the UBS in its early years.

Mr. Charles Baas, Treasurer of the American Bible Society and joint Treasurer of the UBS (New York office).

The Bible Society in action in South America, with "Las Buenas Nuevas" (Good News).

Rev. Dr. Ulrich Fick, UBS General Secretary (1973–1988) successor to Rev. Dr. Olivier Béguin.

Baron van Tuyll van Serooskerken, General Secretary of the Netherlands Bible Society (1950–1975) and Chairman of UBS Council (1960–1963).

Rev. John T. Mpaayei, General Secretary of the Bible Society of Kenya (1964–1971) and Chairman of UBS Council (1980–1984).

The UBS Council meeting held in Addis Ababa, Ethiopia, in 1972. The UBS President, Rt. Rev. Donald Coggan with the Emperor of Ethiopia, Haile Selassie I. The Council theme was "Let the Word Speak."

A short drama at the UBS Council meeting in Addis Ababa, Ethiopia, 1972.

Rev. Dr. Ulrich Fick, General Secretary of the UBS, talking with two Presidents, outgoing Rt. Rev. Donald Coggan (1957–1976) and incoming Rev. Oswald Hoffmann, right (1976–1988).

From left to right: Rev. Dr. Ulrich Fick, Rt. Rev. Donald Coggan, Rev. Dr. Oswald Hoffmann, Rev. Dr. A. E. Inbanathan, Rev. James R. Payne, and Rev. Dr. Kenneth McMillan.

Rev. Dr. Ulrich Fick in China, on the opening of the Amity Printing Press, September 1987.

Delighted faces at the success of the Amity Press: Rev. James Payne, Chairman of UBS Executive Committee (left) with Bishop K. H. Ting, President, China Christian Council and Amity Foundation.

Rev. Dr. Cirilos Rigos, General Secretary of UBS (1988–1990) at the dedication of the UBS World Service Center, Reading, England, 1990.

Rev. Dr. John D. Erickson, General Secretary of the UBS (1991–present).

Rev. Dr. Cirilos Rigos, from the Philippines, appointed UBS General Secretary at the Budapest Council meeting, successor to Rev. Dr. Ulrich Fick.

Delegates at the UBS Council in Budapest in 1988. The theme was "God's Word: Hope for All."

"Helps for Readers will occupy more and more attention, because this is the area of Bible Society work that is so important in those parts of the world where there are few Christians or where the Christian leadership is either limited in its academic preparation or has so few helps that can be provided to believers.[6]

CHAPTER ELEVEN

The General Secretary

———— ◇ ————

The progress of the United Bible Societies from a fledgling cooperative venture to a highly structured world organization owed much to outstanding Christian leaders who brought their talents and their special gifts to the service of Bible work. The roll call is impressive—North, Wilkinson, Berggrav, Rutgers, Nida, Coggan, Platt, and Holmgren, to mention only some of the notable figures who came and stayed with the UBS. Many others came for shorter periods and exerted their influence. But the pilot of the waterways was always the senior executive who lived UBS day and night: Temple, Béguin, and Ulrich Fick, to take the story into the seventies. The UBS had been very fortunate in the caliber and the devotion of its General Secretary.

John Temple

Wilkinson, who with North and Temple may be called the founding fathers of the UBS, worked with John Temple in the BFBS for seventeen years. He learned much from him and observed at close range the quality of his work. Assessing his character, Wilkinson wrote:

His ability was great and his work will stand the test of time, but his personality was greater. His finest work was done through his personal contacts. He could win the affection and respect of others more quickly than any other I have known. He had a genius for friendship, which he used not as a mere means of increasing the number of his friends, but of gaining them for the service of the Lord. His face revealed the strength of his character; you could read both kindness of heart and shrewdNess of judgment in his eyes; his voice conveyed sympathy. The sorrows of others distressed him for he had a very warm heart. I fell under his charm as soon as we met.

The epic decisions that were made in 1932 in London with Wilkinson and North owed much to the contribution of Temple's personality. It was North's opinion that without Temple, the application of the London Conference agreements regarding joint agencies would have been impossible. He embraced with enthusiasm the new concept of cooperation in Bible Society work which eventually brought forth the UBS. This could not have succeeded without friendship between the Societies, and here his genius had full range. There were old rivalries and antagonisms to be forgotten. Although very proud of his own BFBS, he never allowed its interests to impede the wider interests of Bible Society work as a whole. He strove to understand the differing viewpoints of the other Bible Societies and patiently expounded his own. North often told of what he called the "joyful journey" which he and Temple took after the London Conference to the Middle East, in order to establish the new joint agencies from Sudan to Bulgaria. After years of competition and disagreements between ABS and BFBS in the various regions, it was a matter of considerable astonishment to the missionaries and the Bible Society staff in the area to see the two General Secretaries, one from London, one from New York, happily traveling together in full concord on policies governing program and procedure. North always chuckled as he told of this journey. During the war that held up the formation of the UBS, Temple found scope for his gift of friendship among members of the refugee governments in London. He was honored by the King of Norway and the Queen of the Netherlands for his work among refugees from these two countries. At the conference which formed the UBS after the war, in "Elfinsward," he was unanimously invited to become its first General Secretary without relinquishing his position as BFBS General Secretary. He accepted, despite the extra burden it placed upon him, and at a time when he was suffering from a very serious duodenal ulcer. Wilkinson's assessment of him concluded with an explanation of the source of his undoubted strength:

> I have known men of greater endowment who accomplished far less. What then was the secret of his success? From youth he had consecrated his heart, mind, and will to his Lord. That consecration unified his powers and made him a dynamic personality.[1]

In 1949 when Platt was arguing for the continuance of the United Bible Societies with no decrease in its budget or its staff, he paid tribute to Wilkinson in London and North in New York, as well as to the role the National Bible Society of Scotland and the Netherlands Bible Society had played in the formation of the United Bible Societies. And then he added:

> With the coming of Dr. Temple into this widening circle of Bible Society relationships and especially into the development of the joint work, the planning and the setting up of the United Bible Societies, his own particular gifts and spiritual insights were an added asset to what was truly a great conception. The impact upon world Christian leaders in the setting up of the United Bible Societies has been such as never could have been achieved by a procedure which might have aimed only at increased efficiency or wider cooperation. On this subject the testimony of Bishop Berggrav to Temple's industry, insight and vision is eloquent. It was largely this world conception that made a man of Bishop Berggrav's caliber and influence decide to come into this work and to give it a very prominent place in his interest and activity.[2]

John Temple's Last Journey

After the Council Meeting in Dunblane, Temple prepared for a visit to China and Japan. He was not well, and his duodenal ulcer was causing trouble, accentuated by overwork. Wilkinson did not want him to go, but it was what Temple wanted. "I knew he was taking a risk,"

Wilkinson reported, "but he was convinced that it was God's will, and one cannot argue against that conviction." When Temple saw a work to be done, he could be careless of his health. "He hated the thought of the enforced idleness of old age," Wilkinson said, "preferring to 'die in harness.'"

He first visited Japan, where he shared the excitement of Bible Society work and the successful evangelism of Kagawa. After leaving Japan, he wrote to his son, James Temple, from Shanghai on October 6, 1948. The letter was one of encouragement and sympathy. James was going through a difficult period at that time, and it looked as though he would have to cut short his time at Cambridge. All of this he wrote about and also conveyed the excitement of his mission:

> My visit to Japan was most cheering, in fact it was inspiring. The Church is faced with a wonderful opportunity. Thousands of people are asking wistfully if Christ can save them. The Japan Bible Society had a three year plan, beginning in 1949, to produce and distribute ten million Scriptures. When I told General McArthur of this plan, he said, "that is magnificent, magnificent! The Bible is the essential book for the moral and spiritual recovery of Japan." I was cheered also by the things Kagawa told me of the response of the people to his message. Everywhere he goes, great crowds gather to hear the 'Good News' and about 165,000 people have signed decision cards at his meetings during the last two years.

The tone of the letter was so full of hope, that although he commented upon the political situation in China, there was no reference to his health. His strenuous journey so far must have affected his duodenal ulcer, and the crucial decisions he had to make in China would not have helped. But there was no mention of this in the letter. His only concerns were for China and its future government:

> Life in Shanghai at present is very exciting. No one knows what is going to happen, but it seems that Chang Kai Shek's government is tottering and about to fall. Will the Communists gain the whole of China or is there an alternative to the present Government which will be formed to stop them is a question no one can answer. There is great fear and dread in the minds of many.[3]

Such matters occupied his thoughts far more than his own indifferent health. He ended his letter with an expectation of reaching Tilbury, England, by December 27, and seeing his family again for what was left of the Christmas holidays. Throughout October he continued to work and travel in China. His base was Shanghai where there were rice riots. In November he took a Japanese boat to Hong Kong, but because of the riots, the boat did not take on enough food for the passengers. This accentuated the duodenal ulcer, which was already causing trouble. On arrival in Hong Kong, he was taken to the hospital in very poor condition and shortly afterwards died of a coronary thrombosis on November 30, 1948. The saying, "Man is immortal till his work in done," applied only to the great. Wilkinson thought it was essentially true for John Temple: "He could have gone on doing useful work, but his main work was done."

Olivier Béguin

The death of Temple was a shock to the UBS, which was too young to have any plans for a successor. Looking back, it was obvious that the man most prepared to carry on Temple's work was Béguin. He had full knowledge of the workings of UBS from "Elfinsward" onwards and although he was not in a senior position in any major Bible Society, he had worked with the American Bible Society as their representative in Europe during World War II. Temple's death was a shock to him too. He had worked closely with him and certainly did not feel ready to succeed him yet. One of his comments, on hearing the news of Temple's death was "he has died too soon." Many would have echoed that comment, but for Béguin it had a special meaning. He knew that he was the obvious successor, but he was just thirty-four and had been little more than two years working for the UBS in the Geneva office. When he was appointed, he was ready and saw more clearly than anyone, except perhaps Eric North, the way that the UBS needed to take into the future.

Béguin was born in Neuchâtel, Switzerland in 1914. His Swiss origins had certain advantages which became evident in his work. In both wars, his country had been neutral and served those in need on both sides of the conflict. This had enabled him to do much for Bible distribution during World War II and be more acceptable in camps of all kinds after the war. As a Swiss national, he was also able to be objective about differences arising in the growing together of the Bible Societies. He had no imperial pretensions. In the struggles between the BFBS and the ABS, he was a mere observer and remained neutral. In the early years of the UBS, that was a valuable asset. Within that framework, he had experiences to bring which few could match. He was European in culture but not the defender of any national tradition. He was French in his mother tongue, but had mastered English and German with knowledge of other European languages. He acquired a world view easily, and when eventually he went to Asia or Africa he had no sense of Western superiority. One small example was that he treated an African or an Asian as equal in every sense. Britons and Americans tried to do this and often succeeded, but Béguin did not have to try. When a man addressed him as "Mr." he returned the respect by calling him "Mr." and only used the Christian name to those who called him "Olivier." That was no small thing in the difficult and often sensitive relationships between the West and those of the so-called Third World, who had been under British or American colonial domination.

The Making of a General Secretary

Béguin was early involved in the ecumenical movement which had strong support in the World Student Christian Federation and the various national Student Christian Movements. He was a member of the WSCF and there met W. A. Visser 't Hooft.

When Béguin left university he went to England to learn English and later, Visser 't Hooft recommended him to the household of Reinhold von Thadden-Trieglaff to assist him in the study of German and to act as tutor to von Thadden's sons. That introduction and the year he spent in the Pomeranian household of the von Thaddens prepared him for his future task in a very special way. Once the UBS was founded, Germany became one of the priorities. Berggrav, looking back, wondered if that had been wise, but at the time it was clear. Anyone who was to do Christian work in Germany after the war had to know about the "church struggle" and how Christians had coped with the demands of National Socialism. There was no better school for this than the Pomeranian lands of the great Junker families. The Church of the old Prussian Union provided the heart of the struggle against those German Christians who had accepted the tenets of Nazism and supported "the monstrous tyranny." Reinhold von Thadden-Trieglaff was involved in every aspect of the Confessing Church of the old Prussian Union, holding more offices than one could imagine possible. He was committed to the resistance to Hitler, made chairman of the German Student Christian Movement until it was dissolved by Himmler in 1938, and arrested and imprisoned more than once. He served in the German army, largely as an agricultural adviser in Brittany and Belgium, and after the war founded the Evangelical Kirchentag. Béguin was part of that household for the crucial period of 1938–1939. It was not only the German language that he learned in that school.

When the Ecumenical Youth Conference was held in Amsterdam in 1939, Béguin was chosen by Visser 't Hooft for his leadership potential. He was twenty-five, vigorous, and acute in mind. Physically, he was tall and strong, but not aggressive. His smile could disarm any who were ready for conflict. This was not to say that he was always conciliatory. He had firm ideas and was ready to take in and consider new thoughts, but once he had made up his mind he could be persuasive and persistent to the point of obstinacy. It was at the youth conference in 1939 that he met Agnes, a representative of the students of Hungary. The conference was short, and Olivier fell in love. Within three days, he proposed marriage to her.

The Family Man

Béguin was called up for army service, as were all Swiss males who were not exempted by their profession. It was usually understood that a Swiss soldier should not leave the country during this service, but Béguin persuaded his seniors that he needed to go to Hungary. He was able to visit Agnes' family in Hungary in January 1940. Her father's comment on meeting him for the first time was, "He doesn't look like a man who would propose marriage within three days." Beguin retained that ability to hide his feelings.

They were married during the war, in Hungary, September 1941. They had three children, Pierre-Michel, John, and Anne. All three children were born in Geneva where they made their home. Béguin's main task was with the WCC (in process of formation) where he had responsibility for service to prisoners of war. Agnes had to adapt to a new culture and a new language as she brought up her family. It was not easy to do this, but she did not then know that there would eventually be a more difficult change yet to come. When Béguin was appointed UBS Associate General Secretary, supervising the work in Europe, they could still live in Geneva. But his appointment as General Secretary to the UBS in succession to Temple meant a move to London. In September 1949, the UBS Central Office was in London, and there was no inclination to move it to Geneva. At first, Béguin had to come alone to a strange London, which was not the most friendly city in the world.

Agnes's father was ill in Hungary and came to live with them in Geneva. He could neither be left nor taken to London, which meant a painful separation for Olivier and Agnes. Agnes's father died in the January of 1950, and the following month she came with three small children to Barnet, north London. It was a difficult move, a new language, and a new cultural environment. London in 1950 had its own problems with rationing of food still in force. The nation was tired after a grueling war and in no mood to be hospitable to foreigners. The children were Swiss and found the English schools alien.

Against this background, Béguin took up his new task, so very different from the continent of Europe where he moved about with confidence. It was part of his character that he undertook the leadership of the UBS without revealing the family struggle that beset his private life.

Béguin took up the torch of Temple and carried it into the future in ways that Temple had never dreamed of. One example of his early realization of the world potential of the UBS was at the Standing Committee at Sarpsborg, Norway in June 1951, which was preparing for the first meeting of the Council in Asia:

The UBS is still very European-minded. I believe that this is a weakness. The very fact that next year we shall meet in Asia will help to throw a brighter light on other problems which should not leave the UBS indifferent. I believe it was necessary to begin with Europe. Now that the reveille has been sounded, it is important to turn our attention, and the attention of those who are preparing to give their help, towards strategic points to which our common action should be actively and effectively directed. This is a new move and we hope that the years to come will allow us to make it. We would ask God to lead us into it together by his Holy Spirit.[4]

That was not much more than a year after the family had moved into Barnet.

A Quarter of a Century

From 1946 when Béguin and Visser 't Hooft represented the WCC at "Elfinsward" until 1971 when at the Aurora meeting in Canada it became noticeable that Béguin was unwell, he was involved in the UBS for a quarter of a century, half the time covered by the Jubilee, which this volume celebrates. Holmgren, who worked very closely with Béguin over a large part of that time, expressed clearly the role he played in the history of the UBS and conveyed what everyone felt in his last days: "Olivier Béguin has been the master builder of the United Bible Societies as we know it today (1972), an achievement of extraordinary significance for the whole world mission of the Church of Jesus Christ in our time."

But he also added from his memory of long hours with Béguin, a portrait of him which, although brief, perfectly depicted the man:

. . . that solid, good-humoured, dynamic, purposeful man of God whom we knew and loved across the years, whose comprehension of and commitment to the Bible cause was astonishing—and inspiring! Those of us who were often with him in the long hours of preparation for conferences and councils probably never realized the full measure of his greatness, so disarming was his friendly humility.

Béguin had been ill for a long time, bearing the pain of cancer for at least four years before he gave in.

The Last Months

Although seriously ill, he put his energy into the third phase of "God's Word for a New Age," which the General Committee named "Serving the Seventies." He defined the ground on which the campaign would stand or fall. He saw this as two sides of a coin and would let no member of councils or conferences forget that they were committed:

> Actual personal participation in passing the Book from hand to hand, from person to person, and in commending it and helping in its effective use by one's own witnessing word is one side of the coin. The other side is effective support by way of interest, prayer, and money for the worldwide enterprise of the Bible Society movement.

The year was 1970. In that year, he met with the Executive Committee in Canberra in February and in Vienna in September, still clearing the work that had to be done to implement the decisions taken at the momentous meetings of the sixties. Then he had an interim meeting with the chairman, vice-chairman, and European members only in Paris in April of the next year. Only a few of those nearest to him saw the creeping effect of his illness, but by the time the committee met in Aurora, Toronto, it could no longer be concealed. He was evidently seriously ill. At that last meeting he attended, the initial plans for holding a UBS World Assembly in Africa, in the fall of 1972, were agreed upon. He was not to see it. He did, however, see one thing decided for which he had worked: The four Regional Centers were established and the two former administering centers in London and New York were transformed into consultative centers and were later renamed as World Service Centers. Rev. W. A. Hutchinson, General Secretary of the ABS (1969–1977), and Rev. J. G. Weller, General Secretary (Overseas) of the BFBS (1968–1973) were appointed as UBS World Service Officers to coordinate and supervise the new structure. They were given overall responsibility for administering the World Service Budget in their respective regions—Hutchinson handling the Americas and Asia-Pacific and Weller dealing with Africa and Europe. On return to London Béguin entered the hospital where a few months later he died April 1, 1972. It was Easter Eve.

A special issue of the *UBS Bulletin* (fourth quarter, 1972) consisting of tributes from world Bible Society leaders was devoted to the memory of Olivier Béguin, and an Olivier Béguin Memorial Fund was established for the distribution of the new translation in Hungary. In addition, the Bible Society in Australia established an annual endowed lectureship titled the "Olivier Béguin Lectures" designed to increase interest in and support of the Bible cause in Australia and throughout the world.

CHAPTER TWELVE

The Growth of a
Regional Structure

———— ◇ ————

Ulrich Fick

About the time when the conference at "Elfinsward" was giving birth to the UBS, a young German prisoner of war was reading a New Testament provided by the American Bible Society through the agency of Béguin. Without knowing it, Ulrich Fick was making his first contact with the UBS, in process of formation. That New Testament changed his attitude toward life from despair to hope. It also led him to discover his talents as a communicator and sowed the seeds of a ministry of the Word. When he was released, he decided upon the ministry as his life work and applied to his home church, the Lutheran Church of Württemberg. He began his theological studies almost at once. He was able to pay for this from a bonus of 3,000 *Reich* marks which he received for his war services, made up of grants for specific activities. This was helpful at first, but when the Currency Reform came in 1948, his old money lost its value. There was then the need to earn something, and he found work with *Christ und Welt* program of the *Süddeutschen Rundfunk* (the radio station in his region). At first he had to miss a semester to do this, but with enough money earned from broadcasting, he continued his studies. One of the major influences was the very popular preacher Helmut Thielicke. His companion in broadcasting who helped him to get the job was Jörg Zink, who became one of Germany's most popular broadcasters and writer of devotional books. Fick was ordained in 1952. It was not long before he combined his radio experience with his ministry. In 1956, he became the "radio pastor" of his Church. When the Lutheran World Federation won the franchise for an international radio transmitter in Addis Ababa and shared support with the World Association for Christian Communication, Sigurd Aske of Norway, who was the director of the new station (Radio Voice of the Gospel), began to gather highly experienced staff from many parts of the world. He saw in the Rev. Ulrich Fick a man well equipped for the task of program director. Fick was appointed in 1961. He served for six years and raised the standard of radio programming to a professional level. This gave Fick an international exposure from which he learned much about countries throughout Asia and Africa.

When he returned to Germany in 1967, Fick was put in charge of a department of his church of Württemberg, with responsibility for missions, ecumenical relations, church and society, and public relations. He was appointed an *Oberkirchenrat* of the Church. He became chairman of *Dienste in Ubersee* (Overseas Aid) of the Federation of Protestant Churches in Germany (EKD).

As a senior churchman with special experience in many fields and a concern for Bible Society work, he was elected chairman of the Württemberg Bible Society, which for many years had been responsible for the production of the Hebrew and Greek texts of the Bible and scholarly helps. Fick was sensitive to the historical significance of his own Bible Society, which was one of the founder members of the *Verband,* to which most German Bible Societies now belonged. As chairman of the Württemberg Bible Society, Fick helped these other Societies to come into closer cooperation until eventually they united in the German Bible Society. He developed special interest in translation and was soon appointed a member and later chairman of the UBS Europe Region Translations Committee.

In 1972 he was appointed acting chairman of the Bible work of the Federation of German Churches (Evangelisches Bibelwerk). He had all the qualifications and interest to make him a good successor to Béguin.

In Addis Ababa, the Executive Committee took the step which was decisively to affect the immediate future of the UBS. The nomination of Oberkirchenrat Ulrich Fick as General Secretary of the United Bible Societies was approved. The resolution was adopted unanimously first by the Executive Committee and then by the General Committee. It had earlier been referred to all UBS member Societies with his curriculum vitae and had received unanimous endorsement. Fick accepted the invitation, but asked to be allowed to postpone the effective date of his appointment as UBS Secretary to January 1, 1973, because his Bishop had requested him to remain at his present post for the balance of 1972.

Program for the Decade

Fick had said of the Assembly that it provided a program for the next ten years and this soon became evident. The theme of the Assembly was "Let the Word Speak." The implication was that the content of the Bible must be heard and understood. This put the emphasis on translation in the widest sense of the word. Once again the call was for service to new readers. When the "God's Word for a New Age" campaign entered its second phase, the words, "A Book for New Readers" were added to the original slogan. Holmgren showed his broad interpretation of this phrase earlier when he spoke to the Asia-Pacific Regional Conference in Bangkok in November 1967:

Who is the "new reader?" He is a new literate; he is an elementary school child or a high school dropout; he is a man at the shop or a man at the desk; he is a man with his family and a man without a friend; he is a man at home and a man with no place to lay his head; he is a wealthy landowner and he is a migrant worker; he is a retarded child and he is a professor of nuclear physics; he is a new citizen and he is a man in the services; he is a hospital patient and he is a prison inmate. He is a man who is blind, a man who is starving. He is every man everywhere in need of the reconciling love of God as revealed through Jesus Christ our Lord.[1]

To Holmgren he was, in fact, anyone who did not read the Bible. "If he does not have a copy, we must see that he has one." But the Bible

Societies had a responsibility to see also that if he has a copy, he opens it and can understand what he reads. It was the task of the churches to interpret the Bible, but the Bible Societies had to do all they could to help the new reader understand what he reads.

The World Assembly concentrated on those emerging from illiteracy—those who as a result of the widespread literacy campaigns were beginning to read for the first time. The Assembly asked the vital question, "What shall they read?" The Council Meeting, following the Assembly in Addis Ababa set its goal—500 million Scriptures annually.

There was some uncertainty about the wisdom of retaining one slogan for the decade, but no uncertainty about the vital need for partnership with the churches. Bible Societies may sometimes have to pioneer, but there was to be no doubt in any mind that Scripture distribution is primarily and most effectively achieved through the Christian community. To this end, churches had to be encouraged and church members trained in Scripture distribution.

By now the Bible Societies had overcome their reluctance to step outside the mere provision of the text and knew that they had a larger responsibility, namely to provide "helps to readers" (as the Driebergen conference had strongly urged eight years earlier). The Council was prepared to go further than the "Guiding Principles" agreed with the Roman Catholic Church. The World Service Officers specified the need for introductions to all new publications of Bibles, New Testaments and Portions, especially in common language versions, indicating the historical setting and content of each book and relating it to the context of the readers. Such introductions would, of course, be prepared in consultation with the translations consultants concerned. There was, however, the warning that doctrinal note or comment must be avoided.[2]

Mass Media

Among the "new, perhaps risky, experimental, not yet tested" ideas which the General Secretary brought to his first Executive Committee meeting in Teheran, March 1973, was a proposal for a series of workshops, exploring the "translation of the Bible into the language of the media." Bible Societies had used the media in different ways. Bible passages had been recorded for the blind on cassettes or open tape.

One ingenious method for new translations in areas that had no electric power or easy access to batteries was the "fingerfone." The passage was recorded onto a small disc and power provided by the rotating finger. It was not much use for a Mozart Quartet, but it spoke the language of the people, even though the speed varied with the strength of the finger. Other methods had been used by different societies and, of course, the larger societies were able to produce films of Bible use and the influence of the Bible for promotional meetings. The Canadian Bible Society produced some highly professional films and within the UBS family made them available to Bible Societies for fundraising. What was now proposed was different. It was a translation project.

As a postliterate generation arose (the end of the Gutenberg era, as Marshall MacLuhan said) when many people were receiving information not from print but from radio and/or television, it was necessary to communicate the message of the Bible in ways other than print. Fick proposed workshops at which Bible Societies, translations consultants, and media people would work together in different regions to explore the possibility of translating the Bible into the language of the media. This proposal was not at first received too enthusiastically. The cost was considered, and only when Evangelisches Bibelwerk, of which Fick had been chairman, offered to provide 50,000 deutsche marks for the project was it accepted. Eventually workshops were held in Taiwan, Switzerland, and Australia.

They came to some very significant conclusions as to the limitations as well as the possibilities of the various media used—radio, video, television, cartoon, etc. After these three workshops, little was done, and the matter left as "unfinished business" which was taken up again twenty years later by the ABS Translation Department.

The Ethiopian Official

It was inevitable in Addis Ababa that the story of Philip and the Ethiopian Official, found in Acts 8:26–40, would figure prominently throughout Assembly and Council Meeting.

After the World Service Officers had presented the program as they saw it emerging from the Assembly, Fick contented himself with expounding Acts 8. As the Ethiopian court official returned to his home situation, Fick reminded the Council, he had amazingly little to help him build upon his first encounter with Christ through the ministry of Philip, "no gospels, no Christian friends, no pastor, no blueprint for reshaping the administration, no written report." He did have, however, the knowledge that "he belonged to Christ, having been accepted without being acceptable; the confirmation of this knowledge through the sign of baptism and the key to the Scriptures—knowledge of Christ shown to him from the book of Isaiah." Fick concluded that none of the delegates was as "poor" as the Ethiopian official. Each one of the delegates at the Assembly had something to be happy about, something to give and Someone to present to his people, and "go on his way rejoicing."[3]

The Relocation of the UBS General Office

Soon after Fick's appointment, private discussions began about the possible relocation of the UBS General Office. At the Executive Committee in Teheran, in March 1973, Fick raised the question. "The location of the headquarters had to be seen in the overall context of the global and regional structure of the UBS; (but) it was not yet possible to bring any proposal concerning this." Fick had, in fact, intimated that he wanted to bring this matter up, but was clearly not yet ready. It was, however, presented as a firm proposal at the Executive Committee meeting in Brasilia in September of that year. Fick had circulated a paper in advance, and it made out his case for relocating the UBS office in Stuttgart. He maintained that there he could more easily obtain the necessary staff to run a small office; that he could not at present move his family from Stuttgart (he was married with four children); that it was by no means evident that the UBS office needed to be in close proximity to the World Service Office in London or New York, and world communications would not be adversely affected by the move. He proposed that if the main UBS office moved to Stuttgart, the Europe Regional Translations coordinator could be accommodated at the BFBS in Queen Victoria Street, London, and be based at the World Service Center related to Europe. His proposal was to move as soon as possible after December 24, 1973.

There was a very frank discussion by the Committee, but even those who spoke against the move expressed their sympathy for Fick's personal situation. Nevertheless, they urged a different solution. The main line of objection was based upon the assumption that the UBS General Office had to serve as a coordinating agency through the Regional Centers, World Service Centers and World Service Officers. This meant a well staffed permanent headquarters located in close proximity to a World Service Center. Fick, however, sensed the growing power of Germany in a way that the Executive Committee did not. Dr. Hans Florin, at that time chairman of the Europe Regional Committee, raised an unexpected objection—whether location in Stuttgart might create difficulties due to Germany's past history in Europe. The committee did not think this would be a factor. The proposal was that "authorization be given for the removal of the UBS headquarters office from London to Stuttgart as soon as practicable, and that the situation be reviewed in three years time." It was passed by a majority vote, but there were still some misgivings. Only the Rev. J. R. Payne of Australia voted against the proposal, but three members abstained, and it was carried by the four who voted in favor.[4]

A New Chapter

With the appointment of a new General Secretary, it was obvious that a new chapter was about to open in the history of the UBS. The proposal to move the headquarters to Germany signaled this in a very positive way. At the same time, 1972 was a year of many changes in the officers of the UBS. The UBS Council had not met since 1966, but since then the Executive Committee had met thirteen times. As its chairman Holmgren was unrivaled. He always listened carefully and sympathetically to various points of view and then summarized the discussion showing respect for all those interventions no matter how trivial, and he then put before the committee a proposal for consensus which ensured the best decision.

Outside the committee, as well as in, he had a mastery of the English language, and his powerful way of using it to persuasive effect was impressive, both in writing and in speaking. He used it with elegance, style, pace, rhythm, and humor. Nobody has been more effective as an advocate for the Bible cause and he had done this at the highest level of ecclesiastical diplomacy. His contribution to the UBS during this whole period was notable. At Addis Ababa he was succeeded by Inbanathan of India. But Holmgren's influence on the UBS did not cease. He remained an active member of the General and Executive committees until his retirement as ABS General Secretary in 1978 and thereafter as the official consultant to the UBS Executive Committee for ten years more. Without doubt he exercised a considerable influence on the development of UBS policies and programs over a period of twenty-five years from 1963 to 1988.

He came to the ABS at a time when the UBS was only six years old, and the dominant influence in its progress was shared between Béguin and North. In 1952, when Holmgren joined the staff of the ABS and came strongly under North's influence, Temple had established good understanding with North and the ABS, but he was gone and the main link was now with Platt, a very different person from Temple. Platt believed in the UBS and argued for it in the offices of the BFBS after Temple died, but he did not have Temple's unbounding enthusiasm for it nor the openness that saw no threat from America.

While ABS General Secretary, Holmgren continued to involve the BFBS in the work of the UBS, but he met some disappointments in the seventies when the BFBS concentrated on the home front. Although the Rev. Neville Cryer had been appointed general director of BFBS Home Services as early as September 1970, he did not go to Addis Ababa, because it seemed not to be a priority. He served on no UBS committee until 1976, when he was appointed to the UBS General Committee as one of the two representatives from the Europe region. There he argued for the autonomy of the Bible Society in a changing world. Holmgren attempted to persuade him into a more positive attitude toward the UBS and partially succeeded. It must, however, be admitted that Cryer was worried and suspicious about the American dominance in the UBS. The tradition of North-Holmgren, which consistently led the UBS, modified and directed at times by Béguin, had a long history (1946–1988), to say nothing of the outstanding leadership given by Nida and Baas. In the face of this, the BFBS was showing a certain isolationist tendency and Rev. Dr. Tom Houston, Cryer's partner, although giving full support to the Good News Bible was more deeply concerned with the conversion of England and moved the BFBS to become "The Bible Society."

At this time, Cryer began to interest himself in the work overseas, while Houston was very much concerned with the promotion of the Bible in England. Houston brought enthusiasm and competence to the task of increasing circulation and also contributions to the Bible Society.

Regional Organization

By the time Fick became General Secretary, the regional organization worked out at Buck Hill Falls in 1966 was largely operative. That Council provided for four Regional Conferences—Africa, the Americas, Asia-South Pacific and Europe—each of which would meet regularly to "review and consult on all subjects of common interest in the region," and "to consider the best ways of implementing in the region the recommendations of the General Committee or the Executive Committee."

The unity of the UBS was preserved through the Council, which was the ultimate decision-making body. Each member Society sent a voting representative to the UBS Council meeting, which at this time was to be held every six years. Thus, after the Council meeting at Buck Hill Falls in 1966, the next was at Addis Ababa in 1972. This was later changed to eight years. Fick had to wait until 1980 before appearing before the next Council meeting in Chiang Mai, Thailand. Between these meetings, a General Committee did most of the work which the Council did when it met more frequently. It was not, however, appointed by the Council, to which it would have to report, but by the regional committees. Each regional committee chose from its own membership four people including its chairman to be the region's representatives on the General Committee. Once the meetings of the Council were fixed for every eight years, the General Committee met every four years. Thus, meetings of the General Committee were held in the place and about the same time as the Council meetings at which they presented a report, but also once midway between Council meetings. The first meeting of the General Committee was in Edinburgh in September 1969. After that the pattern was established: 1972, in Addis Ababa, just before the Council meeting; 1976, in London, just before the meeting of the Executive Committee; 1980, in Chiang Mai, just before the meeting of the Council. These gaps were long, and it was therefore necessary for the Executive Committee to meet more frequently. This was a committee elected by the General Committee from its own membership, meeting once a year and at other times if needed. When Holmgren concluded his term as chairman of the Council in 1966, he said with confidence that "with all the continents represented on the Council and on the various committees, the UBS could for the first time be regarded as a truly and completely world fellowship."

Two years later, when as Chairman of the Executive Committee, he outlined the global function of the work of the UBS, he defined the role of the UBS Executive Committee as "being asked to assume increasing responsibility in the appraisal and supervision of the total Bible cause in the world." He saw Bible Societies throughout the world gradually surrendering their functions in these matters to the UBS. He charted the growth of "oneness" when he pointed out that "in recent years . . . we have stressed the new *partnership* in our global task, but now a greater attention had to be given to *trusteeship* in this world work." This greatly increased the role of the Executive Committee in subsequent years. In 1968, the threefold task of the committee was expressed as: "to widen the scope of its enquiry, to deepen the exploration of world problems, and to prepare in depth and at length the guidelines for a global strategy of the Bible cause."

The purpose of this regional structure was not to impose control from the UBS Central Office but to enable depots and agencies to become self-governing Bible Societies. The structures were to care for the National Societies, providing them with professional guidance when it was not available locally. This was mainly in the field of management and production, as well as in translation. Holmgren's consistent view was that the UBS needed an adequate *central* organization to safeguard the basic principles and provide a global strategy, *and* a vigorous *regional* structure to provide proximity and flexibility.

Africa Region

There had been considerable expansion of cooperative Bible Society work during the 1950s: In 1957, Salisbury, Rhodesia became an agency both for the BFBS and the NBSS, covering Rhodesia and Nyasaland; in 1958, the Australians became partners in Nairobi, where a Bible House was opened in the same year. In 1958 a new Bible Society agency was created in the Cameroons by BFBS and NBS jointly; in 1960, a joint agency in Madagascar by the BFBS and the Norwegian Bible Society, for which Odd Telle, a Norwegian, was responsible. The Swiss Bible Society, the NBSS, and the BFBS started work together in Mozambique, naming Mr. J. T. Leite, who was Portuguese secretary at Lourenço Marquès. From 1960, the ABS and BFBS formed joint agencies in Belgian Congo, Liberia, and Ethiopia. The BFBS appointed Frank Bedford secretary for Africa, while the ABS named Paul Hopkins.

In 1963, a Bible Society conference was held in Limuru, not far from Nairobi, Kenya. That conference established policy which recognized the new nationalisms of Africa and the need to appoint African secretaries in all offices of the region. Then in March 1967 Hopkins and Bedford played a major role in setting up the first Africa Region Conference in Winneba, Ghana, which was in fact the first UBS Regional Conference. It was a widely representative conference, with some Roman Catholic delegates and almost all the Bible Society secretaries in Africa. The membership was not enough to form a UBS Region at once, but after the Assembly there were sufficient national Bible Societies accepted into membership to form an Africa Regional Committee. The first Regional Secretary, Rein W. Kijlstra, a Dutchman, was appointed in 1968. In 1972 the new delegates from Africa were appointed for the General Committee. Rev. John T. Mpaayei (Kenya) was appointed Chairman, and with him the delegates were Mr. Hailu W. Semaiat (Ethiopia), Rev. Gerrit van der Merwe (South Africa), and Mgr. P. C. Nkou (Cameroon). The first African to be appointed Regional Secretary for Africa was Ato Million Belete, in 1976. Ype Schaaf, writing in 1992, briefly outlined the growth of African leadership in Bible work in Africa and pointed out the difficult problems on the way:

Finding and training qualified people for the posts of Bible Society secretary, distribution consultant, church relations secretary and administrator sometimes is difficult. The UBS regional center in Nairobi is constantly at work in staff training. Although qualified cadres in some countries (and churches) are scarce, there is some progress in this respect. The staff who work in the Bible houses are a varied group consisting of ministers of various churches, teachers, accountants, former civil servants (even one former ambassador) and lawyers. There are also women secretaries, and all Bible houses are now directed by Africans.

In tracing the development towards this position, he added:

In 1993, G. Bimazubute, the Executive Secretary of the Bible Society in Burundi, was murdered in a political row; in 1976, in the tense days before Zimbabwean independence, the Rev. Kachidza was imprisoned for a time. In 1977, the last European secretaries, Leite in Mozambique and Knight in Rwanda, left their posts.

He succinctly showed the growth of the UBS in Africa with two comparisons, looking back twenty-seven years from 1992:

In 1965, South Africa became a member of the UBS and Cameroon-Gabon, Ghana, Madagascar, and Nigeria became associate members. By 1992, there were fifteen African Bible Societies in the UBS, including three associate members, and there were sixteen Bible Society offices in other countries.[5]

Schaaf, in his very careful analysis, showed the difficult steps by which the Africanization of the African work was achieved. It was aided greatly by the international framework of the UBS within which it developed. He listed three historic moments in the growth of Bible work in Africa, when the UBS presence brought its influence to bear:

- 1967—the conference in Winneba, Ghana
- 1972—the UBS World Assembly in Addis Ababa
- 1992—the Regional Assembly in Nairobi

Schaaf did not list the preliminary meeting at Limuru, without which these three could not have happened. It was the first conference of Africa Secretaries for the continent and a groundbreaking one. These conferences brought Bible work in Africa a giant step towards Africanization. Schaaf has his own way of describing the conferences and their effect:

The Dutch, however, had started in 1959 in Cameroon with the aim of preparing the ground for a national Bible Society in five years, and the Norwegians were trying to do the same in Tananarive. The Americans, Scots, and Swiss agreed with this strategy: apart from internationalization, decolonization was also needed. In 1963 a significant impulse was given to this movement by a three-day conference of national African church leaders in Limuru, Kenya, preceding a conference of Bible Society secretaries from the whole of Africa. In Limuru the ABS, BFBS, NBSS, NBS, and the Norwegian Bible Society (NoBS) were also represented. African staff were already working in a number of Bible Societies. At that moment, the BFBS General Secretary, Dr. John Watson, came to Kenya convinced that the structure of joint agencies, agreed the previous year with the Americans, could still be built up for a number of years. However, when the Ugandan Rev. Asa Byara, later himself secretary of the Bible Society in Kampala, thanked the mother Bible Societies for their service in spreading the gospel in Africa and expressed trust in the new impulse that the Americans would be able to give to evangelism with their Bible Selections, but went on in the name of his African colleagues to make a strong recommendation that Bible Society work should become a matter for African churches and Christians, Watson understood the signal. With the hearty agreement of the representatives of the other "mother societies," he declared a few days later to the secretaries that the whole Bible Society work must become a matter for the Africans themselves. Some secretaries, who thought that Africans were by no means ready for this, seemed inclined to rebel, but the old British Bible Society tradition of obedience to London won the day. At the BFBS Annual Meeting, Watson had explained the Buck Hill Falls agreement as a necessary cooperation of all forces in the face of the rapid growth in population. A year later, in the light of the Limuru meeting, he stated that in Africa the time had come for national Bible Society committees and African secretaries.

In these years of expansion, internationalization and Africanization, remarkable things happened here and there in Africa. In 1958 the "million Gospels" campaign was launched, and in 1962 2,676,000 copies, especially of John, that most un-African Gospel, were distributed in many languages.[6]

It is not surprising that the various participants in the tumultuous changes in Africa described events differently. The old colonial powers were loosening, if not losing their grip on their former colonies. Some changes were peaceful, others violent. Belgian, British, French, Portuguese, and Spanish governments gradually had to accept the change. There was not a similar reluctance among Bible Societies, partly because of the work which the UBS had already done. In the storm, the main concern of all in Bible work was that the changes should not destroy the work already accomplished. The role of the UBS in guiding the depots, agencies, and Societies into the new world of postcolonialism was immense, and Olivier Béguin, whose country had no colonies, was the right man at the helm for such changes. Schaaf's three words described the change: expansion, internationalization, and Africanization.

Money, as Schaaf pointed out, was always a problem in Africa, both because of poverty and also because so many African currencies were not convertible. However, the extent of Bible Society work in Africa could be illustrated by facts and figures. Africa in the seventies had a formidable record. Although Africa had no great record of contributions in money to the Bible work in this period, it held its own with regard to distribution. The following world summary for 1972 of distribution of Bibles, Testaments, Portions, and Selections by Regions gave a good position for Africa when one considered the population of that continent. They were as follows:

World Summary[7]

	Bibles	Testaments	Portions	Selections	Total 1973	Total 1972
Africa	1,488,742	1,082,580	3,060,271	4,042,455	9,674,048	7,772,901
Americas	1,804,955	7,454,196	23,423,086	119,890,735	152,572,972	150,609,366
Asia-Pac	1,093,225	3,967,956	13,788,463	56,414,884	75,264,528	51,716,955
Europe	1,516,885	1,455,975	4,494,443	4,173,240	11,640,543	8,330,373
TOTAL	5,903,807	13,960,707	44,766,263	184,521,314	249,152,091	218,429,595

The Americas Regional Conference in Oaxtepec, Mexico

The Regional Conference for the Americas was the last to be scheduled. It was held in Mexico at the Holiday Center of Oaxtepec, December 8–13, 1968. The press release after the Oaxtepec Conference pointed out how widely representative it was and then listed some of those who were present:

> Church leaders and Bible Society Executive Secretaries from North, Central and South America and the Caribbean, together with UBS consultants, fraternal delegates from other continents, and a number of observers. Among the observers were Rev. Walter Abbott S.I., and Rev. Jorge Mejía representing the Roman Catholic Church.

The appearance of a Jesuit speaker at the UBS Council meeting in 1966 in Buck Hill Falls was dramatic enough, but the atmosphere at Oaxtepec was electric. At night Abbott could hear groups of evangelicals praying and discussing his disturbing presence. This was his fourth Regional Conference, and he had a single message for all, but it was much more difficult to put across to a largely Latin American audience which had suffered much from Catholic oppression. His text was the Second Vatican Council and its Constitution on Divine Revelation—two simple quotes: There should be "easy access to the sacred Scriptures for all the Christian faithful," and the Council recommended cooperation with other Christians in making translations in modern languages, and it urged cooperation in distributing editions of the Scriptures specially prepared for non-Christians. Abbott was well aware of the suspicion of Roman Catholic statements by Protestants and nowhere was this more evident than in Latin America. Added to the persecution in such countries as Colombia of quite recent date and a long history of duplicity and hostility, these suspicions were intensified. Abbott did not hesitate to state them clearly, letting his audience know that he understood. He read the minds of Protestants, as he listed four questions:

- Can we take seriously this *conversion* of Rome?
- Will we lose our liberty and our independence if we enter into cooperative projects with Catholics?

- Will our translations not be influenced too much? Will Roman dogma be introduced slightly, since every translation is an interpretation?
- Won't Catholics profit from the financial help of the Protestants?

His frankness, his understanding, and his self-evident honesty won respect, and as he met with Protestants in one-on-one conversation, they trusted him and a miracle of understanding occurred. It was not only his humanity, although that helped. It was the discovery that this prominent Roman Catholic was at heart a Bible man.

It was a conference which benefitted from information from the three earlier regional conferences, and there were representatives from those conferences in attendance. They all spoke and told something of what they were doing. The Americas region, however, had its own particular problems. Some were exactly the same as elsewhere in the world, but others referred particularly to Latin America or to Anglo-America. Meeting in Mexico they were between the two, and it was possible to speak quite freely about the difficulties in the past which were now being overcome. Béguin spoke to the conference and expressed the wish that the people in South America would not only receive but also give to those in North America and that North America should learn also how to receive as well as give. This was to be one region, and something of the solidarity came through in the papers that were read and the discussion which followed. It was a large conference with about one hundred people present, representing some twenty-three different countries.

This conference at Oaxtepec was of very great importance and began cooperation which continued for a long time between many who had been totally separated in the past. This was the first time that the representatives of the Roman Catholic Church and the Protestant Church in South America had met together. They were suspicious of each other, but somehow the conference brought them together as they saw a common work in the production and distribution of the Word of God. It was not viewed as merely a structural change or a new kind of bureaucracy. It was in fact a breakthrough, and the whole relationship between churches and some Bible Societies in the Americas was changed by it. There were many who told stories of how they moved from opposition to a real cooperation as a result of this conference in Mexico.[8]

That did not apply to all. There were still many Societies in the Americas and even in Europe which were exclusively Protestant in both Board and staff membership. Although there was some progress since then, it had been very sporadic. It was time for some of the still exclusively Protestant Bible Societies to have their bluff called.

The Structure of the Americas Region

The Regional Continuation Committee was set up including representatives from a wide range of countries in North and South America. There was also a Regional Secretariat nominated with two people: Alice Ball, regional consultant, based in New York; and the Rev. Dr. Alfonzo Llloreda, regional secretary, based at the Regional Center in Mexico City.

It was unfortunate that Lloreda did not remain long as regional secretary. He was an ideal choice, and his contribution was considerable. He was succeeded by Rev. Ronald Denton, who successfully continued the distribution campaign Lloreda had started, called "Rivers of Living Water." Denton remained as regional secretary until the end of 1972 and then was replaced by Mr. Alberto Cárcamo. Cárcamo had served the Bible Society in Chile for eighteen years, first as accountant and later as executive secretary and had been a member of the executive committee of the Methodist Church of Latin America and chairman of finance and administration committees of the Methodist Church of Chile. The minute for his appointment by the executive committee meeting in Addis Ababa in September 1972 reads:

> That, on the recommendation of the Americas Regional Executive Committee, the World Service Center/New York concurring, Mr. Alberto Cárcamo be appointed Regional Secretary for the Americas as from January 1, 1973, for a period of three years in the first instance.[9]

The Americas Region, although not as large as the Asia-Pacific, either in area or population, was the most prominent in finance, distribution, and leadership of the UBS. It included the ABS, the Canadian

Bible Society, Mexico, the countries of Central and South America, and the islands of the Caribbean. In South America, these included Argentina, Brazil, Chile, Colombia, Peru, and Venezuela as full members of UBS. Bolivia, the Dominican Republic, and the West Indies were associate members.

When Cárcamo took up his duties as regional secretary, he found his work, throughout Latin America, greatly facilitated by the use of a common language, Spanish, spoken in almost all the countries except Brazil and Haiti where Portuguese and French were spoken respectively. The whole area was in the midst of the two-year "Rivers of Living Water" campaign, which was already boosting circulation. The production of literary material, the development of women's work and the training of clergy and laity (Protestants and some Roman Catholics) in methods of distributing the Scriptures, were all proceeding apace. The Penzotti Institute was a particularly good example of this systematic training in Scripture distribution. One special event had been the presentation of the millionth copy of *Dios Llega al Hombre (God Speaks to Man)*, the first common language, dynamic, equivalent translation of the New Testament ever published by the Bible Societies, to the Secretary General of the Organization of American States.

One administrative issue showed the development of regional responsibility. The NBS had long administered work in the Netherlands Antilles from Amsterdam, but now transferred supervision of the program there to the UBS Americas Region under the guidance of the regional secretary. There was every sign of increased activity in the Latin American and Caribbean countries under the new regional arrangements.

Asia-Pacific Region

At its meeting in London in January 1968 the Executive Committee endorsed the appointment by the American Bible Society of the Rev. Warner A. Hutchinson as ABS Regional Secretary for Asia, succeeding the Rev. Dr. John D. Erickson, who transferred to the ABS Ways and Means Department in charge of fundraising. On the recommendation of the Asia-South Pacific Regional Executive Committee the UBS Regional Secretary was named as the Rev. E. A. Cline. Cline was the Executive Secretary of the Bible Society in Vietnam and was himself a Canadian. There was not yet an Asian for the post but Cline came with specific experience in the Asia region.

In November 1967, this vast region, covering half the world and two-thirds of its population, held its first regional conference in Bangkok. There was wide representation: Japan, India, Korea, Thailand, Burma, Hong Kong, the Philippines, Australia, New Zealand, and many others. Among the Roman Catholics were Abbott, Phimphisan (not yet a bishop), and Bishop Gomes. The theme of the papers read and discussed showed the wide range of issues facing this region: "Is the goal numbers or persons?"; "Our translations are not adequate"; "Producing the Book and paying the bill"; "Roman Catholics and the provision of Scripture;" and "Can Churches and Bible Societies really get together?"

Many who came to this conference had little knowledge of Bible Society work, others had been involved in it for years. It fell to Holmgren to sketch in the background and outline the cardinal principles upon which the Bible Societies had historically organized and extended their ministry. He did this under five headings—the Bible work program must always involve large numbers of consecrated laymen, who would invite distinguished and learned clergy to assist in the management of the work; the structure and program must be fully interdenominational in character; ultimate authority should be lodged in committees and boards, not in staff; the intention of all Bible Society work must be deeply evangelical, the range is the world. And Holmgren concluded: "For the first time in history, a systematic effort is being made annually to appraise the requirements of all lands in all languages for copies of the printed Scriptures and to allocate on a global basis the total resources available to underwrite this gigantic task—resources woefully inadequate to serve a world of exploding populations and advancing literacy and learning."[10]

Distribution and New Readers

The challenge issued by the Addis Ababa Assembly was quickly taken up in the Asia-Pacific Region and for the first time ever, in 1973, three Societies of the region (India, Indonesia and Korea) each achieved an annual Scripture circulation of ten million. They aimed now for fifteen million, with special concern for new readers. They soon discovered that new readers were not only those who had just learned to read, but also those who had started to read the Bible for the first time. They needed help to understand what they read.

After Cline, the post of regional secretary was temporarily vacant, and it was not easy to find a suitable and available Asian to fill the post. The Rev. Russell Self was appointed officiating regional secretary and later confirmed in the office. In January 1975, when a UBS New Readers Scripture Consultation was held in Nairobi, he was invited because of his record in Scripture distribution and skill in presentation. He made his mark and later reported on the Consultation: "The purpose of the New Reader Scriptures Program graded series is to take the limited skills of the reader seriously and also help him reach a place where his perhaps distorted understanding of the Gospel can be replaced by a meaningful response to the Good News of Jesus Christ."[11] Reporting to the General Committee in London, 1976, he was quite clear that 70–75 percent of the readers which the Bible Societies target in his region were at the new readers level. For all the money spent on education in Asia and the Pacific, most of "the students going to school emerge as marginal readers."

At the request of the Regional Committee for professional help, Mr. Hendrik Duym was appointed UBS Regional Production/Supply Consultant for Asia-Pacific on July 1, 1976. The flexibility of the regional structure was well illustrated as each region developed in its own way, according to opportunities, need, and vision. The UBS was ready to help and responded, but did not control. Progress in new reader selections had been rapid. Three years after the project was launched in Addis Ababa, 711 new reader selections had been completed or in process of translation in 209 languages in more than fifty countries.

Europe Region

When the Rev. Sverre Smaadahl of Norway started to work for the UBS in Europe in 1967, the General Secretary of the Norwegian Bible Society said, "Learn the 1966 Buck Hill Falls minutes by heart. Do your best to implement them." Béguin wrote, with enthusiasm, "You will be the first area secretary who will not be attached to any one single Society."

Previous area secretaries (Ball, Bedford, Hopkins, and Tidball) had been staff members of ABS or BFBS. Smaadahl (whose title was soon to be changed to regional secretary) was appointed by UBS. He was appointed on the initiative also of a number of supporting Societies in Europe (including Germany, Netherlands, and Norway) who were anxious to participate in Bible work in southern and eastern Europe at a time when BFBS was still administering them as their own sole agencies. The other Societies saw Smaadahl as the person who could get them into the act, and he did. Smaadahl was beginning with the new structures and Béguin saw his appointment, which was then only for northern Europe, as a presage of things to come. He always saw ahead of everybody else:

> There is no doubt in my mind that though at present the area secretaries for Africa, Asia and Latin America, in particular, are administering secretaries of one given Society, this pattern will be disappearing pretty soon to give place to a new formula, by which these area secretaries will also be primarily in the service of the Societies in the area, receiving their general instructions and guiding principles in matters of policy from those Societies and probably themselves living within the area.[12]

This was what Fick inherited and carried through. He also mastered one problem which Béguin saw coming, but could not solve—the relationship of the regions with the UBS headquarters. Béguin recognized the centrifugal tendencies inherent in the new structure. A proper balance would have to be found between centralization and decentralization. Fick went a long way to finding this balance.

For some time, Smaadahl worked in Northern Europe, and he was remembered particularly for his work in Eastern Europe. One outstanding achievement of the Europe region was at a Europe Regional Committee meeting in Bad Saarow in the German Democratic Republic (GDR) in 1973. Church life in that country was difficult and made more difficult by those who smuggled Bibles into the country with worthy intentions, but little regard to the effect upon the churches. The UBS agreed to give its support only "through legal channels." The resolution passed added: "The Committee wishes to place on record its dissociation from Bible work done by illegal means. Furthermore, the Committee dissociates itself from any Scripture distribution linked with political propaganda."[13] This resolution enabled the UBS through its Europe region to continue work in the Communist countries of Eastern Europe. The meeting at Bad Saarow was not only of the Europe region committee but also a consultation of Bible Society secretaries from every Society in the region. Its significance for future work was immense.

The report of the Europe region for 1973 showed wide-ranging activities throughout the whole region and included the move of the remaining regional administration to Bassersdorf in Switzerland, where Smaadahl had been since 1967. The Rev. P. D. Fueter began work as distribution consultant for Europe, at first part-time, then full-time, based at Bassersdorf; and Peter Wigglesworth, the management consultant for the region, moved there in January 1974.

The Unfinished Task

In his editorial to the Annual Report for 1973, which was published as No. 95 of the *UBS Bulletin* in July 1974, Fick chose the title, "The Unfinished Task." He described the problems of 1973, in what he called a rather "normal" year—wars, mutinies, coups, revolutions, strikes, earthquakes, volcanic eruptions, fires, floods, droughts; affluence and abundance in parts of the world, with famine, need and starvation in others; inflationary developments in almost all countries, lack of integrity in political leaders, corruption, etc.—a "normal" year! Against this background, Bible Society work grew and prospered. The year saw increased distribution, new translations, cooperation with Roman Catholics, with "Good News for Ireland" spanning the sectarian divide. The structures of the UBS were tested and found viable.

But Fick freely admitted that structural patterns were not an end in themselves. They were merely means of doing the job, and they had to be kept resilient in order to fulfil that task, which was "to get Scriptures out to the people who need them, Scriptures which they can understand and can afford to buy."

He ended with a quote from a letter Berggrav wrote on the day of his death. It was addressed to the pastors of the Norwegian Church who had to prepare sermons for Bible Sunday 1959. Many wondered if it was worth it. What can people get out of this difficult book, some had asked. Berggrav acknowledged their doubts, but insisted: "People do *get* something out of reading this "difficult" book. It was best expressed by the African woman who said, 'This book reads me.' This cause, the Bible mission, the Bible for all peoples and tribes—this has priority because it concerns the foundation of all Christianity and because it is right *now* that it is important. . . ." Fick said, "The letter was never finished. It was found on his desk when he died that afternoon." And then Fick added, "So is the task: unfinished."[14]

Quadrennial Meeting of the General Committee, London, 1976

After the cluster of meetings in Africa in 1972, the Executive Committee met a little more frequently than once a year because of the rapid development. Apart from Africa it was careful to cover the other three regions as it met in Teheran and Brasilia in 1973, Warsaw in 1974, and in New York and London in 1975 and 1976. The last of these meetings was before and after the General Committee had met, also in London, for the first time since Addis Ababa. There was much to do and many changes to report and initiate. In addition to monitoring the progress of the campaign, "Let the Word Speak" in each region and even each Society, the Committee looked at the problems of distribution in the politically troubled areas of the Arab/Muslim countries. These covered three separate regions of the UBS—North Africa, West Asia, and Turkey (Europe). With three separate regions involved, it was difficult to coordinate efforts. These countries were gradually recognized by their special problems as a subregion and called after the initials of the three areas being served, NAWAT. Decision on this was left until the next series of meetings, including the Council Meeting in 1980 in Chiang Mai There were also serious questions about the role of the two World Service Centers in London (for Europe and Africa) and New York (for the Americas and Asia-Pacific). These two centers were differently related to their host national Societies, BFBS and ABS. The ABS integrated the World Service Center much more into its own staff operations than the BFBS, who while providing facilities and accommodation were more clearly separated from the UBS work. In 1976 the Rev. Dr. John D. Erickson was appointed World Service officer/New York in place of Hutchinson. The closeness of the officer to the ABS was seen in the fact that Hutchinson was a General Secretary of the ABS until 1977, and Erickson was appointed to that office in 1978, while still continuing as World Service officer.

The Rev. John Weller, a Congregational minister in England, had been appointed BFBS General Secretary before the conference at Buck Hill Falls; in other words, before the Society's role as an "administering Society." As a result after Buck Hill Falls he was given the UBS office of World Service officer." At that time all World Service officer appointments had been either exclusively ABS or BFBS initiatives. However, the expectation of Weller's performance from the side of the UBS was quite different from that of the BFBS. Crucially he had now to be able to handle financial and personal questions which in BFBS had always been taken care of in the finance department. Weller was highly skilled in ecumenical relations but was not an administrator. The UBS therefore suggested that as the role was now quite different from what was initially intended, the BFBS should appoint Dean to succeed Weller as World Service officer. This was done in May 1973. Dean was therefore automatically appointed at the same time a BFBS General Secretary. This seemed from the beginning to pose at least a potential conflict of interests, and Dean suggested that he should not continue to serve as BFBS General Secretary but be transferred fully to the UBS. This the BFBS General Committee was quite happy to agree to. Thus he was transferred to the UBS, though invited to sit in on BFBS staff and committee meetings. This meant that he was not as closely involved with the BFBS as his counterpart in New York was with the ABS. Both Fick and Dean always thought that the roles of General Secretary of a major Society and World Service officer of the UBS should be separated but this was only accomplished in 1988 when the general office was established in Reading.

President Coggan

Another important change in 1976 was the resignation of the president. Coggan was nominated Archbishop of Canterbury in 1976. The fact was that Coggan was now so busy as primate of all England and head of the worldwide Anglican communion that he reluctantly decided that he could no longer continue to serve as UBS president. He was, however, delighted when UBS responded to his decision by electing him honorary president. He, since then and right into his retirement, continued to be both interested and helpful in the whole work of the UBS.

Donald Coggan was what the Roman Catholics would call, "A Bible Bishop." During most of the war years he taught New Testament at Wycliffe College, Toronto, Canada, until 1944, the year in which he wrote the *Canadian Lent Book*. He returned to England in 1944 to become head of the London College of Divinity. There, of course, he taught the Scriptures and in fact always had throughout his whole life. He had been about ten years there when the BFBS approached him because the position of Anglican General Secretary fell vacant. He was obviously interested, for he had a high respect for the work of the BFBS, and discussed the invitation with the chairman of his school governors, Bishop Taylor. Taylor advised against it, because he thought it would take Coggan out of the mainstream of English church life, where, to use Coggan's words, "he had some mad idea that I should have a kind of leadership in it one day." So he stayed until 1956 when he was appointed Bishop of Bradford. In the same year, Coggan was appointed a vice-president of the UBS. He attended the Council meeting in Brazil in 1957, and it was clear that Berggrav would soon have to resign. He did that year, and Coggan was appointed president. At first he was content to follow Berggrav; his energies had to go into Bradford. It was one of the most difficult dioceses in the country, very run down, and for Coggan it represented a period of intense work, pouring what resources he had into it to get it on its feet.

The first UBS Council meeting Coggan attended as president was in Grenoble,1960, and he played his part, but his mind was full of the problems of his diocese. He talked of the loneliness of his clergy in remote areas and the lack of communication or encouragement from their parishioners. He was a very pastoral bishop. In December of the following year, he carried through a Bible Week in Bradford in cooperation with the UBS study secretary, who was developing new forms of Bible Study in "the living situation of the churches." Shortly afterwards, he was named as Archbishop of York and he seemed at once to be relieved, despite the heavy responsibilities that York involved. He had heard the challenge of Béguin's call at Grenoble for greater and more effective distribution. When he went to New Delhi to attend the Assembly of the WCC, he responded on the evening devoted to the presentation of the UBS Study with vigor and statistics, showing by unmistakable charts that the churches were losing the battle for the rising population of the world. The need for support of Bible Society work had rarely been so powerfully expressed. His enthusiasm was lit for a major advance in Scripture distribution. This flowered in 1963, when during the UBS Council meeting in Hakone, he launched "God's Word for a New Age" in Tokyo. He saw that such a program was impossible without full cooperation of the churches, in fact, unless the churches adopted the campaign. With this in mind he proposed a Conference of Church Leaders, which was held in Driebergen in 1964, and which he convened both as UBS president and Archbishop of York.

In the following years, the duties of archbishop increased and the UBS Council meetings were spread out to eight yearly intervals. Coggan was always ready to conduct the Bible Studies, which he did supremely well, but he was less involved in the public meetings of the UBS. His influence continued through his close personal contact with Holmgren, Béguin, Fick, and others. When he talked about the UBS, he was always informed even if he had not been at the meetings. This was due to personal contacts and the ready hospitality of Bishopthorpe, his residence as archbishop. When he was named Archbishop of Canterbury, he continued participation as honorary president. He conducted the Bible study both at Chiang Mai (1980) and Budapest (1988). In his retirement at Winchester, and over eighty years old, he had a concern for the UBS as lively as ever.

Dr. Oswald C. J. Hoffmann

The third president of the UBS (1977–1988) was a warm, outgoing man of considerable gifts. Hoffmann came from the Missouri Lutherans, who were somewhat isolated from other mainstream denominations by their strong German background and did more than most to bring them out of that isolation. He was a classical scholar, and many remember his Bible studies at UBS with the Greek New Testament in his hand. When he became chairman of the ABS Translation Committee, he already had a reputation as film producer, broadcaster, and founder of the Public Relations Department of the Lutheran Church, Missouri Synod (1948) directing it until 1963. At the Second Vatican Council, where he was an official observer, he helped create dialogue between Lutherans and Roman Catholics and as president of the International Lutheran Laymen's League, he introduced the first Roman Catholic Cardinal (Cardinal Cushing) to address its convention in 1965. He had an immense reputation as a broadcaster and brought to the UBS outstanding gifts of communication and of sympathetic understanding to people of various theological views. He had a unique work in China with teaching cassettes and understood all that the Bible Societies were doing in their efforts to reach the people of that vast Communist land with the Gospel of Jesus Christ.

A scholar, evangelist, and friend to the UBS, he wore the mantle of Bishop Berggrav and Archbishop Coggan with competence, fervor, and humility.

The Role of Women in the Bible Society Work

For a long time, the administration of Bible Society work was almost entirely in the hands of men. This reflected the all-male leadership of the churches. The growing awareness of women in political and commercial life and their outstanding contributions in academic and medical work, as well as the opening of the universities to more and more women students, had their influences upon the churches too. Women moved into leadership positions with the coming of the ecumenical movement but slowly. There were few women delegates at the WCC Assembly in Amsterdam in 1948, and all of them were on the first section of Committee IV dealing with "The Life and Work of Women in the Churches." The Nominations Committee brought forward the names of one honorary president and six presidents—all men. The ninety members nominated for the Central Committee included two women. This changed later, but it was not surprising that the UBS followed a similar pattern. In 1954, Mrs. Jessie Bader of the U.S. was appointed a vice-president of the UBS—the first women to hold office at the international level.

Of course, women played a part in Bible work from the beginning as Bible women, colporteurs, and secretaries of Societies. On the UBS staff there was one outstanding woman, who was duly honored in 1972 at Addis Ababa—Miss Margaret Sullivan, secretary and later administrative assistant to Olivier Béguin, 1949–1972. Her contribution to the work of the UBS was far greater than can ever be recorded. At times, in the early days, the UBS was Olivier and Margaret, and she stayed with him in remarkably efficient and faithful service for more than twenty years. A presentation was made to her in 1972, when Holmgren commented:

> Our president, the Archbishop of York, frequently reminds us of the large and important place women play in our world work, and he quite properly chides us for not including more women in our deliberations and counsels.
>
> To be sure, we are fortunate in having Mrs. Orsuna de Soto of Venezuela as one of our vice-presidents, but we should be deeply embarrassed that there is only one other woman representative on this large UBS Council, none on the General Committee, and none on the Executive Committee. Moreover, and this is a major scandal, there is not one woman on any of the four regional committees.[15]

This statement had its effect. There was increasing concern, and efforts were made to bring more women into the work of the Bible Societies. Some became translators or experts in fundraising, production, or distribution, and a few obtained major administrative positions, but progress was slow.

Ball succeeded Holmgren on the UBS General Committee, and Executive Committee and also became General Secretary of the ABS. Others followed, but not so dramatically. She was joined by Mrs. Barbara Enholc-Narzynska from Poland, appointed by the Europe Region to the General Committee in 1980. The Africa Region appointed Dr. Mary Khimulu (Kenya) in 1988, and when Ball retired she was succeeded by Miss Maria Martinez. This was hardly rapid progress. The Executive Committee was even slower. Ball alone served on the committee as one of the two representatives from the U.S. from 1980 until her retirement, but was not succeeded by another woman in 1988.

Alice Ball

The first woman chairman of the Council was Miss Alice Ball. She stood in a very distinguished succession, and her appointment was a tribute to her considerable contribution to Bible Society work both through the ABS and the UBS. Her appointment in 1984 meant that she presided over the Council meeting in Budapest. She was also the first woman General Secretary of the ABS, and her portrait hangs in New York among the innumerable portraits of men who held that post.

Alice Ball graduated from Hunter College and was a New Yorker, born and bred. She brought business experience to the Bible Society, having served 1942 to 1955 as an administrative assistant with the Air Reduction Corporation. She was a volunteer in Bible Society work and for ten years a counselor in the New York Bowery Corps of the Salvation Army. In 1950 she was a delegate to the first International Youth Conference of the Salvation Army, which was held in London.

She joined the ABS staff as administrative assistant, supervising stenographers and secretaries, processing Scripture requests for delivery abroad, and handling routine correspondence with overseas agencies. Her tasks in the Overseas Department were expanded, and her responsibilities increased, until in March 1959 she was given special responsibility over the Latin American Desk. From then on, she brought her business experience into ever widening fields—assistant secretary in the Overseas Department, with special responsibility for work in the Caribbean, and later extending this to the whole of Latin America. She assisted in the creation of the Latin American Center in Mexico and promoted the Penzotti Training Institute. By 1979 she was a General Secretary of the ABS in charge of the National Division.

Alice Ball was involved in UBS work quite early. From 1968 until 1971 she was consultant for the UBS America Regional Conference. Because of pressure of work for the Department of Women's Activities of the ABS, she had to resign from her UBS consultant position in 1971, but she was appointed to the UBS General Committee in 1979 and again in 1981, when she was also appointed vice-chair on the UBS Executive Committee. It was therefore a natural appointment to chairperson of the UBS Council in 1984. Alice Ball retired in December 1988 from the staff of the ABS after thirty-three years of service to the cause.

CHAPTER THIRTEEN

Europe and China

———— ◇ ————

In January 1966, Olivier Béguin and Baron van Tuyll, both aware of the growing strength of some of the continental Bible Societies in Europe, met at the home of van Tuyll for a prolonged discussion on the coordinating of Bible Society work in Europe. On January 11, as a result of this discussion, Béguin wrote one of his most influential letters. It was addressed to Rev. B. Mathiesen of the Norwegian Bible Society and Rev. O. Naegeli of the Swiss Bible Society. He urged them to prolong the time they were to meet in Düsseldorf in order to discuss the conversation he had with van Tuyll:

> During the course of our conversation it became clear that the time was ripe for a first consultation between some of the European Bible Societies now interested in supporting the worldwide work regarding the particular contribution which Europe could make in the world planning and world budget of Bible Society work . . . we thought that the four continental European Societies which at present are contributing most to the World Budget (Netherlands, Norway, Germany, and Switzerland) should not delay further in having a first consultation on the subject.

The Continental European Production Fund (CEPF)

In 1967, there was a proposal from the Executive Committee meeting in Geneva that a production fund be established on the continent of

Europe. This was sent to the Europe Regional Conference for consideration, meeting in St. Cergue, Switzerland in September 1967. Holmgren challenged the conference with the proposal that the Continental European Bible Societies should create a joint production fund to the amount of $1 million. The UBS had set a distribution target in Hakone in 1963 of 150 million Scriptures a year, and the amount required to publish this quantity was $6.5 million. Could Europe supply $1 million? There was unanimous agreement in principle, but the organization for such a fund was not in place. A Continuation Committee set to work and decided that the Europe Region should participate in missionary Scripture production within the framework of the UBS World Service Budget and proposed that each European member Society should contribute a nominal sum of 1,000 deutsche marks each year and then decide how much extra to contribute. Even nonmembers of the UBS, including the historic Canstein Bible Society, were encouraged to help. A board was soon appointed and the Continental European Production Fund established (CEPF).

In this rapid move to form the CEPF, Germany played a leading role. It was indicative of her new role that the bylaws for the work of the Board and Directors were in German. Enough was promised from the European Societies to enable the work to begin. Dr. Gernot Winter, at that time the chairman of the Württemburgische Bibelanstalt, was appointed to take steps to have the CEPF legally established in Stuttgart. A board was created composed of Mr. N. P. Wedege (Norway), Mr. Dodeshöner (Germany), Mr. E. Ryser (Switzerland), Mr. C. P. Starreveld (Netherlands), and the Rev. J. M. Alexander (Scotland). The UBS executive also appointed Tattersall and Dean to be ex-officio members of the Board, because they were at that time coordinating the World Service Budget, and hence related to the two principal production funds in London and New York. The CEPF had the following terms of reference:

1. To participate in missionary Scripture production within the framework of the UBS World Budget.
2. To act as coordinating center for the financing and production of Scriptures in consultation with UBS regional consultants and with other production funds.

3. To coordinate on the request of contributing Bible Societies, Scripture production within Europe.
4. To make full use of specialist personnel and machinery available in Europe.
5. To engage in any other activity consistent with the aims above.

This was one further step in what Béguin called, "internationalization and regionalization."[1] The achievement owed much to Dorothea Kindt, Gernot Winter, and Erwin Zimmerman in Stuttgart. In 1968 when the CEPF was established there were twelve contributing European Bible Societies, and the fund stood at a little less than half a million dollars. The target remained $1 million, which was eventually achieved and surpassed.

The placing of administration of the CEPF in Stuttgart encouraged the German Bible Societies in their movement towards unity as the German Bible Society. Winter of the Württemburgische Bibelanstalt was already discussing plans for a new Bible House in Stuttgart. By 1970 he had offers to buy the old site in the town center and plans for a new building further out, in the suburb of Möhringen. Thus when Fick reported to the German Bible Society that the UBS had agreed to move its headquarters to Stuttgart on January 1, 1974 he was able to say that the new building would house the Bibelanstalt, the Evangelische Bibelwerk, the CEPF, and the UBS headquarters.

This made Fick's residence in Germany essential in the early years, and it gave him a Bible Society base which was steadily growing from which to do his UBS work, while the conscientious work of Kindt, Winter, and Zimmerman assured the efficient management and the steady growth of the CEPF.

Eastern Europe

Smaadahl, Regional Secretary for Europe, always regarded his work in Eastern Europe as his most important contribution to the UBS. He began in the difficult times of the Cold War and was recalled later to reestablish contacts in happier times after the collapse of the communist hegemony. Bible Society work had been forbidden in almost every country in the region except Poland, Yugoslavia, and the German Democratic Republic. Béguin worked where he could, but the demands in Western Europe were then also enormous. His reports on Hungary, in particular, showed how far he went. But it took time, and not until the establishing of a Europe Region, with a Europe Center in Bassersdorf in 1967 and a Europe Regional Secretary, did the work of the UBS begin to grow in Eastern Europe. It was Smaadahl's greatest contribution. This outgoing Norwegian with a tendency towards optimism, nevertheless, found it a difficult task. He painted the picture, looking back from 1990, contrasting it with 1967:

> The atmosphere of the Cold War was predominant. It was justified to speak about the Iron Curtain between East and West. There was much tension and lack of confidence between the two parts of Europe. There was no experience to draw upon for the furtherance of Bible work under such circumstances.[2]

But 1967 and 1968 saw the development of a new policy in the Federal Republic of Germany largely inspired by the popular Chancellor, Willy Brandt. He offered to exchange "renunciation-of-force" declarations with the Soviet Union, Poland, Czechoslovakia, and in principle, other interested countries. Brandt's firm belief in the solidarity of the human family gained credence as he declared, "We condemn racism as an inhuman sentiment and as a source of the most terrible crimes; our own history has become our bitterest experience in this respect." He affirmed the universality of human rights. He maintained that a policy based upon peace, solidarity and the renunciation of force was indivisible. "The human capacity for reason had made the United Nations possible," he wrote in his memoirs, "but the human propensity for unreason made it necessary." He believed in the United Nations and pressed his beliefs into policy. His ideal was a world community governed by the principles of the United Nations. But he added, sadly and truly, "I shall not live to see that day." He did, however, help towards its dawn.[3]

During the autumn of 1973 the Helsinki Agreement on human rights and the coexistence of East and West passed through its initial phase at Foreign Minister level, and consultations on mutual and balanced force reductions got under way in Vienna. The dawn was a little premature because of disagreements about the reunification of Germany, but the atmosphere was better for Bible Society work—a little better. As Smaadahl said, "The Iron Curtain was no longer tight." Smaadahl's first step was to develop initial contacts with church leaders in Eastern Europe, and for this he found international conferences of particular importance, especially the conferences of the Council of European Churches. When these conferences were held in Switzerland, church leaders came to the UBS Regional Center, and initial contacts grew into friendships. Béguin was an extremely valuable adviser to Smaadahl. His successor, Fick, continued to be of great help as were Baron van Tuyll and Hans Florin, the two Europe Region chairmen during Smaadahl's time as Regional Secretary. They all understood well the problems of Eastern Europe and gave the Regional Secretary encouragement in his difficult task.

Two Europe Region conferences took place in 1967 and 1970, and between the two there was considerable change in relationships with the Orthodox churches of Eastern Europe. At the first in St. Cergue, Switzerland, only a few eastern Europeans took part, but at the second in Vienna most of the countries were represented. The Russian Orthodox Bishop German, who served in Vienna at the time, attended the conference, contributing considerably to the discussions and urging the other participants from Eastern Europe to have more courage and come out of their ghetto. He convinced the conference that they could be a part of the European scene, pointing out that now for the first time it was possible to write a document about Bible work in Eastern Europe and circulate that document in the West.

Smaadahl found Finland with its in-between position very helpful, especially the services of Esko Rintala, General Secretary of the Finnish Bible Society. After some time and much patient work, a few basic principles were discussed openly. Bible Society work was ecumenical from its beginning, therefore the UBS was aware of the need to respect the elementary ecumenical rules. "For the revitalization of Bible work in Eastern Europe it was a presupposition to work as closely as possible with *all* the Christian churches, and listen to them." The agreement reached by the UBS in 1968 with Roman Catholics on principles for interconfessional Bible translation was especially helpful, while the good working relations with the Russian Orthodox Metropolitan Nikodim in Leningrad opened many doors in establishing new contacts. It was soon made clear to all that the UBS was not in the business of sabotage or smuggling. It was important that all Bible work related to the UBS should be strictly legal and carried on only through official channels. The UBS followed the same principle as that laid down long ago by the BFBS for its staff members working abroad: "In many instances the Society owes its freedom to work to a studied desire on the part of its representatives to keep within the law."

Coupled with this was the longstanding conviction that working with the church leaders in each country, whoever they were, was essential for efficient Bible Society work. Even in Poland and the DDR, where Bible Societies already existed, cooperation with church leaders had to be close. Smaadahl soon found that only they knew the intricacies of the situation in their own country and the conditions under which Scripture distribution could be done. They had to be respected and consulted even if they were unable always to be open about their activities. There was some danger of misunderstanding some of these relationships because outside Eastern Europe, especially among certain constituencies in America, it could appear that the UBS was fraternizing with—and even employing—fellow-travelers, "pink" if not "red." The principle was put down in black and white at the conference in Bad Saarow, German Democratic Republic, in 1973. Again, when matters were somewhat changed politically in 1985 at the UBS Europe Region Conference in Malta, the same principles were reaffirmed whoever the church leaders were and whatever political system was in power. On the basis of Bible work in Eastern Europe since 1973 and paying tribute to Bible Society staff such as Barbara Enholc-Narzynska of Poland and Bohumir Sedlisky of Czechoslovakia as well as the "untiring efforts" of Smaadahl, the resolution was passed which confirmed that of Bad Saarow in 1973. The comment upon their confirmation illustrated its wisdom:

> Since Bad Saarow the work has developed in such a way that it is now possible to supply Scriptures in national languages from Bible Society offices in Czechoslovakia, East Germany, Hungary, Poland, and Yugosla-

via; and the UBS is increasing supply to Romania, and, more sporadically, to Bulgaria and the USSR.[4]

Translation in Eastern Europe

Apart from the obvious need to make personal contacts, Smaadahl had to seek advice on how to begin the new work in Eastern Europe. He took the right decision by beginning with translation. Production and circulation are necessary, but in sensitive situations can sometimes look like the spreading of propaganda. Translation is a scholar's job and looks harmless enough to a politically motivated official. In this delicate task of beginning with translations there were problems enough, but the translation consultants were able to cope in their own quiet way. They were Rudolf Kassühlke (German), Paul Ellingworth (British), J. Margot (Swiss), and Jan de Waard (Dutch). All were scholars with high academic achievements and considerable experience in cooperating with church leaders and with translators in the various countries. They were tactful and commanded the respect of all. No one feared they would exercise undue influence because of their denominational or political persuasions. The translators were very often church leaders themselves, well versed in the Biblical languages as well as their mother tongue. Many were bishops, deans, and professors who knew that they would be using the finished product in their own services of worship, catechetical instruction, pastoral work and what limited apologetics were permitted. They saw the consultants as enablers and worked well together with them. Most of the translations were used ecumenically. This was particularly true of the Czech translation which Catholics used without seeking permission. The Czech translators also wrote a commentary for lay people. Such cooperation was not possible in Poland or Hungary at that stage, though it was to come later. In Russia, there was openness for a new translation. Metropolitan Nikodim led the way with a frank statement, "Russians have the right to read the Bible in the Russian of today."

But he was being far too optimistic. The plain fact was that the Russian Orthodox churches were not usually prepared to accept an "improved" translation. The Orthodox churches generally and the Russian Orthodox in particular believed themselves to be faithful custodians and guardians of the sacred text, entrusted to them down the centuries. This usually meant a text in the ancient style of their own language, and, in the Russian case, in the old Slavonic script. In such a context, reference by a UBS translation consultant to the authority of "best" Greek and Hebrew manuscripts carried little weight. This fact continued to be of increasing importance in the years to come as the UBS sought to encourage good modern translations in Orthodox majority countries.

The Romanian Orthodox church was even more reserved. The Patriarch Justinian, with a smile, explained the situation in Romania: "I think you have observed that we have very many theological professors. You may also have observed that we do not have quite that many theologians." Two different kinds of translation were attempted. The Bible for the altar and the pulpit came first. In some cases, those who wished to evangelize within the permitted limits or to deal with young people who found the church old fashioned, attempted common language translations. These were the days before the opportunities of "Bibles everywhere," of *perestroika* and *glasnost*, and steps had to be taken with care. Considering the limitations, it was amazing how many new translations and revisions were made. Difficulties in Albania did not discourage the translators. There were many Albanians in Yugoslavia, and a new translation of the New Testament into Albanian was done there.[5]

Production in Eastern Europe

Step by step, local production developed in almost all the countries in Eastern Europe, even to a small extent in Bulgaria. Smaadahl gives four means whereby the UBS was able to achieve this in an atmosphere so politically hostile:

1. Pressure from the translators who once having done their work wanted to see it in print.
2. A measure of competition between countries, "If in Prague, why not in Warsaw?"

3. Financially made possible by money provided by the sale of imported Scriptures, because no money could be returned to the sending country.
4. The energetic work of, and high regard for, Erwin Zimmermann, the UBS production consultant, based in Stuttgart.

There is no doubt that these means were the more effective because the UBS had made clear its principle always to act within the law.[6]

The UBS production consultant to whom Smaadahl referred, Erwin Zimmermann, moved with tact and understanding among the delicate problems of countries in this area. He had also been able to gain the confidence of competing groups, whether denominationally or professionally, and where necessary provide the professional help and resources to accomplish the production under very difficult circumstances. For example, the Romanian Orthodox Church in Bucharest had a printing house, but its equipment was very old. Using the UBS resources he was able to supply modern equipment and obtain help for Bible production. He did the same for some state printing houses in other countries, with similar results. Where he found little enthusiasm for Bible production, he inspired it by bringing local machinery up to date. In all communist-dominated countries, a compromise had to be worked out, and Zimmermann was particularly gifted at negotiating such compromises to the mutual advantage of both the local church organizations and the UBS. He was respected because he had technical expertise and was able to offer invaluable assistance. Local production took time in many of the countries of Eastern Europe and meanwhile books had to be imported from Bible Societies in the West, but always within the law. Eventually local production became highly professional and could even compete in the open market with secular literature. The *Illustrated New Testament* produced by the Bible Society of Poland won the prize of the year for the best produced book.

China

Almost any part of the world where political systems were in a state of flux presented problems for Bible Society work. Few countries presented more problems—and challenges—than China. In 1966, the

Cultural Revolution almost destroyed Bible Society work in China. In the 1970s the situation eased a little. Fick reported to the UBS Executive Committee in Chania, in Crete in September 1979, that he had been reading recent reports on China, and he circulated a paper summarizing what he had gleaned from them. His conclusion was that easy access of the Scriptures would not be immediately forthcoming. He recommended that all UBS efforts to promote Bible work should be only at the request of Christian churches within China. The Rev. Dr. John D. Erickson, who replaced Hutchinson as the World Service Officer in New York, read a report from the Asia-Pacific Regional Secretary on the list of various Scriptures which were now being typeset in Hong Kong in the simplified Chinese script which had been officially adopted by the Chinese government. He also gave some details about Christian radio programs, an issue which had been very controversial, because many evangelical groups were supporting Christian radio programs beamed from off-shore islands, the Philippines, and California. These were regarded by the Communist government as objectionable propaganda. The UBS could not be identified with propaganda broadcasts but had been broadcasting Scripture readings without note or comment. The World Association for Christian Communication gave its backing to these legitimate means of circulating the Scriptures, which were distinguished from smuggling Bibles. The broadcasts were often made at dictation speed and received some response, especially from those who were taking the text down in longhand and circulating it locally. Thus radio became a means of circulation, both of content and text. This was not a translation of the Bible into the language of the media, but it was a direct use of radio as a means of circulation. The Asia-Pacific Regional Secretary also gave some information about Bible work in China, including the revision of the Union Version Bible being undertaken at Nanking University. Erickson was able to report that there had been a meeting in New York with two mainland Chinese Christians visiting America for a Peace Conference. At that meeting, it was agreed that help could be given to the translators on the Nanking University revision committee. In particular, this included the provision of Hebrew and Greek texts of the Bible. However, the rule applied that there should be no smuggling of Bibles into China and that Scripture distribution in China should only be carried out by known persons to known persons, preferably Chinese.[7]

The Amity Printing Press in Nanjing

Bible printing in China itself became possible again in the early 1980s. At first, this new opportunity was valuable, but there were no Bible Society presses in China to take advantage of it. However, three million Bibles were printed in China, using different state-run presses. This was not enough, and it was expensive. The UBS then undertook what was described as "the largest single project of the United Bible Societies" and accomplished it in a remarkably short space of time.

The idea was first expressed in a discussion after a dinner in Nanjing on January 13, 1985, arranged in honor of the Rev. Chang Young Choi, UBS Asia-Pacific Region Secretary, and Dr. I-Jin Loh, Regional translation coordinator: During these days in Hong Kong, Bishop K. H. Ting, president of the China Christian Council, announced at a press conference his intention of establishing the Amity Foundation "as part of the services rendered by Christians to the nation." He then added that the Foundation might also include a printing press for the production of Scripture. Within a few weeks, at a meeting in Hong Kong between regional and international staff of the UBS with Bishop Ting and other representatives of the China Christian Council, the feasibility of setting up a printing press was discussed. By March 22, a "Memorandum of Understanding between the Amity Foundation and the United Bible Societies" was signed announcing the UBS's intention to establish and equip a printing plant in Nanjing. The key words in that Memorandum were, "We, representatives of the Amity Foundation and the United Bible Societies, wish to announce that we have come to an understanding which we hope will lead to the establishment of a modern printing facility in the People's Republic of China . . . which will give priority to the production of Bibles and New Testaments."

The proper formalities were followed, and on January 31, 1986, little more than one year after the idea was publicly announced, the UBS announced its "Bible Press for China" project and officially launched a fundraising campaign. The original plan was to set up the

Amity Printing Press on the campus of the Nanjing Normal University, but it proved to be too large to be incorporated in their normal activities. Instead, a further agreement was made with the Jiangning County to incorporate it within the Industrial Corporation. Care was taken to see that the agreement included the same priority to produce Bibles and New Testaments. The foundation stone was laid by Bishop Ting on November 8, 1986, with General Secretaries and fundraisers from ten member Societies. Once completed, the press was officially presented to the Amity Foundation by the UBS in a special ceremony in July 1987. Printing began very soon after that.

On December 5, 1987, a UBS delegation, led by President Hoffmann, assisted at the dedication, and inaugural ceremony of the Amity Printing Press. During the following year the UBS participation became more active, and an agreement for joint venture between the Amity Printing Press and the UBS Publishing Company was signed and the Amity Printing Company Limited formed. The Rev. Peter MacInnes was appointed general manager of the Press. Every move was accompanied by a ceremony. It was at once a success. By the end of September 1988, half a million Bibles had been printed, and the end of year target was set at 700,000 Bibles. At the inaugural ceremony on December 5, 1987 Fick spoke, and his words clearly define the role of the UBS as he saw it at that time:

> Our goal is to enable Christians everywhere to fill the needs for the printed Word of God by their own efforts. It requires different steps here and there to reach this goal. At some places, only consultancy in translation matters is asked for, while at other places staff need technical training. Somewhere else special paper has to be provided. Somewhere else equipment is needed.
>
> You, dear friends, have got the best technical equipment that is on the market today. It is at your disposal so that you can make the Bible truly your own book—not anything foreign or imported, but your Chinese Bible, printed and bound by Chinese here in China, and circulated to the thousands of Chinese who are its potential readers.[8]

Erickson, writing as Chairman of the UBS Executive Committee at the end of 1988, insisted that the UBS had a continuing responsibility for this Chinese press: "The UBS is committed to continue the supply of resources unavailable in China at present, such as Bible paper, and to the development and maintenance of the press."[9]

How the Press Was Financed

Providing equipment and working capital for the Amity Press was a massive financial undertaking. Funds for such a project were not available when the idea was conceived, but the opportunity was grasped and the UBS went to its constituent members asking for their support. Thirty-seven Bible Societies and two UBS Regional Centers responded. The wide spread of Societies, ranging from Uruguay to the United States, was testimony to the world fellowship of the UBS.

CHAPTER FOURTEEN

Global Distribution and Fundraising

———— ◇ ————

After the UBS Council in Hakone, Japan, 1963, mass distribution became a major emphasis and with it a careful attention to the needs of the recipient. Selections, accessible translations, attractive cover illustrations, and advertising were developed among the Bible Societies of the world. Stimulated by the designation of 1979 as UNESCO's "International Year of the Child," the UBS called for a recognition of "the importance of a missionary and evangelistic outreach with the Scriptures to children and youth." At its meeting in Hong Kong, September 1978, the Executive Committee confirmed resolutions which it had prepared at its previous meeting in Nairobi calling upon UBS member Societies and national offices to budget for "the publication of one or several special Scripture publications intended for children and youth in 1979." With this approach in mind it was decided to appoint the Rev. Russell Self to the newly established post of UBS Distribution consultant-at-large. Self, a Canadian missionary, had been UBS Regional Secretary for the Asia-Pacific region until an Asian candidate was found, and it was in this region that he had previously served as distribution secretary.

Russell Self

The flavor of this remarkable enthusiast was caught by any of his regional reports. In 1976 the Asia-Pacific Region spanned war in Indo-

China and terrorism in the Lebanon. In his report, he swept across his region with confidence:

> While 90 million in Indo-China and Burma were often unable to receive Scriptures, we are thankful that the Bible Society office in Saigon is still functioning, and that the Thailand Bible Society has been meeting the needs of thousands of refugees by making available Scriptures in different languages at open border situations.
>
> After twenty months of bitter and bloody civil strife, we express gratitude to God that even though the Beirut Bible Store was blown up, the staff are all safe. The Lebanese office reopened on January 1, 1977, and an extensive pre-Easter distribution has been developed with the new Today's Arabic Version text.

And in that confident vein it continued.

Self went to India as a missionary in 1949. His initial contact with the UBS was when it held its first Council meeting in Asia, at Ootacamund, India, February 1952, and he was invited as a guest. He met Mahanty, the General Secretary of the Bible Society of India and Ceylon, and formed a friendship with him. He was equally impressed by others he met at that Council meeting and recalled Platt and Nida in particular. These men shared his ideals and to a certain extent also his dreams. In 1954 he was invited to be a member of the Allahabad Bible Society Auxiliary. In this way he became interested in evangelism through the distribution of the Gospel Portions then available. During his second furlough as a missionary he was appointed moderator of the North India Synod of the United Church. He was active in the Evangelical Fellowship of India and became secretary of its literature arm. Mahanty died in 1958 and was succeeded after an interval by Inbanathan with whom Self developed a very close friendship. In the early sixties, he encouraged the Bible Society of India to introduce new covers for their *Gospels*, which helped them to put up their circulation considerably in 1962. The design of the covers was intended to introduce the Gospels as Indian. They were all of Indian scenes illustrating *The Way of the King* (Matthew), *The Way of Joy* (Mark), *The Way of Peace* (Luke), and *The Way of Life* (John). Each bore a description in two Hindi characters on the cover. This venture was offered in an attractive way with a leaflet explaining the covers and a shortened form of an article by Mahanty's son-in-law. The leaflet also bore a challenge for Christians: "The Coca-Cola Company has a project whereby they aim to let every human being in the next ten years taste a bottle of Coca-Cola at least once." Then came the challenge: "If this is the aim of businessmen of the world, can we who are in the King's business have a lesser aim?"

Self remembers with enthusiasm the release of the New Testament of Today's English Version at the Berlin Evangelical Congress led by Billy Graham. He and Béguin were both there, and they had enough copies shipped to Berlin for one to be put in every delegate's box. The large press staff also had their copies.

Self worked for the UBS from 1966 until 1981. He described his time as "great fun and hard work." His region was very extensive, and, until the Middle East was assigned to the Europe Region, he had more than half the world from Vietnam to Beirut. What he enjoyed most was conducting workshops on distribution, or rather circulation (like the life-blood circulating through the body). He covered one hundred countries, in 75 percent of which he had workshops. He recalled 107 workshops, 35 percent of them being in India. Their variety was shown in their locations—from plush hotels in South Korea to tents in North Bangladesh, in a variety of languages and the full range of denominations.

Such a man was Russell Self, and it was men like that whom the UBS attracted. They were the frontline troops of circulation. His appointment as UBS distribution consultant-at-large from September 1, 1978 was a natural. He retired three years later, having served the UBS in one capacity or another for fifteen years.[1]

Financial Participation

In the 1950s the ABS and the BFBS consulted on the financial basis largely by an exchange of correspondence between the two Societies, simply listing the total amount of money which the administering Society believed to be necessary to support each agency or Society which the two had agreed to support jointly. After which each agreed to finance a specific percentage of the cost, usually on a fifty-fifty basis.

At the time of the BFBS financial crisis in 1957, the ABS began to express interest in sharing more information, and for a year or two budgets were shared in a bit more detail, although again by correspondence. Then, in 1960, Holmgren came to London for a face-to-face discussion on budgets. It was at that time that John Dean first met him and realized that there was a strange kind of cooperation between the two Societies. He reported, "As a rather junior member of the finance department, who had worked on these budgets, I found myself dealing directly on behalf of the BFBS with the Chief Executive of the ABS. And all because the BFBS General Secretaries, in those days, did not concern themselves with such routine and mundane matters as budgets." Then other Societies began to get interested in sharing in the work. Not only the Europeans but also the Commonwealth Societies wanted to have some say in what happened to their money. (Previously, all money from Australia, Canada, New Zealand, and South Africa had gone to London and disappeared into the BFBS General Fund.)

So the joint meetings, earlier initiated by Holmgren in London, continued each year in London, but began to be attended by what was euphemistically described as a "gallery" of observers from these other Societies. Many had a lot to say but still the ultimate decisions rested only with the General Officers of the ABS and BFBS. What was worse, the budgets came to the table in an unbalanced state, and amounted in total to far more than the sum of money available. Consequently, the first ones to be considered (usually from Africa, as the regions were considered in alphabetical order) were severely cut. And sometimes this went so far that by the end of the meeting there was spare money available which was put into Europe.

The meeting in Buck Hill Falls in 1966 changed all that. Now the ABS and BFBS handed over the task to the UBS which appointed a World Service Budget subcommittee, having representatives from both net *supporting* and net *supported* Bible Societies. Later the approval of the budget became such a smooth routine (all the work having been done by regional committees and then by the global budget "Round Table" to prepare a balanced budget in advance for committee approval) that this committee was eventually disbanded, and the World Service Budget was for many years submitted directly to the UBS Executive Committee (UBSEC) for approval. This continued until 1988 when the Finance subcommittee was established. What had started out as something rudimentary and at times chaotic and limited to two Societies turned into a reasonably efficient and infinitely less cumbersome instrument of collective global decision-making about the optimal use of the limited funds available for the work.

The Subcommittee on Distribution

At the General Committee meeting in Addis Ababa, Hutchinson reported on a Distribution Consultation which had just been held. His report outlined the task of the Subcommittee on Distribution and the Strategy of the UBS for the Seventies. He cleared up at once the role of the Bible Societies vis-à-vis the churches:

> The very center of target was effective distribution of the Scriptures in every possible form. The Bible Societies could not, as many Christians tended to think, fulfill this task alone; it was a specialized function within the activity of the Church. Nor could they become involved in the biblical apostolate—this was the task of other organizations within the Church. The whole Church is engaged in "Bible work," whether in its pastoral ministry, teaching or mission; the Bible Societies' task was to provide the actual Scriptures, in attractive and compelling formats, to be an instrument, through church channels, by the programs and the prayers and the gifts of concerned Christians, of deepening the Church's life and of its mission in the world.

He then asked the question which the Bible Societies had to ask themselves: "How could the Bible Society help to perfect this instrument?" He insisted that this required continual survey of strategy, a willingness to adjust methods and structures, and, in the light of these activities, a readiness to reallocate money, personnel, and energies to meet the present needs of a changing world. "It is here," he added, "that the UBS seems to be failing." He did not hesitate then to put forward precise details of the concerns which the consultation of distribution consultants had identified as matters of real concern: "More intensive concentration is needed on the preparation of dynamic equivalent or common translation, initially in the major world languages, and as soon as possible in the world languages of second and third importance." He pointed out that the urgency was created by opportunity. "A biblical revolution was now taking place," he maintained, "which is unparalleled in the history of the Church. Scriptures are needed which are specially prepared for new readers and new literates." He supported this appeal with figures of world population, now 3,700 million, of whom there were 1,600 million outside the Church. "Scriptures are needed specially prepared to reach young people, who form half the population of the world. The Assembly and the Council are to issue a mandate to member Societies to increase annual Scripture circulation to 500 million by 1980. Scriptures must be produced in more attractive forms." Hutchinson was serious. These were no pipe dreams but urgent concerns, and the General Committee responded. They all knew that he had set a high level of achievements, and he himself pointed out what this would mean to all Bible Societies. "Analyze potential markets and audiences and restructure distribution networks to reach them; select and train the best possible staff; be responsible stewards of their funds; plan at all levels—local, national, regional, and global." Such was the World Strategy for the Seventies which the UBS Assembly addressed.[2]

The Dimmed Vision

It was depressing to look through the Minutes of the Executive Committee and read the reports from the Subcommittee on Distribution. Meeting after meeting recorded that the subcommittee had not met. Perhaps the vision of Hutchinson's appeal in Addis Ababa was caught by the individual Bible Societies, but not by the subcommittee that should have picked it up. It had nothing of the fire of Russell Self in it. But at last there was a meeting in Mexico, January 1977. It was Cryer (BFBS) who introduced the minutes of that meeting to the Executive Committee in March. He was deeply concerned. By now he had been seven years in the office of BFBS General Secretary, and there was no doubt that he had his effect. In eight years the contributions rose from £200,000 to £2 million, and when Cryer left in 1987, it stood at £3.5 million. His colleague as Executive Director, Rev. Tom Houston, a Baptist minister, had concentrated efforts on an evangelistic distribution of Scriptures and had involved the churches. The BFBS was passing through an energetic period, but was inclined to isolation from UBS affairs. In Mexico, Cryer had been disturbed by the lack of preparation for the meeting of the Distribution Subcommittee. Papers had not been circulated beforehand, and there seemed a readiness to leave everything to the national Bible Societies. He was in a fighting mood when he reported to the Executive Committee after the Mexico meeting. He made three recommendations: that there should be women at the regional centers as part of the distribution staff, that more attention be given to distribution, and that national Bible Societies be encouraged to appoint a distribution secretary. The subcommittee had finally come alive and had already published a new journal, *The Bible Distributor.* *The Bible Translator* had established itself and was invaluable to translators through the world. Something similar was urged for *The Bible Distributor.* There was need for help. At the Executive Committee where he reported, it was decided that *The Bible Distributor* continue for another year and that it be prepared by a different region each quarter. This enabled the sharing of experiences.

There was more. The subcommittee had worked on a practical manual for the use of national Bible Societies in developing Scripture selection. Cryer was asked to draft this manual and send the draft to the Regional Secretaries, World Service Officers and the General Secretary for comments. Within the year the Selections manual had been printed, and the new reader manual was in the design/layout stage.[3]

Statistics

Béguin had warned many years before that statistics were deceptive. A Bible Society could have easily increased its distribution by publishing more Selections while the number of Bibles distributed decreased. For a realistic estimate of how far the Bible work in the world was growing, it was necessary to define categories.

In September 1977, Erickson circulated a paper defining the UBS Selections at an Executive Committee meeting in Nairobi. In order to make a realistic statement of achievement, Bible Societies and regions were now required to present their statistics with more details of the type of product: Bibles, Testaments, Portions, and Selections.

The Societies were also encouraged to report separately non-print mass media and Bibles, Testaments, and Portions published by other licensed publishers. The value of this burdensome reporting was soon seen in the statistical tables published each year, where the true achievements of the Societies and regions could be seen at a glance. Self's call for a billion Scriptures by the end of the millennium could be seen in perspective when all categories were listed. In 1976, Bible Societies and national offices were working in 115 countries worldwide. The statistics for that year, not including commercial publishers give a total of 330,900,744. Broken down into regions, it shows a wide divergence between the Americas (175 million), Asia-Pacific (100 million) and the other two regions, Africa (14 million) and Europe (14 million). This divergence is partly accounted for by the large number of Portions, New Reader Portions, Selections, and New Reader Selections. When the number of Bibles and Testaments are compared the divergence almost disappears, but not entirely. It was this that led Cryer, when reporting the results of the Mexico meeting, to urge that attention be called to the request that the Africa and Europe regions take distribution more seriously. The mid-seventies were obviously critical years.[4]

The Meaning of Membership

In 1972 a very serious issue of maladministration had to be dealt with in the Philippines. The Executive Committee had expressed concern about this, and Inbanathan, the Asian member of the Executive Committee and chairman of the General Committee, accompanied Cline when he attended the Board meeting of the Philippine Bible Society. The issue was eventually resolved, but not until the PBS had been expelled from the UBS and subsequently reinstated. The pressure on the Regional Secretary was enormous.

This incident of expelling the Society from the UBS showed how seriously membership was being taken. It was important to maintain certain standards, and quite clearly the Philippine Bible Society fell well below those standards. There had been vote rigging so that a small group of individuals could take over the Board and then proceed to strip the assets of the Society, sharing the spoils among themselves.

After that, the churches in the Philippines, who were horrified at what had happened in the Bible Society, began to show interest in bringing the Society back to the standard required of a member of the UBS. They took it upon themselves to completely reorganize the Society with the help of the UBS, and the result was that a Society was formed far stronger than it had ever been before.

This was the first time that a member Society had been expelled, and it was for the UBS a crucial decision. Over the years, much effort had gone into defining the conditions of membership. These were clearly known to all who had eventually accepted. But the test of seriousness in any organization with standards was what it did when a member, once accepted, breached the rules by which it was admitted. The painful action taken by the UBS put the stamp of integrity upon membership. It was good that eventually the PBS could be readmitted, once certain procedures had been followed. But the significant action was to expel a member that did not operate according to the high standards required of a member Society of the UBS.

The Executive Committee met twice in 1977—at Santo Domingo, Dominican Republic in March and Nairobi, Kenya in September, when the Bible Society of Kenya was formally received into full membership of the UBS. At the Nairobi meeting in September the meaning of membership was much in the minds of the Executive Committee members, not only because of the number of Societies seeking to become a part of the fellowship, but even more because of the action taken in the Philippines. The General Secretary rose to the occasion with a penetrating report, reminiscent of Béguin at his best. Fick, in fact, went back to Béguin's definition of the UBS as a world fellowship for "common thinking, joint planning, and combined action."

While maintaining that a real member of the UBS had no secrets to hide from fellow members, he admitted that this can be seen as a threat—a threat to national autonomy and independence. He then launched into his theme:

> Autonomy and independence are ideas which have to be modified by fellowship. I would claim that as soon as membership in the UBS is accepted as the key fact, independence and autonomy cannot remain absolute principles which are taboo. For some of us, it is a painful

process to adjust, to change, to have others see what we are doing and how we are doing it—but these are things on which any life in a family is based. Fellowship is impossible without the readiness to sacrifice some freedom for the sake of others and their freedom. This is basic for any kind of human interrelationship.

It was a critical moment in the life of the UBS when he could say, "common thinking" as a precondition for joint planning and combined action must have spiritual depth. Otherwise it was only a superficial and temporary pragmatic agreement to follow certain purposes because this was more economic, more efficient, or more convenient in particular cases than to go it all alone. This meant involvement in the worldwide efforts of the UBS: "The national and the global task cannot be separated. No Bible Society can confine itself to the area within the borders of its own nation."[5]

"Paradoxical Predictions of Great Things to Come"

Holmgren retired from full-time work with the Bible Societies in 1978. He had guided the UBS through those decisive years leading up to the historic Council Meeting in Buck Hill Falls 1966 and watched over the implementation of the radical decisions taken there. He had seen a World Service Budget, a European Production Fund, and full regionalization within a structure of an international organization. The tributes paid to him were warm and deserved. He had been the major figure in the UBS for a generation, supporting and guiding two general secretaries. It was a historic moment when he retired from full-time service but continued his influence and interest. At that moment he had something to say about the past and the future. As he looked back, he asked, "What are the signal events in the history of the UBS?" As he listed them he saw them also as portents of great things to come. He chose five examples and described them as movements from the past into the future:

1. More literary/liturgical texts being developed, while at the same time far more simplified texts for new readers of the Scriptures, leading to more activity both in major and minor languages.

2. More full Bibles, many appearing with the deuterocanon (Apocrypha) in order to reach a whole new constituency, while at the same time many more shorter Bibles for first-time readers.

3. A greater variety of printed Scriptures, with more sophisticated techniques of illustration and layout, while at the same time far more production in the nonprint media, a field we have barely touched.

4. Fewer areas calling on world service budget support as Third World countries become more affluent, while at the same time infinitely greater resources being needed to meet opportunities in presently closed areas.

5. A greatly strengthened central administration with the general office offering far more services, more guidance, and more global strategy than at present, while at the same time much greater vigor, initiative, and self-consciousness at national and regional levels emerging.

He described them as "paradoxical predictions." They were creative paradoxes, with the tensile stress of dialectics. Each part tuned the other and enabled this creative tension: literary and liturgical texts were balanced by texts for new readers; full Bibles with Apocrypha were balanced by shorter Bibles for new readers; elaborated and sophisticated print material was balanced by use of the nonprint media; less need for help to Third World Societies was balanced by new opportunities demanding greater resources; and a strong central administration was balanced by new initiative at national and regional level. Earlier in that meeting in Hong Kong, he had already listed five "signal events" which were historical milestones and in the nature of achievement rather than prediction:

1. The Greek New Testament (begun in 1956), which marked a new phase in the Bible Societies' cooperation with one another, their first major cooperative world effort being this beginning to the series of the aids for translators.

2. Today's English Version New Testament (begun in 1960), which became the model for scores of common language dynamic equivalent translations and has opened the way for the New Readers program.

3. The use of Scripture Selections (authorized in 1963), which marked a new global effort to reach the unevangelized.
4. Conversations with the Roman Catholic Church (1964–1968), which had strengthened the mandate of the Bible Societies to serve the whole church in the whole world.
5. The World Service Budget (1966–1979), which represents the UBS "coming of age" in a new day of global partnership and commitment.[6]

Holmgren was so rooted in the life of the UBS that it was impossible to let him go as soon as he had retired from the American Bible Society. As Fick pointed out there was still some unfinished business: "The revision of the UBS bylaws had not yet come to a conclusion," and he had been asked by the Asia-Pacific regional secretary to assist in negotiations in the Philippines and by the Europe regional secretary to assist in the development of relationships with Orthodox churches. It was clear that Holmgren still had work to do with the UBS, and he was willing to do it. The Executive Committee, therefore, resolved "to appoint the Rev. Dr. Laton Holmgren special consultant to the UBS Executive Committee for a renewable term of one year, effective October 1, 1978."[7] The procedure then was that he should report to the Executive Committee and have his assignments coordinated by the General Secretary, with consultation as appropriate. It was left to Dr. Kenneth MacMillan of Canada to record a tribute to Holmgren:

In expressing our appreciation for the life and work of Laton E. Holmgren as he relinquishes his major responsibilities, we wish to record our appreciation for the truly distinguished service he has rendered to the whole fellowship. His missionary zeal, born out of a deep and abiding faith, far from diminishing over the decades, has grown and has been the motivation for his concern to place God's word in the hands of all readers. His reputation as an able preacher was recognized when his sermons were selected in successive years for inclusion in the volume "Best Sermons for the Year.

His ability to recognize the importance of detail and of clarity of expression coupled with a clear vision of the goals of the UBS fellowship have enabled him to make an invaluable contribution in constitutional matters. It can be said of him that he is not only a key architect of the present form of the UBS, but he is in addition one of the workers who has actually built our present structure.

His gentle persuasive manner has established him as an international diplomat for the UBS and our most valuable ambassador in the midst of the variety of cultures, languages, political systems, churches, and theological traditions in which Bible Society work is carried out. The giant strides made in the whole area of interconfessional relationships is but one example of what he has made possible by his good judgement and wise decisions.

Words cannot capture or express all we feel about the life and work of Laton E. Holmgren. We thank him for what he is, for what he has done, and for what he means to us. We shall remember him in many ways, but most of all as a friend, as our friend and as a friend of the One who has been his constant companion and who we pray will go with him and bless him for many more years of service.[8]

Distribution in the Eighties

Before they left Hong Kong, the Executive Committee agreed to the holding of a meeting of the distribution subcommittee early in 1979. This meeting prepared a strategy for the eighties. Cryer, who reported, wanted the meeting in association with a meeting of the regional secretaries in January 1979. He explained that four papers had been requested and they would form the basis of discussion at the meeting:

1. "What Do We Mean by Effective Distribution?" by John Dean
2. "How Do We Motivate the Churches?" by Russell Self
3. "Where Are We with the New Reader Program?" by Dr. Edward Hope, Asia-Pacific translation consultant
4. "How Far Beyond the Print Media?" by Neville Cryer.[9]

The meeting was held in Nairobi, January 24–27, 1979. All four papers were presented and discussed. The second paper on motivating the churches led to the request for a distribution training program. This was predictable since Russell Self had presented the paper. Details of this proposed program and of an expansion of the New Readers Program were presented to the Executive Committee in September, when it met in Chania, Crete. Both were approved for further discussion and financial assessment. What was becoming evident was that the growing opportunities could not all be met with the UBS limited resources. Perhaps the clearest indication of this is in the general secretary's report to the UBS General Committee when it met in Chiang Mai, Thailand, September 26, 1980.

"Years of Growth, Years of Testing" (1976–1980)

During the period 1972–1976, the UBS had put almost all its resources into distribution and was now suffering a lack of capital. There were many production funds—Fick listed the European Production Fund, the Scripture Supply Fund for Nigeria and other areas of need, later transferred to New York to become the UBS Scripture Supply Fund, the Americas Production Fund, and now an appeal for contributions to an African Production Fund. All this was good but needed better coordination. He pointed out that some funds were tied up in countries from which they could not be exported. He also pointed out that some national Bible Societies had considerable funds they might make available on loan to the UBS. The question he asked the members of the general committee was, "To what extent are we ready to allow our spending on our own needs to be governed by the needs of others?"

Fick then went on to deal with the question of competition in Bible distribution. Sometimes it was most helpful that other organizations supplement the work of Bible Societies, but in other cases free distribution of some organizations damaged the sale of Bible Society books. Sometimes translators needed for common language translation projects were invited to work for Living Bibles Incorporated, as in Iran, and Fick urged a plan and new steps to avoid such overlap and competition. Sometimes the opposition was deliberate and so it could not be avoided, but in the areas where cooperation was possible, efforts should have been made to coordinate. He quoted the example of a meeting of the Lausanne Committee at Pattaya in June 1980 when the suggestion was made "to invite representatives of the major Scripture distribution agencies to an informal meeting in 1981 with the aim of establishing better information and coordination." Fick supported this move, because it gave hope of a better use of the "total resources of the people of God."

Another reason for the strain on resources was that the growth of Scripture needs in the Roman Catholic Church had not been matched by increased contributions. Fick put the issue quite clearly:

> We had a springtime in this relationship when in 1967 the "Guiding Principles" were formulated. The names of the persons who achieved this are well known to you: foremost Olivier Béguin and Laton Holmgren on the side of the UBS, and Cardinal Augustin Bea, followed by Cardinal Willebrands and Walter Abbott at the Vatican. These contacts and agreements resulted in a vigorous program of joint translations. Out of 751 translations projects which are at present under way, 140 have the full participation of Roman Catholic translators and reviewers, and are carried out with the intention of making these translations available to Christians of all traditions. Many Bible Societies, especially our friends in Latin America, report that the majority of the New Testaments—and presumably soon of the Bibles in the Versión Popular—go to Roman Catholics. Subsidies which are needed for this distribution, however, are still largely funded by the traditional supporters of the Bible Societies.

Despite this, Fick defended the efforts to make Bibles available in the Catholic and Orthodox churches. His argument was clear: "I know from reading the minutes and reports made by the fathers of our movement that it was the original plan and desire of the Bible Societies to make God's Word available to all." Finally, he dealt with the question of whether the UBS could reduce its elaborate organization. He defended the organization and the structures worked out over the previous decade, but insisted that it was necessary to reexamine with economy in mind. "We have expanded and improved on the services which the UBS as a global fellowship is rendering to national societies and offices," he said, "but no complacency. A new decade needs new questioning."[10]

Raising the Money

Bible distribution on the principle of making it available to all at a price the recipient could afford was like no other business. The greater the success the greater the loss. Bibles were subsidized, and somehow the money had to be found. Member Societies had worked out their own methods of fundraising over a long period. The BFBS, for example, had formed a network of associations in towns and villages where churches could be persuaded to raise money locally for the cause. Legacies were encouraged and outright gifts, which were often of considerable proportion. Membership schemes were widespread. Success brought demand for more than could be raised by traditional methods. Dr. Robert Taylor of the ABS employed a professional organization to help develop means of fundraising, including direct mail appeals. Houston of the BFBS did much the same in his own way. Every new challenge called forth new methods. The most effective way of raising large sums proved to be by direct mail. That was more than finding a list of interested people and mailing an appeal to them at regular intervals. This was done, but it still proved inadequate. Thanks to Taylor's efforts, the ABS was more successful when it used commercial people sympathetic to the Bible cause to put ABS fundraising on a professional basis. The European Bible Societies saw the value of this and invited the Americans to help. The NBS, who was already into direct mail appeals, took the lead.

In 1972, Erickson was executive secretary of the Ways and Means Department of the ABS. At the invitation of the NBS, he brought three professional men with him and led a seminar for the European Bible Societies, at Breda, from May 30 to June 1, 1972. He had experience in the ABS, both in the ways and means department and in the church relations department, but he needed support for what was to be a symposium. He brought the three members of the panel.

Lester J. Harmon, who had been in advertising twenty-six years, was at that time vice president of the Philadelphia Agency. He was sympathetic to Bible Society work and as director of Religious Communications Division of his Agency, he serviced the ABS and other religious bodies, as well as producing the film, "Billy Graham in Vietnam." Edward N. Mayer, Jr. was regarded as the most knowledgeable expert on direct mail in his time was also a consultant to the ABS. Murray Miller was president of the OEI Computer System, which for more than fifteen years had specialized in computer fulfillment of direct-mail services.

It was clear that the NBS was firmly behind this project, and eight of its staff attended, including the General Secretary, Baron van Tuyll. Other Bible Societies were also well represented. The BFBS had Cryer, its general secretary for home affairs, and Mr. Alan Gardner, who was responsible for promotion and information. The Bible Societies of Scotland, Germany, Norway, Belgium, Austria, as well as the Europe Regional Secretary, Smaadahl, the UBS Treasurer, Tattersall, and two representatives of Catholic organizations—the Netherlands office of the Catholic Mission Council and the Roman Catholic Bible Foundation in the Netherlands. What is obvious from the composition of the symposium is that the Netherlands Bible Society took this venture very seriously indeed and that the other Bible Societies of Europe saw some hope in a new method of fundraising. Many, like the NBS, had done direct-mail appeals before, but what was on offer was training in a professional way of using this method with the experience of commercial firms available.

Introducing the Conference

The conference was hosted by the NBS and led by Erickson. He was at once aware that this conference must not appear like the Americans speaking to the Europeans in any superior kind of way. He recognized that the NBS had considerable experience already and that the BFBS had looked at this method carefully. The conference, he said, was not the know-all Americans telling the Europeans, but a sharing of experiences. He illustrated this attitude by describing the direct marketing symposia which Murray Miller had conducted over the previous years in Switzerland. At the beginning, the commercial people in Switzerland wondered what they had to learn from these "aggressive, brash, know-it-all Americans," so, few came to the first conference. Later it grew, and by the third year they were writing to say, "Would you be sure to bring some of the most recent things that are happening commercially in the Americans' experience?"

Erickson was skillful in drawing upon his own experience of inadequacy when he was moved over from the program side of the ABS to the promotion side. In his confusion, which he described in a way that must have won the sympathy of the participants from the start, he had said to Baas, "I don't know anything," and got the reply, "We know that, but you can learn."

It was a Bible Society conference, and fundraising could not seriously be discussed without reference to the purpose for which the funds were raised. Smaadahl in the opening prayers spoke of the "variety of gifts with the same Spirit" from 1 Corinthians 12. He concentrated upon the offices God had appointed in the Church, in verse 28, and pointed out that "administrators" were among the gifts of the Spirit, although it came second from last. Erickson knew that this conference would only take a method of fundraising seriously if its purpose was clearly defined and within the God-appointed mission of his Church. With pounds and dollar signs on one side and the Japanese character for people on the other side, he put Bible Society in between, adding:

> We have a *transforming* responsibility. We have the responsibility to transform money into message. Now in the Bible Society we talk about books. . . . It does often seem that we are caught in the middle. We are being pressed from both sides. We cannot get out. But . . . we are in the middle, we have a transforming responsibility. We are a conduit, we are a pipeline. We are the thing that makes things happen.

Then he quickly passed over to the self-evident three things that would keep this conduit open and persuade those who want their money to be transformed into the message that the Bible Society can do it:

1. A credible cause—we must close the credibility gap.
2. Implementation that is proven—show that you can meet the need by evidence of what you have already done, that you are established and dependable.
3. Continuing communications—go back constantly to your donors, show them that by the help of their money you were able to meet the need; you are the conduit, keep the flow going in both directions.

The Program

That first session had been a general introduction over the whole range of direct-mail appeals. Examples were given; success and failure discussed. It was an opportunity for the conference to question the experts and test them each against their own experience. Much of the time was spent on "lists," the way in which you compile lists of addresses. The second session was taken by Ed Mayer on "Basic Objectives," but again it was not an uninterrupted lecture. Mayer had much to give, but he wanted to share and enter into dialogue. He did. The content of his presentation was stimulating. Acknowledging that the overwhelming amount of mail in the U.S. was consumer mail, he gave the result of a survey of how it was received. Of 100 persons who received such:

- Fifteen get mail that is not wanted and thrown away unopened.
- Thirty-three love to get mail.
- Fifty-two decide upon each piece of mail—whether or not they will look at it.

Now, that last proportion, more than half, was the key to success. How did they decide? Honestly, they responded that it depended upon whether they had a good breakfast, quarrelled with their spouse, got stuck in a traffic jam, or were bored. But they also said that it could have depended upon "if they liked the feel of the piece or the name of the organization, although some were made curious by the fact that there was no name on it." Something could be done there.

But Mayer insisted that the important thing was that 75 percent of the people opened the mail.

Then he went on to talk about what can be done to make people read it after they had opened it. What kind of mail did people want? A simple example raised a few questions, like the desire to tell them about the organization, but they were not yet concerned with those details. Erickson provided him with an example, a recent experiment in which an identical mailing was made to large contributors to the ABS. In one, a printed folder was included with an appeal letter; in the others, just a letter. With the large donors, the letter alone "pulled" better responses. All this was done in dialogue, questions and answers from different members of the panel and as though everyone had something of his own to offer. Gradually the necessary skills were described and partially already learned. There were closing sessions on research and testing. Throughout, questions were encouraged and answers given quite frankly.[11]

The Follow-Up

After three days of conference, most of those attending were appreciative of this team of Americans who had brought their skills and expertise and shared their long experience with the European Societies. They were also aware that they had learned much from each other. But the days had also shown them that they now had experienced friends to whom they could write if they found problems in carrying out their own direct-mail appeals. Erickson offered his continuing help as mediator and announced that Ed Mayer would come into the ABS office each week to dictate answers to queries sent in.

Van Tuyll, chairman of the UBS Europe Region, and Sverre Smaadahl, its Secretary, agreed to work out other ways of following up the conference. As Cryer was chairman of the UBS subcommittee on promotion and information, he saw that the effects of the conference were taken into the structures of the UBS.

Similar conferences were held in subsequent years. If contributions to the UBS World Budget in 1974 were compared with that in 1977, some idea of the effect was presented. Of course, other factors were involved, but the growth was significant in some European Societies:

Society	1974	1977
NBS	$319,811	$508,500
NBSS	63,069	102,000
Austrian Bible Society	41,672	61,111

These figures did not include the additional money raised in these countries for work within their own borders.

◇ CHAPTER FIFTEEN ◇

Dressed for Action with Lamps Lit

—— ◇ ——

The UBS Council met at Chiang Mai in Thailand from September 28 to October 5, 1980. The Executive Committee and the General Committee scheduled meetings immediately prior to and following the sessions of the Council. This cluster of meetings focused attention on the work of the UBS for the eighties.

More than two hundred persons from eighty countries gathered in this moated city of Thailand, representing forty of the forty-two national Bible Societies in full membership with the UBS; nineteen of the twenty-three associate members; twenty-one national officers, fraternal delegates, special guests, and extra officers of the region, together with UBS officers and staff. Many had never attended a UBS meeting before.[1]

The theme of the Council was "God's Word Open for All." The paper which the delegates made the basis of their discussion and the substance of their commitment became their call to action and the demanding project of the Bible Societies of the world. The Council set itself to strive constantly toward achieving certain specific objectives over the next ten years, defining those objectives and aims in the context of "national opportunities and possibilities." The document was conceived as a working paper for the UBS fellowship. It had six sections:

1. *The Bible Societies and the Churches*
   Objective: To involve all churches and the whole Christian community in the vigorous promotion of the Bible cause.

   The Conference of Church leaders held in Driebergen, Holland
   in June 1964 made this a prime aim of the UBS, which echoed
   effectively in the UBS Assembly in Addis Ababa in 1972. Now
   each Bible Society was committed to specific action relating to
   this objective. Cooperation with all churches in the region was
   emphasized, an objective not yet fully achieved. The national
   Bible Societies committed themselves to finding new ways of motivating Christian churches, organizations and other groups
   which had hitherto shown little interest.

2. *Bible Translation*
   Objective: To provide the Holy Scriptures in the languages of
   today.

   The experience of the UBS so far had shown the value of
   "dynamic equivalent translations" which were not only accurate
   but understood in terms of contemporary culture. Many translations still remained in the languages of an earlier generation or
   in a remote "religious" language. The objective now was clearly
   defined as "all languages with more than one million literates,
   and all officially designated national languages" should have a
   whole Bible in "clear and comprehensible versions" within a decade. Portions and Selections should be available for "new
   readers" in all major languages, enabling them to move towards
   common language translations. For this, 1985 was the target date.

3. *Production and Supply*
   Objective: To ensure that Scriptures produced attractively and
   economically are available for all.

   This objective required a careful review of present administration and proper safeguards for the best use of resources. In production, this also meant attention to price, quality, durability,
   etc. In supply, it meant maintaining a smooth and uninterrupted
   flow of Scriptures, matching local needs.

4. *Distribution*
   Objective: To provide easy access to the Bible for all.

   The duties of each society were clearly spelled out—to determine needs and develop appropriate programs; to direct programs to clearly defined targets on the basis of continuing audience research; to develop adequate distributing patterns for those groups, such as ethnic and social groups, who did not have sufficient access to the Scriptures; to make special efforts for those who do not read, through cassettes, radio, television, posters, and cartoons; to determine distribution targets each year for the next five years.

5. *Resources*

Objective: To confront the supporting constituencies with the urgent need for greatly expanded financial resources to meet the growing demand for Scriptures.

The paper spelled out the need to pursue new and compelling ways of mobilizing support as well as an openness in accounting, so that supporters could see where their money was going and what more could be accomplished with more resources.

6. *Enablement*

Objective: To mobilize human and spiritual resources and develop organizational structures to fulfill the purpose of the Bible Societies.

Regular reading of the Bible and prayer headed the list of proposals and thus to "strive to become a spiritually motivated fellowship." Then followed staff training, regular review of structures, a continuing program to enlist and train volunteers in the Bible cause, and new ways to involve youth in every aspect of Bible Society work.

This was a very representative Council, and it committed itself to this detailed effort. There was an urgency about the decision:

> The task is pressing. Action is urgent. Within this program each Society will determine its goals and establish a timetable for launching and developing them. Achievements to date will be reviewed at the next meeting of the UBS General Committee (1984).[2]

Fick added that for him the great new fact in this working plan was that the widest possible representation of the member societies of the UBS accepted this paper as a "starting point for detailed national programs."

Message to the Churches

The determination of the Council meeting at Chiang Mai was conveyed to the churches in a message which contained two crucial paragraphs:

> The Bible Societies are ready to produce editions of Scripture that will support the spiritual life and mission of all branches of the Christian Church. The Bible was, is, and always will be the basis of the worship and work of God's Church. Today many churches are reexamining the use of Scripture both in their own fellowship and in their evangelistic and missionary outreach. We, the Bible Societies, pledge our openness to assist every Christian church with Scripture publications that support, deepen, and intensify the church's life and mission.

That was about as open as any statement could be. It contained none of the hesitations that had earlier marked the "protestant" Bible Societies. But it needed the cooperation of the churches for which the second paragraph asked:

> Only through full and frequent consultation will the Bible Societies learn how to serve you best. New translations may be needed. Perhaps Scriptures in different formats are needed in order to reach specific groups. New ways and methods of distribution must be established. Please let your Bible Society know.[3]

This was a reaffirmation of the long-standing conviction that the Bible Societies need the churches and the churches need the Bible Societies, but now the interdependence of the two had become more manifest and, in fact, essential. The work to which they were committed in the Bible Societies of the world must never be the "special concern of just a few."

Translation Work in Africa

At the age of 87, still alive to the cause he had served all his life, Platt wrote to the Council at Chiang Mai, calling upon the delegates to be "realistic, not romantic." He had been a missionary in French West Africa before he joined the staff of the BFBS. He pointed out that in that francophone region which included, at that time, six self-governing territories and 27 million people, the only Bible Society staff consisted of one African secretary, who was a retired Methodist minister. He asked why the Western-based Bible Societies were still so "Anglo-Saxon minded." He called for African Bible Societies to fill in the open spaces with new translations and for distribution staff to move around carrying the gospel for sale to millions of Muslims. He was not at Chiang Mai, but his voice was heard, and it met with sympathy.[4]

So far as his appeal for distribution to Muslims was concerned, Schaaf had a valuable summary of the attitude of the churches towards Muslims. Their missions had been largely to followers of traditional African religions, avoiding missions to Muslims. This changed around 1960. "The history of Bible translations intended for mainly Muslim peoples," he added, "reflects the position of churches and missions to Islam. With the change in the churches' attitude, Bible translations intended for Muslims have grown, taking account of Muslim thinking." But there were problems.[5]

NAWAT

For many years there had been concern and action taken with regard to those areas in North Africa, West Asia, and Europe (Turkey)—NAWAT—where the population was predominantly Muslim. The work was hampered by political instability and religious opposition. There were common problems across the whole area in which three UBS regions were involved, making coordination of work difficult. There was a proposal to make the whole area a fifth region, but this was rejected, and it became a subregion attached to Europe. A NAWAT consultant was appointed: Rev. Samuel Yeghnazar.

After World War II some Orthodox churches reopened their seminaries and academies and were in need of scholarly editions of the biblical texts, which the Bible Societies were able to supply. Gradually a partnership developed, especially among scholars. This partnership went far beyond the supply of texts and even included the provision of printing presses and technical aid. Consultancy in translation soon followed.

Although this was not an approach to the Muslims, it was a necessary prerequisite. As Smaadahl discovered in his relations with the churches in Communist countries, it was soon found necessary to accept the similar limitations of a minority church in Muslim-dominated countries. The Orthodox churches in these lands had learned to survive by accepting the limitations and keeping within them. As in Eastern Europe, the UBS kept firmly within the law and were thus no threat to the security of the Orthodox churches.

The work among Muslims in this subregion was difficult enough, but also hindered by the failure to find a successor to Yeghnazar for the Bible Society in Lebanon. The conditions of appointment had been that Yeghnazar would start his work in NAWAT as soon as another general secretary could be found for Lebanon. At last in 1980 the Rev. Lucien Accad was appointed to the office in Beirut, and Yeghnazar began with NAWAT on April 1, 1980. Shortly after, a budget workshop was held in Istanbul with Florin, by now the regional secretary for Europe, in the chair. This was the first experience of attempting to look at NAWAT as a whole and to recognize that they must have their own budget rather than relate separately to three different regions. It was not easy, but the participants agreed that the areas had common problems, and the exchange of ideas was well worthwhile.

Inadequate Resources

Expansion soon brought added problems. Finding the funds to meet increasing budget demands became a constant concern. As the UBS program expanded there were inevitable pressures for it to expand even more. It seemed that the desire and need for Scriptures throughout the world was almost unlimited. A special meeting of major fundraisers was therefore held in Lisbon, February 1984, to assess the situation in the light of the Chiang Mai working plan. One of those chosen to give information was Lucien Accad of Lebanon:

We are grateful for your support and prayers in these difficult times, and for the financial support that has enabled the work of Scripture distribution to carry on as in the past. We are particularly grateful for our new premises. (The old premises had been blown up.) The Bible has a relevant message and speaks to the people of Lebanon, Syria, and Jordan today. . . Yet at our budget workshop last year we looked at all our distribution opportunities—realizing that they were all excellent opportunities for distributing the Word of God, but knowing that they could not all be included in the budget because of lack of funds. Some really wonderful opportunities for spreading God's Word in this troubled part of the world had to be excluded—and this at a time of greatest need.

In a similar vein, Mr. B. U. Khokhar, General Secretary of the Pakistan Bible Society, spoke and ended with an appeal:

In the past some of our volunteers have had to face difficulties—even to the extent of being beaten up. One of our volunteers was distributing Scriptures in a bus and he was actually thrown out of the moving bus. Fortunately the Lord protected him from serious injury, and now he is back distributing Scriptures in buses again.

Then he added, "Somebody is willing to risk his life for the sake of the Gospel. Is there somebody, somewhere, Lord, who is willing to risk his money for the sake of the Gospel, so that the Good News may be shared in Pakistan?"[6]

The meeting in Chiang Mai also focused attention on the approach to other religions. Thailand was overwhelmingly Buddhist, and, although that did not present the problems of a Muslim-dominated country, it did affect methods of distribution and required appreciation of other people's faith. In fact, most of Asia was something other than Christian. Clearly a different approach was made to one who fervently held to another religion than to one who sought a faith or was even careless of faith.

Approaches to People of Other Religions

In Chiang Mai it was evident that Scriptures should be produced and presented in such a way as to command the respect and the attention of those of other faiths. That was the birth of WASAI, which under the leadership of the Rev. Kenneth Thomas, helped Bible Societies to prepare Scriptures for the peoples of West Asia, South Asia, and Indonesia.

This was under the guidance of the newly created UBS Asia-Pacific Region WASAI Texts Committee. The full development had to wait a few years, but it was one of the most ambitious strategies of the UBS—to present the Christian Bible to Hindus, Muslims, Buddhists, and Jews. By 1991, "A Guide to Scriptures Prepared by Bible Societies in West Asia, South Asia, and Indonesia" was issued.

The guide went into detail about the necessary research and development needed to produce the Selections with helps that would be useful at various states of contact. Then for fifty pages it outlined the nature of approach to people who may have their own preconceived ideas about the Christian Bible. The WASAI Scriptures were adapted to relate to the predominant religion of people in the area and sought to discover the common ground on which people of faith could meet.

The special issues for these countries were so far based upon felt needs of the Muslim audience and were chosen to address these needs. In addition to designing and selecting appropriate Portions or Selections, there was the need to have the right kind of calligraphy, colors, formats, and designs, which appealed to the particular audience. In addition, the methods of presentation and distribution were based upon experience and recommended to those who were going to distribute them.

It was, however, soon recognized that the most effective approach to WASAI audiences was through several stages, with Scriptures, given in progression according to the increasing interest and understanding of the recipients. These stages were initial contact, follow-up, study, and then nurture.

The sensitivity of this UBS subregion had shown positive results. Similar work had yet to be done for Buddhist audiences but this was already started.[7]

New Technology

The world was changing, and new technology was making its impact. In 1983, the Executive Committee meeting in Canberra appointed a computer task force. The role of computers in translation was already established. The General Secretary saw this use widening and explained the possible development in his annual report for 1983:

Computers are now not only a management tool for accounting, stocktaking, and fundraising. UBS translations staff have discovered how much time, energy, and money can be saved when computers are introduced to the process of translation and manuscript preparation. Instead of retyping the script of a New Testament or Bible four to six times, as hitherto, from the first draft through the various stages of revision to the final script, now only changes will need to be keyed in, and the computerized text can go straight to the typesetter. It can be predicted that within a short time not only all full-time translations consultants will be trained and will readily use this tool, but also that all translation teams working on major projects will be equipped with computers from the very outset of their work. . . .[8]

At this stage, Europe and North America were able to give the greatest help to the UBS fellowship in the initiating of this plan.

The Fortieth Anniversary

The conference center known as "Elfinsward" in Haywards Heath was gone, but some thirty former and present leaders of the UBS gathered near the site in the library of Newick Park on May 9, 1986. They had met to recall the "Elfinsward" meeting in 1946 which gave birth to the UBS and to commemorate forty years of growth. One person was present on both occasions—Rev. Dr. William J. Platt, the BFBS Home Secretary in 1946, but on this second visit, at age 93, the retired BFBS General Secretary. The giants of the movement who came on the scene in the decade after "Elfinsward" were remembered for their significant contribution—Baron F. L. S. van Tuyll van Seroosker-ken of the NBS, Dr. Laton E. Holmgren of the ABS, and Dr. F. Donald Coggan, formerly Archbishop of Canterbury. All these and others were there at the celebrations, joined by the new leadership of the UBS. They all, past and present, affirmed their commitment to the Bible cause. North, Wilkinson, Berggrav, Temple, Béguin, and many others were honored in the thanksgiving of forty years of witness. The acorn had grown to an impressive oak. They recognized that the task to which the pioneers had set their hands in 1946 was not yet done. From Newick Park there went out a tribute to the past and a challenge to the future:

Today the task is even greater than it was then. The world population has grown enormously. There are more young people than ever before in human history. The readiness of the Christian churches to base their spiritual life and their witness on the Bible is more evident than ever. The Bible Society family has grown over the past four decades not only in numbers but also in mutual understanding and effectiveness, and for this we thank God. Still, what has been achieved by the UBS over the past forty years is just a beginning.[9]

Baron van Tuyll

The NBS played a significant role in the formation of the UBS, especially in its translation work. This was largely due to its powerful General Secretary. When Rutgers eventually retired, he was succeeded by a no less powerful young man who became one of the most colorful figures in the UBS. "The Baron" as he was called or "Fritz" to his friends, was impressive—both in size and manner.

He went to the Swanley Horticultural College in England (1928–1930) before beginning his military training in field artillery. While holding the rank of lieutenant in the army, he studied at the University of Utrecht in the faculty of law and was employed for two years as a civil servant in the municipality of Veere in Zeeland. In 1937 he was appointed Mayor of Domburg, a position he held from 1937 to 1941. After the invasion of the Netherlands by German armies, he was quickly in the resistance and carried out his underground work while working for the Social Services of the Netherlands Reformed Church. After the liberation of the Netherlands he was a major in military service, with special duties in The Hague. For a few years he worked for the Netherlands Reformed Church, representing them to the government as deputy. Thus in 1950, he came to the Bible Society with considerable and varied experience, and used it in subsequent years.

He was married to Jonkvrouwe Henriëtte Antonia Elizabeth Prisse, who had all the grace of the Dutch aristocracy. They lived in "Valkenberg," an impressive country house of the old style in Ulvenhout. Fritz was born in 1911, which meant that he was only 39 when he succeeded Rutgers, and although shy, he commanded a presence in the beautiful Bible House, on the Herrengracht, one of the principal canals of Amsterdam. He remained General Secretary for twenty-six years and played a leading role in the progressive drama of the UBS.

The NBS was already fully committed to the UBS, and the Baron had no problems there, because he was essentially ecumenical and his vision was global. When the study secretary was appointed and guided from 1956 to 1962 by a committee, Van Tuyll was one of the four representatives of the UBS on the advisory committee. The others were Béguin, North, Platt, and Paul Collyer. So he was among the giants from the start. That group which played such an important part in the study of the place and use of the Bible was later to include Holmgren. Van Tuyll, about the same time, started a department in his own NBS for "the better use of the Bible." He held many offices in the Netherlands Reformed Church and such social bodies as the Red Cross in his own country and travelled widely, becoming particularly well acquainted with Indonesia. He served on many UBS committees.

Van Tuyll was always convinced that the European Bible Societies could together constitute a third force between the two major Societies, ABS and BFBS. In this connection he encouraged the continental Societies to respond when the appeal went out from the meeting of the Standing Committee in Sarpsborg, Norway in 1951. "This is a critical hour. There is a desperate need for Scriptures in every part of the world today. From every quarter there comes a pressing and reiterated cry for Bibles." This was accompanied by an appeal to all Bible Societies to help. From that date onward he saw hope in Norway and Germany, which he believed would ultimately help constitute a third fund. It was not surprising that upon his retirement from the chairmanship of the Council, and no longer having the duties of General Secretary of the NBS, he was appointed Chairman of the Continental European Production Fund. He would have taken a particular delight in the response to the appeal for the Amity Printing Press in 1985, when the combined Continental Bible Societies raised a sum about halfway between that of the ABS and that of the BFBS. As General Secretary of the NBS, he greatly increased the support of churches and members in the Netherlands. In 1950 when he was appointed, the NBS had less than 40,000 members; at his retirement in 1976, it had 260,000.[10]

CHAPTER SIXTEEN

Coordinating the Advance

———— ◇ ————

Fick recognized that the new decade which opened for the UBS at the cluster of meetings in Chiang Mai in 1980 was to be one of consolidation. What was now required was an advance in which all the member Bible Societies were going forward together. The regional structure enabled the center to know what was going on in the member Societies, but it also voiced the complaints and the disquiet. This was evident at many points: cooperation with the Roman Catholics, printing of the deuterocanonical books with the accepted canon of the Bible, modern translations, and finances. All of this was made clear at the meeting of the Executive Committee in Guatemala, in February 1981.

Cash Flow, Production, and Modern Translations in the Americas

Cárcamo spoke first of cash flow. His main concern, he said, was "to pre-finance" Scripture supplies. The World Service Budget appropriation was released monthly but did not provide the funds needed to pay for printing on demand. The Versión Popular was straining the production capacity, while there were heavy demands from many churches for the older Reina Valera Bibles. Failure to meet these demands damaged the credibility of the Bible Societies in many of the countries of South and Central America, particularly among those

churches which did not want the Versión Popular. Such churches felt
that their own needs were not being adequately met.

Funds and cash flow were the problems. The complete New Testament in the minority languages also suffered delay because of shortage
of funds. In cold figures, $8 million was required and only $4 million
was proposed in the appropriation for the region. The responsibility
for directing this production program was assumed by the Regional
Center, because of the use of Spanish as the common language throughout much of the region.

The size of the ABS as the major national Bible Society in the region
inevitably raised the question of undue influence. The Scripture Supply
Fund and the World Service Budget were both administered in the
offices of the ABS in New York. Questions were asked about confusion
of roles and whether the ABS unduly influenced decisions regarding
the region's production program. Baas, who was both treasurer of the
ABS and UBS assured them that "the ABS had no share in making
these decisions."

These were the growing pains of a regional structure, and they were
pains. Although finance was at the heart of Cárcamo's worry, it was
further aggravated by the fact that some Versión Popular editions contained the deuterocanon (still referred to as the Apocrypha by many
Protestants). The Boards of the Bible Societies in Chile, Paraguay,
Venezuela and Argentina had officially ruled against distributing these
editions. At the same time, the Episcopal Conference of the Chilean
Roman Catholic Church expressed the wish to use the Versión Popular
text for the Bible readings in the liturgy for Sunday and festival masses.
They required the inclusion of the deuterocanonical books.

This meant that the Regional Center or neighboring Bible Societies
agreed to supply these Catholic editions to those churches which had
ordered them in countries where the local Bible Societies were unable
or unwilling to supply them. There were those who felt that such
division had a negative effect upon the image of a Bible Society, and
also saw the action as overruling decisions by national Bible Societies.[1]

Production Problems in Africa

In 1981 Million Belete reported slow progress from Africa. Most of
the Scriptures in his region were produced outside Africa, a situation

which, as he said, "is unique to this region." Even when facilities are found for production in Africa they were beset with problems:

> Production is possible in Egypt, but paper is hardly obtainable; production in Zimbabwe is very slow; production in Madagascar is inefficient because of the need to import paper, which is very slow clearing customs; South Africa can produce bound books, but not enough for all its needs; some New Testaments are being produced in Ethiopia, but that is related to the necessity for local typesetting.

Of course, Portions and Selections were produced in many more places, but very often the cost did not permit local production even where the facilities existed, as in Nigeria, for whom the "Adventures of Jesus" booklets in the vernacular had to be produced in England. Belete added that there were other countries where no production of any kind was possible—Cameroon, Sudan, and Angola, being but three examples. This situation delayed production and added greatly to the potential cost, because of transport, for example, in Togo the expenses for transport and customs clearance amounted to 46 percent of production costs.[2]

The Overwhelming Needs of Asia

In 1981, the Rev. Chan Y. Choi, regional secretary for the Asia-Pacific Region, reported on the immense opportunities of this vast region, in which, apart from Australia, New Zealand, and the Philippines, only 2 percent of the population were Christian. There were 100 million Christians in his region, but 60 million of these were in Australia, New Zealand, and the Philippines. Mainland Asia faced 500 million Confucians, 750 million Buddhists, and 500 million Muslims, with a mere 40 million Christians. Tremendous opportunities existed throughout the region, but the financial resources were meager. Asia was the poorest part of the world, with 80 percent of the population economically depressed. The urgency and the size of the task sometimes led to hurried and inadequate production. Choi had to report, as in the Americas region, that a desire to produce enough Scriptures quickly led to editions being published with many errors. When asked about the errors in the Today's Chinese Versión, he admitted, "Either we were rushing production too fast, or had inadequate procedures for checking them."

There was no doubt that the poor quality of these books created serious problems for the image of the Bible Society. Choi explained that it was a combination of technical difficulties in printing, for which a Singapore printing press was liable (60 percent of the run was considered to be defective). In Taiwan, for example, unachievable target dates were set so that dedication services were left with insufficient supplies of books. The first corrections of the TCV were made rapidly, and out of 20,000 copies printed in Korea, 12,000 were supplied to Taiwan in three weeks and sold out immediately. He commented, "Clearly more care must be taken in the future in editing and finalizing these productions." His region, however, did not have the problems that Latin America did with the deuterocanonical books. Apart from a small number of extremely conservative Protestants in Korea, there was no serious criticism of interconfessional translations or so-called "Catholic edition."[3]

Socialist Europe and Migrant Workers

In 1981 Odd Telle, the Regional Secretary, reported lively progress in Europe, addressing the opportunities in Protestant Majority, Protestant Minority, and Socialist Europe. In the first, contributions had grown steadily; from the second came news of increased activity among Catholics and Orthodox; but most news came from Socialist Europe. East Germany had a well-functioning national Bible Society; Poland, a well-established national office in a good position; Czechoslovakia, a dramatic increase in distribution, largely due to the new interconfessional translation; in Hungary, Scriptures available all over the country; in Yugoslavia, a stoppage of production due to a legal complexity; in the USSR, the 25,000 Bibles donated by the UBS in 1979 enabled the Baptists to print 20,000 more locally from returns of sales, with another 20,000 due soon; in Bulgaria, good church contacts, paper supplied by the UBS, and 30,000 Bibles to be printed soon; in Romania, very slow progress. Telle concluded, "In this subregion, more Scriptures were distributed in 1980 with the help of the UBS than ever before—356,000 Bibles, as against 194,000 in 1979 and 173,000 in 1978."

Unfortunately, contacts with the Russian Orthodox Church developed slowly. UBS overtures had met with little response and this church was neither requesting government authorities for permission to import Scriptures, nor encouraging its own translators to produce a revision of the Russian Bible.

One matter remained as unfinished business—the migrant workers in Europe. The size of this problem was illuminated by two examples— one sixth of the Swiss population was migrant workers; there were more Muslims than Protestants in Belgium. This was then, and remained, a major problem which in 1981 had not yet been tackled.[4]

The Working Plan from Chiang Mai—1980 to 1984

At the meeting of the UBS Council in Chiang Mai in 1980, a working plan was outlined in detail and it was agreed to monitor achievements, which would be reviewed at the next meeting of the General Committee to be held in 1984 in Cuernavaca, Mexico.

After studying the report of the structure task force, the Executive Committee recommended the formation of NAWAT as a subregion of the Europe Region, and later established an annual day of prayer (May 9) and set up a special fund to finance such high-subsidy items as scholarly editions for theological students and Braille Scriptures for the blind. In 1983, in Canberra, the committee reviewed in detail the current translation program, especially in the light of the Chiang Mai translation goals, discussed the increasing role of computers in Bible Society work, and authorized a meeting of major fundraising Societies for early 1984.

Fick reported that the Societies had taken the working plan seriously and had begun to implement it in a way that surpassed expectations. It was recognized that each Society had to do this at its own speed, and devise its own national response to the working plan in the light of its own situation and possibilities. One common denominator throughout the fellowship, however, had been the interest in tackling chapter one of the plan concerning church relations. Many societies were asking themselves whether they really were serving all the churches and whether their image conveyed that message. In some cases this questioning had resulted in changes in the constitution of Societies.

Regional Views of the Future

The regional structures of the UBS made it essential to look at the Chiang Mai working plan and what it had achieved, not only regionally, but in consultation across regions. This was done at Cuernavaca in 1984 by a regional symposium, with contributions from all four of the UBS regions, dealing with the question: "What are the main tasks ahead in our part of the world?"

The Americas

The chairperson, the regional secretary and three regional representatives made the presentation.

After presenting the problems and the opportunities, they looked at specific goals for the future, which included learning to think big in order to meet the vast needs and future opportunities; undertaking a number of new translation projects; giving special attention to serving the Roman Catholic Church; discovering ways to meet the needs of the rapidly growing youth population; preparing Scriptures in formats which respond to the political, economic, moral, social, and spiritual problems experienced by people in the region; developing volunteer programs as strengthening for staff work; making the best possible use of new technologies, the new media, and market research; and most of all, deepening faith, prayer, and a sense of calling.

This was spelled out in detail under four headings—translation, with direct reference to five new translations; new fundraising initiatives; the New Reader program, which was a priority for many Societies in the region; and new distribution and volunteer programs.

Africa

The regional secretary and three regional representatives made the presentation. For them the main tasks ahead were meeting the needs of the growing churches, reaching Muslims, preparing new translations in English and French for children, who constituted 46 percent of the population, and of course trying to implement those "national working plans they drew up after the Council meeting in 1980 and the Africa regional assembly in 1982."

In central and southern Africa the great need was for attractive formats and easy-to-read Selections for the growing number of new literates. The work was hindered by shortage of foreign currencies. In many cases cash could not flow out of the country, and the growing balances of blocked local currency dissuaded some people from giving to a prosperous Society which appeared to have more money than it could use. Political unrest and military activity brought a sense of insecurity. But despite all this, the work developed. The use of computers in translation and manuscript processing speeded up production. But even this program suffered from a lack of initial capital investment. The challenges in central and southern Africa, in francophone Africa (south of the Sahara), and in anglophone West and East Africa were presented.

Of the twenty francophone countries, only nine had a Bible Society. Fourteen of them have literacy rates below 50 percent. Only eight had a growing Christian majority; six had a Muslim majority; five had a majority of people with traditional religious beliefs. Children under fifteen years of age constituted 45 percent of the population. Against this background the regional committee set itself the following urgent tasks:

- To establish Bible Societies in the eleven countries where there were only Scripture depots.
- To develop the five national offices into associate members of the UBS, and the two associate members into full members.
- To develop pilot programs including cassettes for new readers.
- To help the Roman Catholic Church to become fully involved in Bible work.
- To improve relationships with churches in the Christian-minority countries.
- To recruit and train staff.
- To increase local financial support.
- To work with the churches to change the political situations.

This was a massive program, but one which the working plan of 1980 had required. In the anglophone West and East Africa area, one of the most urgent challenges was to convince the churches that it was their responsibility to assure adequate Scripture supplies. They needed to be weaned away from the idea that donors abroad would take care of this for them. And something of progress could be minuted. In Ghana, local income had more than doubled every year in the last three years, but that was the exception. In Ethiopia, censorship and limitation on Scripture distribution seriously affected the work. The political changes from a Christian emperor who was a patron of the BFBS to a left-wing republic, accompanied by revolution, inevitably affected the Bible Society work. In Kenya, local income was not increasing, and Scripture prices had to be lowered because of severe loss of purchasing power among the people. In Sudan, the churches and the Bible Society had to face up to the problems of a country living under Islamic law. In Uganda, the Society was hampered by a very poor economic situation. In Nigeria, although things looked better with local income increasing steadily over a period of four years, the financial restriction had prevented the Bible Society from making use of this increase and resulted in only 20 percent he need being met. Sierra Leone showed signs of hope as the result of Bible Week celebrations, which tried to help the churches understand the work of the Bible Society.

Asia-Pacific

The regional secretary and two regional representatives (one a Roman Catholic bishop, Bishop Phimphisan) made the presentation.

The fact that there was a tiny Christian community in this vast region had not discouraged the Bible Societies. In response to the Chiang Mai call to provide easy access to the Bible for all and to direct every distribution program to a specific target audience, the region had looked specifically at the very large Muslim population in five countries of Asia Pacific: India, Indonesia, Bangladesh, Pakistan, and Malaysia. These countries contained one third of the 900 million Muslims in the world. Different approaches and formats were needed, and a task force had recently evaluated and approved sixteen texts and one new reader series for publication. Each of these texts carried clear recommendations as to translation, types of design, target audience and methods of distribution for the national Bible Societies involved.

The region could also report on 300 translation projects in process, many common language. The variety of this region was shown in that it was necessary to produce 204 different New Reader Portions, seventy-nine of which appeared for the first time in 1983. The region had also looked at the use of cassettes and prepared a trial edition for testing in Bangladesh, which included the Gospel of Luke.

Europe

The presentation was made by the regional secretary, the chairman and a regional representative.

In Western and Northern Europe, which is 90 percent Christian, there were strong professional and well-established Bible Societies. But this part of Europe was in a post-Christian secular environment with church attendance steadily declining. There was an important admission that, while the Bible Societies of this part of Europe had been started by lay people, they had later become professional organizations, and tended to lose touch with the lay people who used to identify with the Bible work. These things were recognized and efforts made to correct the trend.

In Southern Europe where the small Protestant, evangelical groups had been and still were the main supporters of Bible Society work, there was a tradition of hostility to overcome between Catholics and the minority Protestant groups. On the one hand was the memory of persecution and on the other, a fear of proselytism. The region saw the challenge and was trying to meet it by building bridges, learning to serve all the churches, and develop boards which were more representative of the entire Christian community. Success in these efforts, they saw, would depend upon openness on the part of the majority churches to Bible work, and good Bible Society leadership. It was important that when new Bible Society secretaries were appointed, they should be theologically well-trained in order to be able to relate effectively to the majority churches. Flexibility was needed, and a broad outlook, with courage to initiate the necessary changes. The object was to serve all the churches.

Eastern Europe presented quite different problems, but again it was important to work with all the churches. Atheistic governments were inevitably unsympathetic to Bible work, but the churches and the Bible Societies had established a *modus vivendi* with most of them—but not Albania.

North Africa, West Asia, and Turkey (NAWAT) presented totally different problems. The subregion consisted of strongly Islamic states, boosted by new wealth, with small minority Christian communities which were among the oldest in Christendom. There were, of course, widespread differences within this subregion. Egypt had 80 percent of the subregion's Christians, mostly Coptic, all served by a well-established Bible Society; Lebanon had experienced eight years of war, but the Bible Society had kept its operation going; while operations in Iraq were closed down, Bibles were supplied from Jordan; the Bible Society in Israel, then changing its name to Bible Lands Bible Society, served tourists freely; in Algeria, the Bible Society was allowed only to serve the Christian minority; Turkey, as a secular state, forbade evangelization, but the work proceeded. For the Europe Region, this subregion has a special concern, because it was the area from which most migrant workers come to Europe.[5]

Facing the Future

The General Secretary emphasized the need to think globally, as he put Bible work issues in the context of a world in tension. The two major tensions were those between East and West, which was mainly political; and between North and South, which was mainly economic. The first tension arose from World War II and was initiated at Yalta when the victors divided up the world between spheres of interest and gave the world two super-powers, the U.S. and USSR. This world of tension meant that resources which were needed for the building up of a prosperous world were used for defense and aggression. Even the developing countries felt the influence, because, poor as they were, they spent an undue amount of their resources on armaments to keep the powerful in power and the powerless in their place. Each superpower readily sold arms to extend its influence. At the same time, the "imbalance between the affluent industrial nations and developing countries," Fick pointed out, "was getting tenser."

With his firsthand knowledge of Africa and the experience of the work of Bible Societies in every part of the world, Fick thought in terms of developing countries when that was necessary, and now it was. The South was going through a period of rapid population growth coupled with severe economic problems. He was not alone in seeing this as resulting in overall political instability. The cold war was coming to an end, but the North-South conflict was growing in intensity. Willy Brandt had already given the world a vision of peace which was more than the proscription of war. "It must be a peace rooted in interdependence and nourished by common interests; a peace that will help us human beings to bear cojointly the burdens we still unfairly divide— a peace associated with hopes for a worthy mode of survival."

Such a vision resulted in the Brandt Report, which the industrial West did not care to adopt, to its loss and that of the whole world. Fick was realistic and yet did not lose that vision. It was not, however, an encouraging picture he painted. The North was paying the price for affluence, with its flexibility getting more limited and "responses to tensions in other parts of the world more difficult as long as there are large numbers of unemployed in the industrial countries, and more and more strings are attached to aid that is given."

There had been a period when the developing countries had the idea of creating an identity of the Third World, to neutralize the conflict between the First (Capitalist) and Second (Communist) worlds. Sukarno (Indonesia), Nasser (Egypt) and Nkrumah (Ghana) had thought of this, but it collapsed.

But what had all this to do with the work of the Bible Societies? This was the world to which they offered "God's Word," and they needed to understand it, Fick insisted.

Population Growth

In such a world the population was growing at a staggering rate. Africa, the Americas, and Asia-Pacific had all referred to this growth. Only Europe did not, "for good reasons." Fick illustrated the extent by turning to Mexico City: in 1984, 16 million, but by 2100 it would be 31 million; Sao Paulo would have 26 million; Shanghai, 23 million; Bombay and Djakarta, each 17 million. The once-great cities of New York, Tokyo, Los Angeles, and London would be dwarfed by the cities of the Third World. He continued his list, which could only be falsified by a major nuclear catastrophe.

And during the same period, per capita food output would decline, fuel supplies would be used up, and schooling would be poorer in quality, while job opportunities would depend almost entirely upon qualifications.

The goodwill that after World War II led to the formation of the United Nations appeared to Fick to have evaporated, while its efforts to solve the problems of a world in conflict were again and again doomed to failure. Fick assumed that no essential change could be achieved, beyond a slight lessening of tension here and there. He deplored the fatal simplifications of finding a scapegoat. The plight of the world was such that everywhere there was a search for new attitudes, concepts which make the world more habitable, which do not exclude but include one's neighbor.

Activities of Other Religions

Geoffrey Fisher, while Archbishop of Canterbury, was reputed to have said that, "only Communists and Christians know what they are after," adding that all others were "amiable nonentities!" But this was no longer true, if ever it had been. The Muslims knew what they are after, namely the propagation of Islam as a world religion which offered peace to the whole world through a God-given law for all humans. "Muslim missionaries are on the road," Fick said. "There are timetables for the Islamization of Europe and of all other continents. Mosques are going up almost everywhere!"

Buddhism, also, he saw as grasping its world meaning. Its impact upon intellectuals and especially young people in Europe was considerable. Hinduism also had become more missionary minded. These were no longer "nonentities." For these reasons, missionary activities by Christians were seen with suspicion, were hindered, or even suppressed and outlawed.

Fick forecast increasing difficulties—blocked cash for more than economic reasons, restricted travel, and the refusal of awkward passports. International work as a whole would become more difficult. There would no longer be the protection of Western-supremacy. But this latter he saw as a gain. A gospel which can no longer be identified with one culture was more persuasive in a world of confrontation. Taking all this into account, Fick set forth the challenge of this new world:

> In this situation there will be a growing need for a universal message. The gospel is this message, addressed to all, intended to save all. The mission of the Christian church universal has to strip off its western costume very fast and to show a genuinely intercultural face if it is not to become just another factor in the international network of tensions. That's why it is so important that Bible Societies work both in the East and in the West, both in capitalist and in Marxist-Leninist countries.

The Youth Program

"The world of tomorrow will be a world full of young people." The population figures assured us of that. Already in 1984 there were countries where half the population was under 15. Fick stressed the essential nature of seeing that these young people encounter the Word of God. The UBS Executive had already proposed to launch, "a program of advance, a major campaign for the years 1986 to 1988, aimed at reaching the new generation with the Good News."

Fick was aware of the need and also aware that Bible Societies were going to find it hard to make the changes necessary to satisfy the new youth. There was by 1984, a youth culture, and it was universal—very much the same music, taste, fashion, and feeling in many parts of the world. He pointed out that in Singapore, Rio, Nairobi, and Stockholm, the same music and posters could be found in all the shops which youth visit. Bible Societies could not ignore, nor could they afford simply to disapprove of this secular youth culture:

> The children who are growing up today will not only be looking for work and food, for shelter and clothing, but also for orientation, for a

purpose in life. Many answers given in the past will no longer be sufficient. A new world situation will bring things into sharper focus and will complicate matters. These young people are our challenge because we who have found the truth in the Gospel of Jesus Christ owe them an encounter with this message.

The Readiness of the Bible Societies

By 1984, Fick had been General Secretary for twelve years. When he faced the General Committee with the question of what has to be done to be ready for the tasks which lie ahead, he could draw upon that experience, and he gave some practical suggestions which in themselves amounted to an assessment of the readiness of the Bible Societies. He used the "Working Plan for the Eighties" as his model and listed "several major areas of tension" which could delay the work:

1. The tension between national identity and fully cooperating in a global fellowship.
2. The tension between being an interconfessional agency and retaining the confidence of an historical confessional constituency.
3. The tension between seeing the work as a mere job and as a mission done in the name of the Lord.
4. The tension between the older leadership team in a Bible Society and the younger junior staff. Fick comments,

> 1988, when the next term for global officers and governing committees begins, will be a time of major personnel changes. With this meeting here I have entered my last term of service with the UBS. Other UBS officers and some members of the present General Committee are nearing retirement age. We have to see to it that within the next four years young people will be prepared to take over where the older ones will leave and go. Changes are always an opportunity for renewal.

Over the years, the UBS developed organizational structures as they were needed, but there was always an inherent tension between these structures and the flexibility of a movement. Fick admitted that to the point of nagging, he would constantly put before the committees the need for change when he saw it. The life of the UBS depended upon that flexibility of structure which enabled it to remain a movement. He quoted the interconfessional acceptance of the Bible Societies, which had required a great deal of rethinking, as evidence that the UBS was a movement, adding, "Discussions which have been going on concerning involving Roman Catholic and Orthodox majority churches in Bible work, such as in Malta and Cyprus, are indicators of a new plateau of understanding our task which we have reached."

That address to the General Committee in Cuernavaca in 1984 gave the essence of Fick's contribution to the UBS. His was a fresh mind, and he had proved a worthy successor to, although quite different from Olivier Béguin.[6] But he had four more years to go, and much more was to be accomplished before he retired at Budapest in 1988.

CHAPTER SEVENTEEN

God's Word Open for All in the Eighties

———— ◇ ————

In 1980, the UBS had set a target for Portions and Selections to be available in all major languages for new readers by 1985. The translations subcommittee was given the task of helping the regional committees to compile a schedule to meet the requirements of this target. The schedule was to comprise a listing of the languages to be considered for each category, an evaluation of the progress made to date, a calculation of the personnel and financial implications for the entire program, and a set of priorities for the next budget year.

The subcommittee met under the chairmanship of the Rev. Dr. Hans Peter Rütger in Crete in May 1981. It consisted of the four regional translations coordinators, the UBS Translation Research coordinator, (Rev. Dr. Heber Peacock), Nida as special consultant, and the Rev. Dr. Paul A. Vanderbroek as liaison with the Executive Committee.

Before his retirement in 1984, Peacock was asked to present to the UBS Executive committee in Canberra, September 1983, a major review of the entire UBS translation program. He began by listing a number of areas where he hoped for help from the Executive Committee and then circulated a chart of the present levels of work, showing the structure of the translation program at local, national, regional, and global levels. He also showed how these were interrelated. He made clear that the national level was the heart of the program and that all work should begin from that point. Peacock gave a great deal of attention to this relationship of the UBS consultant to the national Bible Society. Regional and global help was *for* the national Society— giving professional aid in training, for example. The greater part of Peacock's report concerned the extent to which the translation work since 1981 followed closely the Chiang Mai translation goals of 1980.

Bibles

In Chiang Mai, he reminded the committee, it was agreed that by the end of the decade entire Bibles would be available "in at least all languages with more than one million literates, and in all officially designated national languages." Further, they should be available in "clear and comprehensible versions." He reported progress on this region by region and asked for clarification of these goals. The difficulties he listed were various:

- Does "Bible" mean with or without the deuterocanonical books?
- In some regions it would be more appropriate to speak of "one million speakers" rather than one million literates.
- In some African countries, the resistance of the churches to new translations makes it impossible to reach the Chiang Mai goals.
- In the Asia-Pacific region there are so many island nations with tiny populations that it is unrealistic to translate the Bible into all designated national languages.
- The NAWAT languages did not appear on the Europe region list— they should be added.

After some discussion of these difficulties the Chiang Mai goals were modified.

New Readers

The target date of 1985 for the translating and publishing of Scriptures for new readers in all major languages raised the question of what was a major language. Nida was requested to provide assistance in identifying "major languages" in sociolinguistic terms. He agreed to present a paper in 1984 at the UBS translations workshop on this theme. Peacock also reported that as they began to evaluate the new reader program they made a number of discoveries:

- New reader material was best prepared directly on a language-specific basis and not from a "model text" in a major language.
- There was confusion between Scriptures for new readers and Scriptures for new Bible readers—two distinct groups with differing needs.
- The breakdown of new reader material into five levels proved too artificial—"more flexibility will have to be used in future."
- The goals set for new readers could only be achieved if priority was given to it—too many times it was regarded as a sideline to the common language translation project.
- Too often the new reader project had been started without involving the churches or assessing the extent of literacy work.
- Research was needed on the effect of the new reader project—how far does it lead on to the reading of a common language New Testament?

Peacock saw much room for improvement in the new reader program and promised that this would be addressed in the translations workshop in 1984.

Non-Print Media

Peacock was able to report that several pilot projects in communicating the content of the Bible to those who could not use the print media were underway in Bangladesh, Sudan, and the NAWAT subregion. He made two complementary proposals:

- Because of the high technological competence required in cassette, radio, and TV production, the translation staff should not be expected to engage in it.
- However, for the translational aspects of this work, the translation staff must be involved in any audio Scripture project.

He commented, "It is already clear that it is much more difficult to translate into nonprint media than into print media. The possibilities to skew the meaning of the text are very numerous and sometimes very subtle."

Helps for Readers

Peacock circulated a paper on Study Bibles for the Today's English Version and another paper on one for the Versión Popular. There were, he said, several study Bibles with a theological stance. He therefore questioned the use of the term for UBS products which insisted upon "no doctrinal comment."

Fick, at this point, reminded the committee that the Vatican and World Catholic Federation for the Biblical Apostolate had expressed their interest in a study of the possibility of interconfessional notes, to become part of interconfessional translations within the framework of the "Guiding Principles." A consultation had been requested on this, but not surprisingly, the committee decided that the UBS itself should first clarify what it considered to be the legitimate extent of notes and helps for readers in its own publications before entering upon a consultation with the Catholics. Again, the translation workshop was asked to look at this when it met near Stuttgart in 1984.[1]

Study Bibles

A very significant document was written in the aftermath of Chiang Mai by Dr. Gunther Metzger of Germany. At Chiang Mai the UBS seemed to move away from the attitude of "how far can we go," in helps and notes to "what do the readers need?" In fact, it was said that "helps are an essential part of the text itself." Metzger's paper after these meetings concluded with a paragraph headed, "Tasks Ahead":

A Study Bible . . . is not one that explains the doctrines of the churches, but one that presents background information about the biblical text in the wider sense. The potential users of such a Bible are people who not only want to read (the Bible), but also wish to penetrate to a comprehensive understanding of the Bible as a whole. Not interested in simply being told what they are to believe, they wish to discover the relevancy of the message for their lives by studying biblical passages, and by learning more about the context and coherence of biblical books. This is an audience that is already motivated for both individual and group studies. Future steps should be to collate available experience and then perhaps present a carefully elaborated model for national adaptation.

He added, of course, that this must be done as a joint venture with the churches, although the Bible Societies may have to "pave the way."[2] After that statement in the semi-official document by Gunther Metzger, the idea of a model Bible was explored and then abandoned. The reason was that the needs of different readers in different parts of the world were too diverse to make a universal model useful.

Metzger's paper was issued in 1981. Stine drafted "Guidelines for Bible with Study Notes" for the translations subcommittee meeting in 1985 and after revision issued it from the UBS General Office in 1986. An important section in those "Guidelines" was on the audience, which began: "Notes to include with a Scripture publication cannot be prepared without there being a clear idea of the intended audience," which led to the recommendation, "National Bible Societies should work with translation personnel to identify particular audiences for whom they want to prepare Scriptures with notes." In dealing with the nature of the notes, the prescriptive factor appeared again: ". . . there should be no attempt to discuss the prehistory of the text," and further, "In general, comments of a historical-critical nature are to be avoided unless they are absolutely necessary to explain the meaning of the text."

However, the April 1986 "Guidelines" go a long way, at least in theory:

> The notes would . . . describe various views that different theological traditions have held regarding passages, not prescribe a particular or specific position. If readers are to make up their own minds about the meaning of a passage, then we can only prepare notes that give readers enough information to do this, without at the same time imposing any belief on them.[3]

Excellent as that advice was, it presented formidable problems in practice. Nida, commenting some years later, assessed the Study Bibles as "likely to be one of the most important aspects of Bible Society work during the next twenty years." He was then looking beyond the second millennium.

He recognized the problems, but was confident that they would be overcome. Speaking in 1993, he said, "People felt that it was simply impossible to put out a Study Bible in cooperation with Roman Catholics and Protestants, but this has been accomplished. Study Bibles will be published in 1993 or early 1994 prepared by a committee of two Roman Catholic priests and two Protestant scholars. And this in Latin America!"[4]

UBS Triennial Translations Workshop, May 1984

Already in the Sixties Nida was bringing translators together from a a wide region to give them intensive training in the various aspects of translation and the skills needed.

Something of the work load of the first translation workshop under the leadership of Dr. Philip C. Stine, appointed World Translation Research Coordinator in 1983 at Canberra, can be seen from the special edition of the *UBS Bulletin* for the Third and Fourth Quarter, 1985. It was a double issue given the title, "Current Trends in Scripture Translation."

The first article is by Dr. Daniel Arichea, Jnr., a UBS Translation Consultant, originally from the Philippines, but then based in Indonesia. Following Peacock's suggestion, he wrote on "Theology and Translation."

One of the most interesting papers in this collection is by Dr. Kenneth Thomas, UBS consultant-at-large for the Asia-Pacific region, but with major responsibilities for the WASAI countries. For many years before joining the UBS he was involved in theological education in the Middle East and he draws upon that experience in his paper. He examines the question of whether there are ways to approach biblical material which on the one hand interpret the text faithfully and on the other hand present it in a way that people of other faiths will hear and understand them. He shows that this is possible and poses the question, "How can the Church decide which portions of Scripture are most effective in working with other groups, including Muslims?"

There is a rich variety of subjects dealt with in this collection of papers from the Translation Workshop, showing with what thoroughness the UBS examined its important task of translation.

It is clear from these articles that in 1984 the translation personnel were wrestling with the problems outlined by Arichea in his article. They did not take their work for granted, as though they were confident that they had found the right way. Arichea asked, "What do we translate? How do we translate? Why do we translate? Is there any theological basis or justification for the task of Bible translation, and particularly for the whole program and strategy of dynamic equivalence and its logical results of audience-centered translations of the Scriptures?"

Stine, in his editorial, hazarded a guess at the kind of concerns the translation personnel would have over the next few years:

- Questions about the use, or disuse, of the translations prepared, and if they are used, in what ways and why?
- Identification of particular audiences and an attempt to prepare translations for them.
- Research on the preparation of translations for different age groups of children, related to the UBS special campaign for youth, 1986–1988.
- Preparation of more and more aids for readers, tailored to the particular audiences in mind.
- Much current research by linguists will become more relevant to making UBS translations more useable.

Stine concludes, "Whether working in these areas or others, one can be sure the UBS translation program will not simply be standing still in the years to come. There are too many things we do not understand yet about translation, too many factors that impede the clear transmission of the message for that to happen. Some of the most interesting research is still to be done."[5]

That quote from Stine is amply illustrated some years later by his plans for such a triennial workshop in 1994 in Chiang Mai, Thailand. Speaking before that meeting took place, he said, "The Triennial in Thailand will have three different parts. One part will be workshop.

There will be five or six working groups on particular topics and we expect them to come up with something. For example, at the last triennial in Zimbabwe (1991) we had a group that was working on poetry. And they had been exchanging papers for two years. They did not read their papers at the workshop, but spent their time hammering out principles and procedures which came together in a syllabus for training in the translation of poetry. Another group was working on the name of God; and yet another on audio translation principles. And so the workshop is an essential part of the triennial. The second part is the discussion of papers. Everyone attending has to have written and circulated a paper. Discussions are on the basis of requests. In the third part we bring in outsiders to stimulate consultants."[6]

Braille Scriptures for the Blind

Although contacts between Bible Societies and other organizations that work among the blind had been established in several countries a long time ago, there had never been an attempt to bring these people together on a global level. Only in 1983 did the first widely representative gathering take place of people from agencies which produce Scriptures for the blind and the UBS.

Dorothea Kindt, who conceived and convened this conference in Darmstadt, was UBS Braille production and supply coordinator and a member of the German Bible Society staff in Stuttgart. At the conference, she pointed out the immensity of her task and suggested ways in which the Bible Societies of the world might do more for the blind. On the size of the task and its current inadequacy, she said:

> Providing some of the world's 42 million blind (a very conservative estimate according to the World Health Organization) with Braille Scriptures is a huge task. The UBS has demonstrated its willingness to take up this challenge by the creation of a Braille Scripture Fund, out of which expenses for the production and distribution of Braille Scriptures can be financed for those Bible Societies in need. Considering that Braille Scriptures are available in eighty-three languages only, while the sighted have access to Scriptures in many hundreds of languages, much is still to be done.

Her own address to the conference gave a great deal of information about the UBS involvement, but indirectly. She continued with "What the Bible Societies Can Do for the Blind." She addressed three different areas:

- Where biblical Scriptures in Braille are available.
- Where a Braille code in the local language is available.
- Where neither biblical Scriptures nor Braille code is available.

Apart from good advice about attitudes to the blind—blind not to be equated with darkness, the blind not contrasted with "ordinary" people—she described what could be done when Braille Scriptures are available in practical terms: publicize Bible Society activities, offer to provide Braille Scriptures and cassettes, so that churches become used to approaching the Bible Societies for Braille Scriptures. Roman Catholics, she pointed out, would be interested to learn of the availability of Braille Scriptures in interconfessional versions.

Bible Societies Kindt said, should watch what is being done by organizations working with the blind and attend their conferences, contact the ministry of education and offer new reader material in Braille, and contact schools for the blind, eye hospitals, rehabilitation centers, welfare workers, etc. with similar offers. She advocated seeking out blind people through the pastors and health workers to let them know what was available. If, as was likely, the Braille correspondence which arrived could not be handled by the Bible Society staff, the Society should arrange with an organization for the blind to handle it.

This was all good, sound, common sense. It added to the workload of Bible Society staff, but it was the work of the Bible Society if God's Word was to be available *for all* in the Eighties.

There were greater difficulties in the second category, where although a Braille code existed, no Braille Scriptures were available. Kindt advised approaching organizations and schools for the blind to find out whether someone, possibly a teacher, could prepare a Braille manuscript for New Reader Selections. In other words, the Bible Society should take the initiative even when it did not have the specialist staff. If neither Braille code and therefore Braille Scriptures were available, it was still possible to find out if an international language was taught in the schools and use that. There was a need to prevent chaos if new codes were invented, but the UBS appointed Kindt coordinator to prevent this. All Bible Societies agreed to work through the Braille coordinator when seeking a new code. The paper was describing what some Bible Societies were already doing and others could do.[7]

UBS—Braille Scripture Availability List

In December 1986 Kindt produced an up-to-date list of Scriptures available in Braille and itemized those portions ready or in preparation in eighty-three languages. Some were produced by Bible Societies and others by organizations working with the blind, some of which were specifically Christian organizations. There were thirty-nine Bible Societies involved and forty-three other organizations. The conference at Darmstadt attempted to bring together as many as possible of these various groups and sought to develop the work for the blind as a cooperative effort. The list published by the UBS in December 1986 showed both the extent and the lack of Braille Scriptures.

Whole Bibles were available in Afrikaans, Chinese, Danish, Dutch, English, Finnish, French, German, Greek, Italian, Japanese, Korean, Norwegian, Chichewa, Spanish, Swedish, and Urdu. Europe and the Americas regions were clearly predominant. Portuguese, despite Brazil, had only a New Testament. Many of the other languages had separate books from the New Testament, and also New Reader Scriptures. The traditional translations seemed to dominate, but there were some common languages, colloquial, popular interconfessional, interconfessional, modern, and even Living Bible translations, not all produced by a Bible Society.

Miss Dorothea Kindt

Among the many women who have played a significant part in Bible Society work throughout the world, Dorothea Kindt had a distinguished record. She joined the staff of the Bible Society of Württemberg in 1962 and served the German Bible Society and the UBS for thirty years. In 1968 when the European Production Fund was founded she began to work for the new fund on a part-time basis, and from 1970 was involved full-time. The thanks of the UBS at the time of her retirement, July 1992, was heartfelt and indicated her wide range of service in the print media:

> Throughout her entire service, Miss Kindt unfailingly carried out her duties with grace and charm as well as with great efficiency. Like Lydia in the Book of Acts she combines a quiet faith in the Lord with a high degree of business acumen. This juxtaposition of God's gifts in her, which she has so readily made available to the Bible cause, was a very significant factor in EPF being able over the years to supply many millions of Bibles, Testaments, and Portions to Africa and Eastern Europe.
>
> In addition to the print medium, Miss Kindt has a heart burden to provide Braille Scriptures for the blind, and she has greatly developed this work in recent years. This ministry has brought her into contact with blind people all over the world, many of whom lift up their hands and say, "Thank God for Dorothea Kindt."[8]

Kindt was appointed coordinator for Braille in May 1982 and for ten years that was the work that held her greatest interest. On her retirement she helped to draw up a job description for her successor, which indicated the extent of UBS involvement in Scriptures for the Blind at the end of the eighties.

'

CHAPTER EIGHTEEN

Budapest—1988

—— ◇ ——

Reporting on his last Council meeting, September 1988 in Budapest, Fick wrote: "One day someone might write a history of the United Bible Societies by taking the UBS Council meetings as the main chapters of the presentation." He had in mind, not so much historic moments but the opportunity to look "before and after" which these meetings enable the UBS to do. They all ask two questions: "What have we done since we last met?" and, "Where does our future lie?" Fick put this in different words: "These regular gatherings both focus on the developments that took place up to the date of the meeting and concentrate on plans for the future." He maintained that both *"experience gained"* and *"visions projected"* determined the nature of each UBS Council meeting.[1]

Experience Gained

The experience of the past eight years had been that it was right to hope and project great plans, but those plans should be realistic; otherwise failure would lead to disappointment and a loss of nerve. This had not happened, but there were warning signs. However, it was clear that God did not leave all his work to the UBS. Things happened in the period from 1980 to 1988, which could not have been foreseen and which could not be explained by human efforts or natural development alone. Much came to the UBS as a surprise, as a gift:

The changes that occurred in several socialist countries affected the attitude of the authorities in these countries towards the Christian churches. "Glasnost" . . . turned out to mean not only more participation of the citizens in reaching government decisions, but also a new appreciation of the services which Christians in these societies are able to offer. This gave the UBS new opportunities to offer assistance to Bible Societies and churches in socialist countries in carrying out this task of translating and producing the Bible.[2]

But the 205 representatives of Bible Society work in 105 countries who had come freely into Hungary needed no persuading of the change. Full support for the meeting was extended by the authorities. No one faced any difficulty in entering and leaving the country. All saw the Hungarian Bible Society selling Bibles and New Testaments by the thousands from a pavilion in Calvin Square, right in the center of the city. Neither was Hungary alone. Reports came in from other socialist countries of a restless sense of freedom.

The second gift to the UBS was the wider acceptance of their services by churches of various traditions where formerly they had been suspect. The presence of Cardinal Carlo Maria Martini, archbishop of the largest Catholic Diocese in the world, at the UBS gathering was evidence of a new relationship with the Roman Catholic Church. Metropolitan Pitirim of the Russian Orthodox was also present.

The new opportunities, of course, produced new problems. The Bible Societies had been rooted in the Protestant tradition, with their principal support coming from evangelical Bible-loving Christians. Now that their services were accepted by other traditions, they needed to assess how far they were able to go. New opportunities do not always bring new resources. But most of the delegates saw this widening range of opportunities as a sign of God's hand, a fruit of the Holy Spirit who can change hearts.

The Youth Delegation

The emphasis during the eighties on children and young people led to the introduction into the meeting of a youth delegation. It was composed of twenty young people, drawn from different countries, with four from the host country, Hungary. The other sixteen were carefully balanced—four from each of the four regions of the UBS.

These young people were not accessory to the main meeting, but were involved in all the business of the UBS Council as well as presenting a plenary session, when they challenged the UBS to new thinking. The general feeling was expressed that no UBS Council meeting would again be without a youth delegation with a plenary session to hear what a new generation had to say. In Budapest they said plenty. The stage was overshadowed by a huge cross, and the actors wore masks. Their masks were used to show how an individual's uniqueness and true identity are hidden, not only in the world but also in the Church. They portrayed the loneliness and insecurity which people feel when masks are worn and the true self cannot be revealed. Into dramatic scenes of fighting between supporters of different political ideologies and authoritarian attitudes within the Church which stifle youthful initiative, they sang the song of hope:

> In this world of broken dreams
> a ray of hope shines through . . .
> In this world of dimming lights
> a mighty candle burns.

Their theme was that this light of hope was "God's Word: Hope for all mankind." They pleaded for more involvement of youth in Bible Society work. Much was severely critical, but it was presented in an entertaining way. The session ended with the member of the group from Sri Lanka, speaking for them all:

We are not here just to entertain or to be entertained. We are here with hearts full of important things to say. You have just heard that we are at the beginning of a new era, where young people need to be reached with perhaps a whole new language. A language which maybe translates the Bible into the medium of drama, of music, of poetry. This is the "now" language the young people understand and want to hear.

We would like to talk to you about yet another powerful type of communication our peers around the world just cannot resist. And this is to translate the Bible into the medium of *people* who embody the Scriptures. People who are dynamic advertisements of the Book of Life.

This may seem a rather irrelevant statement, but we say it here only because we *know* young people want to hear, and do respond to, this powerful language. Young people may not read books and selections but they are looking for genuineness, sincerity, and truth in people. And when they see the genuine stuff in action, they know it and are deeply interested. Is building this kind of person merely the concern of the Church? Can we not do everything possible within the Bible Societies to make ourselves and our staff powerful embodiments of the Bible? Again, I stress, we say this for one reason alone. And that is because lives that practically characterize Jesus, lives that embody the Scriptures, form an actual language, so powerful that youth cannot resist it. A language so powerful everybody around the world hears it loud and clear—they must hear it—life to life.[3]

On the effect of this youth group Fick reported: "The presence of the 'youth group' was like a breath of fresh air, a tonic, an eye-opener to new opportunities and styles. 'Never again a Council meeting without young people,' said many delegates at the end."

A Critical Look

The theme of the Council meeting was "Hope," not just optimism. Hope had to be grounded in experience, and this was made evident, not only by the unexpected intervention of history in giving Bible Societies new opportunities in socialist countries, but also by the careful work of cooperation after the Second Vatican Council—from both sides.

The Council took a critical look at what had been accomplished by the Bible Societies since 1980 in Chiang Mai. This was examined under seven headings:

1. *The Bible Societies and the Churches*
   Mr. Emmanuel Kibira, the General Secretary of the Bible Society in Tanzania, was able to give encouraging examples of initiatives taken by the Bible Societies in what was called, the Third World to develop closer relations with the churches. The Rev. Ole Christian M. Kvarme, the General Secretary of the Norwegian Bible Society, reported on steps taken in North America and Europe.

He traced four trends: broader representation on Bible Society Boards to include Roman Catholic and Orthodox; a new emphasis on Bible use which brought churches and Bible Societies together in cooperative work; Bible events in parishes to focus local attention on the Bible in the churches, and a slow discovery that the churches represent an essential marketing and distribution network for the Bible.

2. *Bible Translation*

The Rev. Jaime Goytia, General Secretary of the Bible Society in Bolivia, reported some progress toward the Chiang Mai goal of the translation of the whole Bible into all languages with more than one million literates. He gave the statistics and added that they had included also some languages where less than one million were in fact literate. His quote when reporting the dedication of the Quechua Bible in a Catholic Church in Bolivia, which was a comment overheard, lit up his report:

> O God, our forefathers taught us to worship the sun, the moon, and forces of nature. Then came the white man who taught us to worship you in a language we neither knew nor understood. But now we have your Word in our own language, and no one can take that away from us.

3. *Production and Supply*

Mrs. Violet Wong, General Secretary of the Hong Kong Bible Society, reported that some good production programs had been achieved, but there was much more to be done. She emphasized the value of human resources and of experienced people in the Bible Societies sharing their experiences. "Human resources are the most expensive items," she said, and, "Experience is one of the most valuable resources of all."

4. *Distribution*

Miss Maria Martinez, a General Secretary of the ABS, was able to report impressive figures and to list the three groups which at Chiang Mai and since had attracted the greatest attention—new readers, young people, and ethnic groups. For new readers there had been a 38 percent increase over 1979. Formats designed especially for young people had greatly increased in number and ingenuity. Many Bible Societies had work among ethnic groups, so that countries where once the Bible had been in one or two languages now were concerned with several, even to the extent of new translations. All was very encouraging, and Martinez' conclusion followed:

> As we assess the last eight years, we must look at them not only in terms of history, but in light of the great challenges before us—the work yet to be done. While the increase in distribution was impressive, we must continue to remind ourselves that there are five billion people inhabiting this earth, and of those five billion only 1.6 billion are Christians. . . . Last year's impressive distribution of 624 million Scriptures reached only 11 percent of all the people in the world.

5. *Resources*

The Rev. Dr. Siegfried Meurer, General Secretary of the German Bible Society, was able to report increases in contributions from all regions except Africa: over the period from 1980 to 1987 the Americas region by 91 percent, the Asia-Pacific region by 83 percent, Europe by 65 percent, but a decline in Africa by 63 percent. When he examined the way this money had been used, he commended the many new translations but questioned the way in which distribution was going over the period: 2 percent New Testaments, 2 percent Bibles, 8 percent Portions, and as much as 89 percent Selections. With the church growing throughout the world he wondered how they were progressing with Coggan's appeal in Hakone, 1963. Then the formula was a Bible in every Christian home, a New Testament in every Christian hand, at least a Portion for all who learned to read. Meurer added:

> That is an ambitious goal. The UBS has not been able to achieve that goal, and I have my doubts that the UBS will achieve it in the future. But if this is the case, then I think we need a new formula, a realistic strategy, and policy for the distribution work of the UBS now and in the years to come.

6. *Training and Enablement*

Mr. Peter J. Frude, from the Asia-Pacific Regional Committee, applauded the high percentage of those Societies making efforts to train their staff (60 percent), but many fewer were attempting to train volunteers and youth workers. The Asia-Pacific Region, he reported, had recognized the need for more sophisticated training and over a wide field, skill-oriented and custom-tailored training. They had negotiated a plan with Lee-Snow Associates of the U.S. and, after three years studying the needs, the plan was being prepared to go into operation in 1990. He argued convincingly for the plan and described it. When complete and working, the plan would be available for all Bible Societies. The UBS had world rights.

7. *Global Goals*

The Rev. James R. Payne, retiring chairman of the UBS Executive Committee, reminded the Societies that a UBS fellowship at world and regional levels had flowed from Chiang Mai. He recalled the attitudes and determination and appealed for greater resources and better management, reminding the Council that their purpose was clear, and he demanded full support:

> There has been a steady and upward progress in World Service Budget contributions. We thank God for that, but we are very conscious of the fact that resources are not sufficient, that millions of people who long to have a copy of God's Word in their own language are deprived of the privilege.[4]

The Mid-Life Crisis

Béguin was fond of comparing the history of the UBS with the growth of a child. By 1988, that child had reached middle age and was beginning to ask if the epic days had passed. In 1986, the UBS had celebrated 40 years of history where once "Elfinsward" stood. A great history had been recalled; but at this conference where the global leadership was about to change, it was possible to be demoralized by an epic past. The giants of the past had built an impressive structure. Who could succeed them? It had been difficult enough to envisage a successor to Olivier Béguin, but Fick had carried the succession well. Would it be possible to retain that standard? And could anyone replace Nida in the translation work of the UBS or Holmgren, who, after

North, had been the leading statesman of the movement? Although less public than Nida or Holmgren, Baas had played a major role in defining the management, not only of finances, but the whole structure. As UBS treasurer since 1960, he had dealt with the various financial crises that the UBS faced as its structures changed. After the UBS Council meeting in Buck Hill Falls in 1966, the management of the World Service Budget became a major task. When the regional structure was fully worked out and regional committees formed and allocations agreed on consultation with the World Service Officer responsible for the region, problems of cash flow could easily arise. The cost of producing the Bibles often had to be met before the payments for the Bibles came in. It was this particular problem which led Baas to draft a manual for policy making and administration. This passed through various revisions until the more or less final form was presented to the Council in Budapest on September 22, 1988. In the following April after further consideration by the Executive Committee in Reading, England, where the new world offices were in future to be established, the manual became official.

The document now called *Manual for Policy Making and Administrative Procedures (MAPMAP)* contains descriptions of the assignments and functions of the several UBS units and their officers. It has forty chapters in five sections, with an additional section for UBS by-laws and regulations. Every office is described in detail with responsibilities and powers. It is unlikely to be replaced, although it is bound to be revised. This was largely the work of Baas in consultation with senior officers within the UBS.

Dr. Charles Baas

Time and time again in discussion, Baas brought the committee back to its proper purpose. He never lost sight of the real intention of the UBS to see that the Bible passed from hand to hand. His story was worth telling. He boasted that he was never recruited but offered his services for Bible Society work, not drafted but a volunteer, although, of course, he received his salary.

The man who first inspired him to volunteer for Bible Society work was the Rev. J. Chapman Bradley, D.D., who had been Administrative

Secretary of the Greater New York Federation of Churches, a Presbyterian like Baas, and ecumenical. He joined the Bible Society staff in October 1944, and in the following year assumed new duties which included the stimulation of the "Use of Scriptures." The ABS thus added to its familiar three dimensions of Translation, Publication, and Distribution the fourth dimension of Bible Use. He was engaged in promoting a Worldwide Bible Reading Program when in 1946 he spoke at the Presbyterian church where the young Charley Baas heard him and decided to seek employment with the ABS. He approached Gilbert Darlington, a quiet but determined and highly gifted Episcopalian minister, who had been treasurer of the ABS since 1920. Darlington had no hesitation. Baas was sure of himself, and Darlington recognized possibilities. Baas still remembers the dark rooms into which he went with men at high desks wearing green eyeshades, bent over six-foot ledgers. But, behind all that, he saw the purpose of the Bible Society, and he believed in it. He had been married only two years. Darlington, who employed him at once, moved on to new adventures in Bible work.

Baas acquired further qualifications than those of accountancy with which he began: a distinction in his Bachelor of Science in 1950, and a Master's in Business Administration in 1954. In that same year he was appointed assistant treasurer of the ABS, still undertaking projects which Darlington had wisely begun, but often left unfinished in the press of other duties. Darlington retired in 1957, and Charles Baas was appointed ABS treasurer in 1958. On his appointment he made quite clear that he regarded the Bible Society as "an act of faith."

By 1960 he succeeded Darlington as treasurer of the UBS. In name, Darlington had been associate treasurer, but that fiction was dropped with Baas. Lord Luke continued until 1969, but the main part of the work was in the hands of Darlington and later Baas. In 1969, Bernard Tattersall replaced Lord Luke, who became Honorary Treasurer. Baas and Tattersall carried through the administration of the finances as the World Service Budget emerged and Regional Centers developed their role in the years following Addis Ababa.

Bernard Tattersall

When Bernard Tattersall died on March 16, 1978, from a heart attack while sitting at his desk in London Bible House, the obvious person to write a tribute was John Dean. Within that tribute, he allowed himself a personal word:

> having worked for and with Bernard for over twenty years and having grown up in the Bible Society movement under his inspiration and leadership, I would like to express how very much I have owed to Bernard's always-available, always-trustworthy, always-constructive experience, encouragement, and objective criticism—at first as a great boss to work for, and later as a true friend to cherish.

In 1950, Tattersall left a successful career in banking to respond to a call from the Bible Society of India and Ceylon (then a recently accepted member Society of the UBS) for a general manager. He guided the new Society for two years until it was firmly established on sound business principles. Then he returned to London in 1952, to become financial secretary of the BFBS. It is a mark of the quality of his work that he was the first layman to become general secretary of the Society. On Lord Luke's retirement in 1969, Tattersall was appointed one of the two treasurers of the UBS with Charles Baas. With Baas, he made considerable contributions to the worldwide work of the Bible Society movement at a critical period of its development, in the field of management and general administration.

Tattersall was described by everybody as kind, thoughtful, understanding of the needs of others, and constantly open. He was therefore an ideal choice, which the UBS Executive Committee made when they asked him to become chairman and convenor of the UBS Personnel Subcommittee. John Dean commented: "Colleagues around the world learned that they could depend upon Bernard to ensure that their concerns were effectively discussed and dealt with by the Subcommittee." His wife, Anne, who had supported him since the first decision to leave a lucrative banking career for Bible Society work in India, had inscribed in the crematorium Book of Remembrance words recalling those of Micah 6:8: "He did what is just, showed constant love, and walked in humble fellowship with his God."

Global Changes

At Budapest Baas was replaced by Geoffrey Hill, appointed not as treasurer, but as finance director. The two World Service Officers before the Budapest meetings had been John Dean (Africa and Europe-Middle East) and John Erickson (Americas and Asia-Pacific). John Dean continued until 1992, but John Erickson was replaced by Rev. Philip N. Oliver. John Erickson became chairman of the UBS Executive Committee. Erickson's position was a key one. The Executive Committee met frequently and handled the main global business of UBS, reporting to the General Committee which met at four yearly intervals, and to the Council at eight yearly intervals. The chair had been held by only three people before him: Holmgren (1966-1972), Inbanathan (1972–1976), and Payne (1976–1988). It was the most involved appointment among the officers of UBS.

John D. Erickson

Erickson was born in Wesleyville, Pennsylvania, a Lutheran, educated at Augustana College in Rock Island, Illinois, and proceeded to Augustana Theological College, from which he graduated in 1959 and was ordained as a Lutheran minister. He served as a missionary in Japan from 1960 to 1962, after completing graduate work in East and Southeast Asian studies at the University of Minnesota. When he returned to the States, he became Assistant Pastor of the Elim Lutheran Church, Robbinsdale, Minnesota, and remained there until 1965, when he joined the staff of the ABS. He came with enough experience of Asia to be appointed secretary for Asia in the Overseas Department. His administrative skills were noted, and within two years he was appointed executive secretary of the Ways and Means, a post he held for seven years. In that position, his responsibilities were for the promotion of direct and deferred gifts from individuals, foundations, corporations, and other prospective donors. He was also in charge of relations between the Bible Society and more than eighty church bodies, denominations, and agencies which contributed to the ABS. With that experience he was a natural choice in 1976 for UBS World Service Officer responsible for Asia-Pacific and the Americas regions. In that capacity he was involved in talks with Amity Foundation which led to the "Bible Press for China" project. He was appointed General Secretary and recording secretary of the ABS in July 1978, providing day-to-day direction to the Society's International Division; but he continued to serve the UBS as World Service Officer until the UBS Council at Budapest. He had meanwhile been awarded the degree of Doctor of Divinity by Virginia Theological Seminary, Lynchburg, in 1973.

When Erickson was appointed chairman of the Executive Committee, it was recognized that the UBS was going through a period of radical change. The Global Office was to be moved to Reading, England, to include the General Secretary, the Finance Director, and both World Service Officers, plus coordinators for translation, personnel, information, finance, and computer services, which with secretarial assistance made a team of thirty-two. These were radical changes with new global appointments. It was all the more necessary, therefore, that the chairman of the Executive Committee should be a person of long and wide experience in Bible Society work at the international level. Erickson's appointment was crucial to the working of the new administration.

The Budapest Declaration

At the end of the Council meeting in Budapest, the representatives of the member Societies expressed their determination to expand the work of the UBS and they confidently believed that they could do it.

Accepting the principles laid down at Chiang Mai in 1980, which they had so far tried to implement, they went further. Under the slogan of "God's Word: Hope for All," they indicated advance on six fronts:

1. *Scriptures for Young People.*
   Assessing the number of young people to be born and survive to the age of 12 by the year 2000, they accepted responsibility "to make accessible to each one of them by the year 2000 specially prepared Scripture in printed or other form, and translated in a manner they will readily understand.
2. *Youth and the Bible Cause.*
   The necessity of full involvement of young people in Bible Society work meant that the Bible Societies themselves must encourage young people to be fully involved "in ways that they themselves find to be productive and worthwhile." Experience and youth had to learn from one another. It was agreed to call, within the

next two or three years, four regional conferences of young men and women "who will be leaders of tomorrow."

3. *Scriptures for the Churches.*

Accepting the estimate that by the year 2000, 450 million people will have joined the Church, the Bible Societies, "in partnership with the Churches and with other Scripture translating, publishing, and distributing organizations," accepted responsibility to ensure that all the needs of these new Christians would be fully met.

4. *Our Spiritual Commitment.*

An admission of failure in the past, both in the work and in personal life, led to a renewed commitment to prayer and "to Christ and His Kingdom."

5. *Resources for the Work.*

The work demanded greater resources than were then available. The Bible Societies committed themselves to a more efficient use of these resources and appealed for "the generous prayer and financial support of many more churches and individuals who love the Bible and want to share it with others."

6. *Service to the Churches.*

Thanksgiving for more effective use of the Bible and a commitment again to the task of "serving all Christian churches and confessions, and also of challenging them with the task of using the Bible in their work of evangelism and Christian nurture."

Outlining "The Task Before Us," the UBS Declaration included, "We pledge ourselves to develop global and regional strategies which will provide creative assistance to each Society."[5]

Financing the Work

One of the six booklets which every delegate to the UBS Council received as background material was entitled, "Financing the Work." Like the other booklets, it was partly historical and partly explanatory of the current situation. The story of the World Service Budget and the subsequent regional structures was described. The philosophy was easy to understand—every society was a giving society, and each region decided how the money should be spent in its own area. But there was never enough money.

The booklet described in detail how the World Budget was compiled. To do this, a number of charts were printed to show how the budget had grown over twenty years in order to meet the growing need. It was impressive, not only because of the amount, but because of the way in which so many national Bible Societies, which were once wholly dependent, had also become giving Societies as Malelu pleaded.

In 1967 there were fourteen Societies contributing to the World Service Budget; in 1987, contributions came from thirty-four Societies, of which twelve were Societies which might be called "net-supported" Societies, and twenty-two "net-supporting" Societies. Over the years no less than forty-eight Societies have made contributions at one time or another to various world service projects.

There was a chart of growth in the World Service Budget over the twenty years, rising like a mountain side from $6.3 million to over $37 million, but when the figures were adjusted by the IMF inflation index to give the real value, the chart lingered among the foothills and revealed the truth that growth had only been 2 percent per year in real terms over that period. The UBS had set up special funds to meet the need of specific projects which could not be supported from the main budget. These had been encouraging—the UBS Revolving Fund, the UBS Production Fund/Supply Fund, the UBS Capital Projects Fund, the UBS Short-Term Support Fund, the UBS Priority Scriptures Fund, the UBS Education Fund, and like any organization employing a growing staff, the UBS Pension Fund. All this was handled efficiently and effectively. But there was never enough money to meet the need. Special efforts at fundraising were constantly devised. Fortunately, the reputation of the Bible Societies and the noncontroversial nature of its work attracted many donors and legacies. At the conclusion of this booklet there were a few tentative suggestions which have in a measure been taken up since 1988.

The New General Secretary

At this crucial time in the history of the UBS, with expanding structures, reorganization, new global officers, and the movement of the global office, the man or woman appointed to succeed in the line of John Temple, Olivier Béguin, and Ulrich Fick might well hesitate before the task and ask, "Who is able to enter into this heritage?" The Rev. Dr. Cirilo Rigos was appointed.

In the course of the closing worship service at Budapest, Rev. Dr. Cirilo Rigos stood with the other three who were newly elected to global offices, the only Asian among a company of Anglo-Saxons. He, more than most, must have listened to the words of induction. It was conducted by the kindly Honorary President, Dr. Coggan. To the Council he said:

> Dear sisters and brothers, we present to you these global staff officers, elected and appointed to serve the global fellowship of the UBS.
>
> It is your task to uphold them in their ministry with prayer and honest advice, and to assist them in applying all that they know and can do for the good of all. Are you ready to do so?

And each of the company responded, "I am."

While the company stood, Coggan called the four officers forward and asked them:

> Cirilo, John, Geoffrey, Philip,
> Before God and in the presence of your co-workers, I ask:
>
> Are you ready to dedicate yourself entirely to the service of the Word of God, and, to that end, to the service of the world fellowship of the UBS?

Their answer was, "With the help of God, I am." And Coggan prayed for strength, enlightenment, wisdom, and understanding from God.[6]

In all the movement of the next few months, only one of those four had to pull up his roots and move into a totally different culture, a provincial town in England, from the warm weather and fellowship of the Philippines. Rigos had an established place in Manila, honored and successful. In England few knew him. He had a mammoth task ahead.

The Rev. Dr. Cirilo Rigos

When Rigos was appointed, he was 56 years old. He had been a successful pastor and an influential church leader in the Philippines. In 1955, during his final year in Union Theological Seminary, Manila, he was asked to become junior pastor of Cosmopolitan Church. Within a year he was appointed senior pastor. The church grew under his ministry, and its worshippers included some of the most distinguished members of Manila's political and cultural society; the families of Jovita Salonga, Narciso Ramos, and Melquiades Gamboa, to mention but a few. During his twenty-two years at Cosmopolitan Church, he built a new sanctuary, ladies' dormitory, and a parsonage. He also filled the church. In 1977 he moved to a smaller church, the Ellinwood-Malate Church, which in his eleven years there grew from eighty worshippers to more than three thousand, making it the largest Protestant church in the country. There was quite a cult following for his preaching which was described as "down-to-earth, laced with sarcasm." Others noted the considerable research that went into a sermon which lasted never more than eighteen minutes.

Rigos was also much involved in the political life of his country. When he was general secretary of the United Church of Christ in the Philippines (1968–1972), he saw that the Church was too much dependent upon funding for projects from American churches, and he guided it towards financial independence. Under President Marcos, the church suffered, as a number of its pastors and laymen were accused of subversion and the church itself branded as communist. When martial law was declared, Rigos was back as pastor of Cosmopolitan Church. He was now a recalcitrant prophet. One of his most powerful organizations was the Wednesday Forum, a breakfast meeting designed to help ministers and church leaders in central Manila understand the issues affecting the life of the people. It became the venue for the truth over against the slanted reporting. The issues discussed and the truth declared ranged widely. The ministers took their stand against the military bases and called for their removal from the country. Eventually this Wednesday Forum became a center of the Opposition to Marcos: political leaders, such as Gerry Roxas and José Diokno, and many others who later joined Cory Aquino's government when Marcos was overthrown were members of that Forum. After the revolution, Rigos spent five months in constitution writing, an experience, which he said he would treasure for a very long time.[7]

Rigos took up his position as General Secretary on January 1, 1989. He moved the office to Reading and settled there with his wife, Lydia, a registered nurse, his son who became a student at Reading University, and his daughter Leah who was working in London.

A new chapter in the story of the UBS was opening, and a totally new chapter in the life of Cirilo Rigos.

A New President

The UBS President has always been a person of distinction in his own church: Berggrav, the Primate of Norway; Coggan, the Archbishop of Canterbury when he retired from UBS Presidency; Hoffmann, Lutheran Hour Preacher and president of the Lutheran Laymen's League. Norway, England, America—there were two Lutherans out of three! Hoffmann continued in office until the end of 1988. Then a third Lutheran was elected President—the Rt. Rev. Dr. Eduard Lohse, an academic, Bishop of Hannover until his retirement in June 1988. Lohse accepted the invitation to become UBS President and succeeded Hoffmann on January 1, 1989, the very day that Rigos started.

Lohse served in the German Navy during World War II, ending as commander of a motor torpedo boat. He began to study for the ministry in 1945, first at the theological seminary at Bethel, then the University of Göttingen, where in 1949 he became assistant to a professor in the theological faculty. In 1950, he was appointed dean of the student hostel of the theological seminary in Hamburg, his hometown. Hamburg, at that time, had no theological faculty. He remained at Hamburg for three years, combining his work with students and as assistant pastor of one of the Hamburg churches. His academic career began in 1953, when he became a lecturer in New Testament in the University of Mainz. In 1956 he became Ordinarius Professor of New Testament in the University of Kiel. In 1965, he returned to Göttingen University, once again to specialize in New Testament. His first administrative experience came when he was appointed Pro-Rector and later Rector of Göttingen University until 1971.

In 1971, on the retirement of Bishop Hanns Lilje, Lohse was elected bishop of the Lutheran Church of Hannover. As bishop of one of the largest Lutheran Churches in Germany, he was soon appointed to the Council of the Evangelical Church in Germany (EKD) and was presiding bishop of the Union of Lutheran Churches in Germany (VELKD). As one of the principal churchmen in his country, with wide-ranging responsibilities in leadership and administration, he nevertheless accepted the invitation to become Chairman of the Board of the German Bible Society in 1975. This was no sinecure. During his tenure of office from 1975 to 1987, he took the German Bible Society through several stages of consolidation until a national Bible Society in West Germany and Berlin was formed. Despite his considerable involvements in German church administration and the Lutheran World Federation, Bible work remained close to his heart. Those who served in the Bible Society during this period paid tribute to the way in which he prepared and chaired board meetings and annual assemblies of the German Bible Society, following closely the work of the staff. High office in the German churches never deflected him from his interest in the Bible Society. Even when appointed Chairman of the Council of EKD, 1978–1985, he did not give up his Bible Society work at once but continued until 1987. In the following year he retired as Bishop of Hannover, returning to Göttingen where he had retained an honorary professorship. He intended in his retirement to lecture on New Testament topics in Göttingen and in universities abroad where he was in much demand. With a less heavy program than he had for years he renewed his involvement in Bible Society work and allowed his name to go forward as a nominee for UBS President. He was unanimously elected.[8]

Facing the Future

One of the most significant addresses given at the UBS Council in Budapest was written by Sir John Marshall, formerly prime minister of New Zealand. As a vice president of UBS he had been asked to look beyond 1988 into the future, both for the world and the work of the UBS in it. He died in England on August 30, 1988 on his way to Budapest, and the address had to be read by Mr. Peter Frude. It was to be the keynote speech of the meeting. His first observation about the future concerned the rapid growth in world population, unevenly distributed: the growth was considerable in Africa, Asia, and Latin America, while it was small or even declining in the prosperous countries of North America and Europe; the balance of age was not uniform, with the growing populations principally young and the West ageing; movement into the cities for higher standards of living was depopulating the countryside in many areas: medicine and improved hygiene was keeping older people alive longer in the areas where these were available. Only war, famine, and poverty check the growth. Marshall added that "almost half the world's population lives in the countries that have an annual income per head of less than $500." This meant that 70 percent of their income must be spent on food. Then he recalled the meeting to its main concern when looking into the future: "You might well ask how we are going to reach another billion people when five billion is already beyond our resources."

His answer to this was a closer attention to the opportunities presented by the new technology, which extended the means of communication of the spoken and written word and pictorial materials through electronic devices which now and in the years ahead can be readily adapted to presenting the Bible and its message of hope for all. He spoke of cassettes, videos, the compact disc, and the computer, "already put to use by many Bible Societies." The Word of God circulated more freely now than ever before in the whole world. Resources were the main problem as Meurer had already shown clearly. They must for some time come from the richer countries with static populations and declining church membership. Two questions arose: "Can the close interconfessional cooperation with the Roman Catholic and Orthodox churches, particularly in those countries where they are the majority churches, bring in greater resources?" "Can the rising middle-income developing countries in Latin America and Asia provide more resources for their own budget if not for the World Service Budget?" It was a realistic look into the future and a hopeful one.[9]

The retiring General Secretary also sounded the note of caution and joy in his sermon. Fick was always impressive on such occasions:

So joy is the first and last word. You will take many impressions home with you from the meeting. Each person who participated will take home a highly personal mix of memories, and different impressions, words, discoveries, and sentiments which will be important to each one of you. You will take with you also a new commitment to the task. Let us not see this commitment as a heavy duty, a burden, which, in addition to other things we must do, we have let ourselves be talked into at the Budapest meeting! See your commitment to the Bible cause with all the joy that your hearts can hold. Be happy about not being forced to extend, extol, and exaggerate yourselves. Be happy about being part of a work which gives honor to Christ. Be happy about seeing so many around you who share this joy. Yes, we have a thousand reasons to tell one another what Paul told the Philippians: "May you always be joyful in your union with the Lord. I say it again; rejoice!"[10]

The next Council meeting would be the year of the UBS Jubilee, 1996.

The UBS in the Nineties

The UBS Executive Committee meeting in Hong Kong, at the beginning of October 1986, recommended the appointment of a full-time finance director, bringing the number of full-time global officers to four. The committee also found it necessary to define the role of the General Secretary. It was proposed that there be one global office with four general staff officers, of whom the general secretary should be *"primus inter pares,"* not senior executive officer. These proposals were accepted, but Vice President Sir John Marshall expressed his concern at the unusual practice of a major organization operating without one person having overall responsibility. He was not arguing for a dictatorship, but a director with a senior key staff group whom he could consult. Marshall then outlined his view of the proposal: "The alternative which the subcommittee is recommending is government by consensus at the global level. This means that everyone must agree, which means acceptance of the least common denominator, which is not usually the best decision."

This vice president, whose paper on "Facing the Future" was to be so pertinent when it was read at the Budapest meeting after his death, was already facing the future when he continued: "In the 1990s, the UBS should consider whether it doesn't need a more positive, dynamic leadership, without disparaging the great work done so far. This decision also greatly affects the selection of a general secretary, since the kind of responsibility he or she is given will affect the person we look for and who would be willing to accept the job."[1]

Despite his intervention, or one might say, prophetic warning, the recommendations were carried. A nomination committee was set up to look for a new General Secretary, but not before Holmgren had been asked to circulate a proposal for guidelines: "The General Secretary exercises leadership as spokesperson, representative, and advocate for the cause of the UBS at the global level in its relationships with member Societies and with international organizations, coordinates and partici-pates in UBS policy-making and decision-making processes, and ensures the follow-up of decisions of UBS world bodies."[2]

The General Office

The "global office" was to be composed of four general staff offi-cers—the general secretary, two general staff officers responsible for relations with assigned regions, and a finance officer—together with their associates and support staff, altogether about thirty-five to forty persons.

The size of this staff to operate in one building made it necessary to consider suitable office accommodation. After careful study of details, it was agreed to settle in new offices in England, not London, but Reading. This was well placed in relation to London and the airports. Reading had developed office accommodation in various large build-ings, and one seemed most suitable because of nearness to the railway station and availability. The UBS took possession of the seventh floor, which gave the space required.

The first task for Rigos as General Secretary (designate from August 1988; in office from January 1, 1989) was to move the whole UBS General Office into the new offices in Reading. The responsibility for this move was left largely in the hands of Geoffrey Hill, with the assistance of John Dean who was in London. This meant moving people and documents from Stuttgart, London, and New York. Apart from a serious fire which destroyed a considerable number of docu-ments from Stuttgart, the move was accomplished successfully. The UBS General Office now had the sense of independence in no way overshadowed by a major national Bible Society. The four global officers, now officially referred to as general officers, were very quickly operating an efficient General Office and had staff with special training in computer use.

The Historic Events of 1989

Although the Soviet Union still remained communist under Gorbachev, the cold war was over. That was evident in Budapest, but it was in 1989 that the Soviet empire and its satellites began to collapse. During the summer, masses on holiday camped in Western embassies and crossed over to the West from Yugoslavia, the German Democratic Republic, Romania, and other former communist lands. Then in November, the Berlin Wall came down, and a whole new world was open beyond the torn iron curtain. Yeltsin later replaced Gorbachev, and the Baltic states asserted their freedom from Russia. They were heady months in which Rigos helped to chart the Bible Societies through history. Opportunities spoken of in Budapest enlarged beyond the resources of the UBS. The four general officers had much to do in advising and husbanding as well as increasing resources. The Bible Societies responded beyond their dreams to the new openings.

A very clear example of this came in the autumn of 1989 after the extensive earthquake in Armenia. Twenty thousand Armenian Bibles were delivered to Etchmiadzine, near Yerewen, the central point of the Armenian Church. The Chancellor of Holy Etchmiadzine expressed his gratitude, but asked for more. "Can you provide us with another ten thousand New Testaments and ten thousand Children's Bibles?" The whole project, from printing to delivery was funded by the German Bible Society. The story illustrated the new openness of the Orthodox Church and of the Soviet Union.[3]

Some preliminary work had been done earlier by the Norwegian Bible Society in September 1987 when Russian theologians from Leningrad and Zagorsk, together with a Russian archbishop, were invited to Oslo. There they met with representatives of the UBS in a consultation on "The Bible in our History and Culture." Much of the discussion focused upon the original text and modern translations. There was a little uncertainty about the text, but harmony came when

Ole Christian Kvarme, General Secretary of the Norwegian Bible Society, told the Russians of the possibility of printing the Russian Bible with the Lopulkhin commentary. The printing was to be in three volumes, and it was agreed to import 10,000 copies of this work. After the presentation of this gift, eventually 50,000, in the Moscow patriarch in 1988, there was more openness to the UBS.

The Turning of the Tide in Eastern Europe

The UBS monthly *World Report* for December 1989 began to include a rapid survey of events under the title "Window on the World." The information office of the UBS in Reading was fully staffed, and this new feature was one of the changes it made.

Not all situations could be fully reported in *World Report*, but this summary enabled the UBS to draw attention to many more projects needing prayer. The very first "Window on the World" began: "All eyes are looking to Eastern Europe as Czechoslovakia and even Bulgaria follow East Germany, Hungary, and Poland on the road to democracy. In the space of a month the world has watched the two halves of Europe begin to grow together."

Within another month, the January issue of *World Report* was itself given over mainly to Europe, whose region occupied more than half the thirty-page issue with the overall title "Eastern Europe: The Turning Tide." A better simile would have been "the avalanche" for what happened, because "the turning tide" was too gentle. The seventeen foolscap pages of the January *World Report* burst with action throughout Eastern Europe: supplies to Romania—3,000 Hungarian Bibles to the flashpoint of the Romanian revolution; the Baptist World Alliance cooperating by providing 50,000 Romanian Bibles; the Patriarchal asking as a priority for 50,000 Orthodox Bibles and 50,000 books of Psalms; $750,000 requested for unbudgeted projects in Romania; plans for a national Bible Society in Romania.

So much was happening that the BFBS sponsored two representatives to visit Czechoslovakia, Poland, and the German Democratic Republic. Everywhere they found the church at the center of the revolution. They were caught up in the 300,000-strong demonstration in Wenceslas Square in Prague, where people were "shouting, praying, or just walking in silence." Later the economic problems would arise, but for the moment, they could only remember Wordsworth's lines: "Bliss was it in that dawn to be alive,/But to be young was very heaven."

The UBS did not ignore other parts of the world, such as Nepal, where there were new openings, but Europe and the tottering Soviet Union took center stage. It was no surprise, therefore, when the Executive Committee meeting in Reading in April 1990 issued a record appeal. It asked that the present target of $34 million be raised to $58 million! This was the largest appeal the UBS had ever made. Erickson, as chairman of the UBS Executive Committee, put the case clearly and frankly:

> While the task ahead appears daunting, there is such a great thirst for Scriptures in what was formerly known as Eastern Europe, we feel it is our responsibility to motivate Christians throughout the world to take part in bringing the Word of God, the "bread of life," to those people who have been starved of the Scriptures for so long.[4]

The goal was to be 30 million Scriptures for Eastern Europe, and that was not all that was needed but only the figure which seemed to be achievable. Rigos was confident that there would be an enthusiastic response from the Bible Societies and churches worldwide to this unique opportunity. That confidence was built upon the experience of the previous year when the UBS appeal had exceeded its goal by 45 percent. There was enthusiasm in the air.

The New Structures

As the new team of global officers proceeded with their work, the decision not to appoint a chief executive officer was beginning to be questioned more and more strongly. In April 1990 the UBS Executive Committee met in Reading and listened to a report from its subcommittee on structure and administration. Before the report was discussed, the Executive Committee held an executive session without staff present. Then Erickson presented a summary of the report's recommendations. He explained that Rigos, on behalf of the UBS Executive Committee, wrote to all Bible Societies last October (1989) to comment on various proposals for restructuring the UBS, and he asked them to share their reactions with their Regional Committees. The four Regional Committees had put the subject on the agenda of their March meetings and then sent in their reports to the subcommittee.

The result of discussing these reactions was a series of recommendations laid before the UBS Executive Committee at this April meeting. These recommendations amounted to the dissolution of the General Committee in favor of a new Executive Committee, which would then be called a World Committee, composed of three representatives from each region (including their chairpersons) and an additional Executive Committee chairperson. This change was expected, but what was new was the recommendation that the General Secretary should incorporate the functions of chief executive officer for the global office. This had the support of the BFBS and two regional committees (Europe-Middle East and Africa). The Executive Committee resolved: "to accept the principle that the role of the UBS General Secretary be modified to incorporate the functions of Chief Executive Officer, and that this shall take place as soon as possible." (UBSEC 90.09)[5]

Rigos had strongly supported this proposed change of status, but he was not interested personally in becoming chief executive officer. He therefore resigned, as from before the end of 1990. There was an immediate need to form a search committee for a chief executive officer. That was done, and the following asked to serve: The president of the UBS (Lohse), the chairman of UBSEC (Erickson), the chairpersons of the four regional committees with the finance director (Hill) as liaison staff member.

That committee was also asked to reexamine the job descriptions of the World Service officers and consider what changes might be necessary in the light of the appointment of a chief executive officer. Having first resigned from the search committee, Erickson was later appointed General Secretary in succession to Rigos.

The 1990s in Czechoslovakia—New Patterns

The earlier contacts between the BFBS and Czechoslovakia were difficult after 1938 and were completely severed when the World War II started in 1939. After the war, the communist government made it very difficult to start Bible Society work again. Even Béguin doubted whether anything could be done, but the wise guidance of Pvale Simek, the lay reader of the Evangelical Church of the Czech Brethren, and the positive interest of virtually all the churches, led to a fully ecumenical Bible translation. Work started early on this translation, and before the Communist government fell it was launched. Czech translators took part in the translation seminar held in Arnoldshain, Germany, in 1968. Simultaneously, translation work proceeded in Slovakia. Scriptures were also imported, and Bible work continued as a division of the Czech Ecumenical Council. Pvale Simek had saved some material from the old BFBS office of Bible work from before the war, and there was a natural movement to involve the BFBS, but only as part of the UBS work. The Advisory Committee for Bible Work met for the first time in 1986; nine representatives from different churches, including the Roman Catholic Church, discussed the current situation and future plans. Before Christmas, they received permission to print in their own country, in 1988, 60,000 copies of the New Testament with exegetical notes and explanatory material prepared by the New Testament Ecumenical Translation group.

After the "velvet revolution," a Partnership Consultancy was established in September 1990. The objective was for BFBS to provide the Czechoslovak Bible Society, as it was then called, with professional help in the formation of its constitution, aims, objectives, strategy, structure, publishing program, etc. All this would be bound together in a business development plan. In October 1990, Richard Worthing-Davies, chief executive officer of BFBS, took with him his marketing manager, Roger Russell, and visited Prague. There they took stock of the situation, met the key people, and began the process of Partnership Consultancy with the Rev. Jiri Lukl, General Secretary of the CSBS. Over the next eight months, Russell visited Czechoslovakia four times, at first as marketing manager of BFBS, and, after he had set up his own company, as consultant. Lukl also visited England twice during this period. All the expertise of the BFBS was made available, and Russell produced a business development plan, covering the period from November 1990 to October 1995. It was an ambitious plan which would put the CSBS on the level of an efficiently run national Bible Society, fulfilling the qualifications for membership of the UBS.

The only question was whether Czechoslovakia could rise to that standard of business efficiency within a measurable time—in particular within five years. It was fine and practical on paper, but Russell soon discovered that in comparison to Western countries, Czechoslovakia had a relaxed attitude to work, but once he saw the conditions under which they had to work, he could sympathize.

By July 1991, Russell saw lack of organization, lots of honest goodwill in a fog of confusion, and inadequate facilities. He as yet saw no signs of the implementation of the plan, but few had seen the plan, and if they had they could not read it in English. That plan, however, was the hope of the CSBS, and its General Secretary followed it carefully as it showed him a possible future.

Czechoslovak Bible Society

By the time the report was prepared in July 1991, it needed the subtitle, "Incorporating the Czech Bible Society and the Slovak Bible Society." The division into two countries, which came into effect on December 31, 1992 at midnight, did in fact solve one problem. The UBS could only have one member society in any one country.

Russell drafted a constitution for the federal Bible Society, but pointed out that until the beginning of 1990 there were no full-time Bible Society workers in Czechoslovakia. He optimistically drafted a staff plan which he said should be in place by the end of 1991.

Looking beyond 1992, Russell saw the need for more staff and facilities for staff training. The rest of the report dealt with constitutions and clear definition of aims, policy and strategy statements, public relations, church relations, publishing, technical support, marketing, and finance. It was a very thorough report which was probably asking too much for the period up to October 1995. The report ended with the following paragraph:

> To reach this position UBS will need to plough in some $2 million (including capital support), but it must be understood that CSBS is commencing operations from a base where the local economy is in a shambles and pricing and foreign exchange is totally unrealistic. A key to achieving the desired break-even or surplus will be in the regulated pricing strategy

proposed. One could argue that financial improvements would be made if the pricing regime were harsher, but it is our judgement that already we will be pressing the buyer and if we went any faster the market could not and would not sustain it. The other key of course will be the steady progress of the Czechoslovak economy in reversing its present bankruptcy. There are too many imponderables at present, other than to voice the opinion that if anyone can do it in this new post-communist world, then the Czechs and the Slovaks must have the best fighting chance.[6]

Sverre Smaadahl

During his period as Regional Secretary for Europe-Middle East, Smaadahl built up extremely good relations with the churches in the communist countries and after the collapse of the USSR and its satellites his experience was invaluable. He was therefore appointed in 1991 as UBS honorary consultant to the region, working with and responsible to the Regional Secretary, who defined the required areas of activities, in consultation with the Norwegian Bible Society. Secretarial help was provided by the Norwegian Bible Society so that he could do some work in Norway.

Terje Hartberg, who was the UBS coordinator for Bible work in the countries of the former USSR and its satellites, worked with Smaadahl and between them they visited all the countries concerned. The Nordic countries had a special interest in this region and supported the work there. Gunnleik Seierstad, Regional Secretary of the Europe-Middle East Region from Norway, also visited the area.

Smaadahl made several fact-finding tours of these countries from 1989 immediately after the introduction of *Glasnost*. The Nordic Societies were strongly supportive of these visits, which were undertaken in full knowledge of the UBS Europe-Middle East Regional Center at Crawley, England. This service was formalized with the UBS in March 1991, and, although only for one year, he has since continued as honorary consultant.

His main task was to advise churches and organizations involved in the establishment of new Bible Societies in certain specified areas where he had previous contacts. He presented guidelines and explained UBS policy. He worked in countries of the former USSR, either remaining in the Commonwealth of Independent States, or fully independent and separate from the CIS. He helped draft the constitutional basis for national Bible Societies and developed their relationships with the UBS and other Bible Societies. He worked on objectives and programs, and completed the preparatory work for a Gospel Portion for the various language groups in the former USSR. He remained until the end of 1992, dealing with specific areas. Some of this work was followed up by John Dean when he chose to end his long period as World Service Officer and wished to get more involved in national Bible Society work. For this purpose John at once went to Moscow to learn Russian, get experience at the grass roots and even learn a little Ukrainian.

John Dean

Dean was one of the most persistent figures in the history of the UBS, an Anglican, who was with the Bible Societies almost all his working life. He was given special responsibilities as regional training and development consultant to the Europe-Middle East Region in a number of the states of the USSR in 1992. As a young man he was a photographer in the Royal Air Force in Cyprus, and there he became a Christian. At the end of 1956, when he returned to England, he applied for work at the BFBS and started in the Finance Department on December 31, 1956.

Dean had met the General Secretary of the Bible Society in Cyprus, Barnabas Constantinopoulos, and was impressed by the consecrated efficiency of his work. The year 1956 had been a very disturbing one for the finances of the BFBS, and the situation did not improve during 1957 when Dean was assigned to assist with budgets and financial records of the BFBS Agencies overseas. He studied accountancy, and for most of his career with the Bible Societies he has been concerned with finance, until his recent appointment which gave him an opportunity to extend his interest in languages. In 1967, he was assigned to the UBS as World Budget Coordinator. He was thus in at the beginning of the World Service Budget, which had been agreed the previous year at Buck Hill Falls. As such, he worked from New York for two years, with responsibility for the coordination and development of some of the UBS financial and administrative procedures. By 1972 there were two World Service Officers with responsibility for specific regions—Warner Hutchinson in New York, for Asia-Pacific and the Americas; John Weller in London, with responsibility for Europe-Middle East and Africa. Dean succeeded Weller in 1973, and in 1976 Erickson succeeded Hutchinson. When Erickson became General Secretary of the UBS in 1990, Dean had already been serving for two years as World Service Officer for the Americas Region and was asked by the newly appointed ABS President, Eugene Habecker, to serve as consultant to the ABS, in order to review the work of the Society's International Relations Department and to give advice on other aspects of the ABS/UBS relationships.

International Relations: A Historical Survey

Dean had seen the development of the UBS from its dependence upon the major Bible Societies to a central office which included all its main functions under one roof. He was aware that developments over twenty-five years (1966–1991) in the worldwide work of the UBS had, of necessity, significantly affected the work of the ABS International Relations Department. The change had accelerated over the last three years with the move to Reading. Dean showed in his report to Habecker how differently the BFBS and the ABS had been affected by these changes over the years. Until the mid-sixties, there was growth but little change. In 1966, however, largely at the initiative of the ABS, the UBS regional structure was initiated and administrative responsibility was largely transferred to UBS regional committees and regional staff. Gradually that responsibility moved to the growing number of autonomous national Bible Societies. The BFBS and the ABS reacted differently to this change. Dean explained this in terms that were both authoritative and clear: "The eventual reaction of BFBS to these developments was to withdraw for a while from major direct involvement in UBS decision-making, except through limited participation in UBS committees."

Dean gave as an example his own experience. He was both World Service Officer for UBS and General Secretary of the BFBS. In 1977, he resigned as BFBS General Secretary and was transferred fully to UBS, while the BFBS Overseas committees were disbanded. The effect was that for a number of years, the BFBS was little involved in UBS affairs except through its financial contributions to the World Service Budget.

The situation was quite different with the ABS, many of whose key staff served in UBS roles, while continuing as ABS general officers. The ABS International Committee continued even though most of its decision-making functions had been transferred to the UBS in 1966. Most significant of the differences was the relationship with the World Service Offices in London and New York. That in New York was staffed almost entirely by ABS staff, some of whose salaries were paid by the ABS. The World Service Office in London, however, was an exclusively UBS office, even though for many years it was housed in the London Bible House. Also, New York was the home of the World Service Budget Office and of the UBS Scripture Supply Fund. Dean made his personal comment upon this situation:

> It might perhaps be helpful at this point to explain that many of the major developments in UBS over the past 25 years were in fact initiated and/or supported and maintained by ABS officers (usually also holding UBS positions)—Baas, Ball, Erickson, Holmgren, and Nida. With some help from others, these people largely developed and implemented UBS policy, and ABS resources were generously put at the disposal of UBS in meeting common aims.

Dean points out that this meant ABS and UBS agendas were very often largely synonymous.

The ABS President and the Society's International Work

Habecker wanted to know what his role should be in relation to UBS. Dean made his suggestions that "the ABS president should reflect in his work, his priorities, and, to a certain extent, in his staff, the two-pronged approach of the domestic work of the ABS on the one hand and the Society's worldwide approach through the UBS on the other." Dean saw that as chief executive officer of the ABS, its president would inevitably give the lion's share of his time to the domestic work, because of its immediacy and size. But in order to ensure that a pattern was established from the start, Dean recommended that the International Service Unit become part of the office of the president. This, he claimed, "would itself reflect an international as well as a national agenda for the Chief Executive Officer." Although this would make demands upon his time, it would "provide him with close and effective support in carrying out his international role." With some hesitation, Dean also suggested some changes in the ABS committee structure in order that "all ABS committees have the UBS on their agenda." He concluded by suggesting that ABS develop closer links with the Americas Region of the UBS.

It was a brave report after only a few weeks in New York, but Dean wrote it with years of Bible Society work experience and with the knowledge that the ABS had played a major role in the UBS in the past, a role which should not be lost in the future. Habecker greatly appreciated this guidance as he set about his new task as president of the ABS and chief executive officer, aware of the significance of his (and ABS) relationship with the UBS.

The UBS in the New Areas

An example of the new areas in which the UBS found it possible to work more freely was the Ukraine, where the first proposal for a Bible Society came in a report from Smaadahl that the president of the Baptist Union in the Ukraine had told him that Protestants had discussed this and had been in touch with the Council for Religious Affairs. Smaadahl's report to the Publishing Consultant and Chairman of the Europe-Middle East Region was dated June 19, 1990. He said further that they wanted an international contact with the UBS. Unfortunately, it was entirely Protestant, and Smaadahl urged contact with the majority Orthodox Church. Although he emphasized the need for ecumenically based Bible Societies, he was aware that they were not used to ecumenical cooperation and also that the Protestants—Baptist and Pentecostal—played a significant part in the Ukraine. The Baptist president talked of forming a Charity and Evangelism Association of which the Bible Society should be a part. Smaadahl urged the Europe-Middle East Region to send Terje Hartberg, the Regional Publishing Consultant, to the Ukraine. They needed advice and had asked for it. Hartberg went to Kiev in October 1991. On October 4, when he arrived, he found matters very much advanced. The new Ukrainian Bible Society statutes were later endorsed and the registration process was completed by November 21, 1991.

The Catholics had not at that time taken up the invitation to fill their two places on the Board, but Bishop Ablondi (from Livorno, Italy) planned a visit to Lvov in Western Ukraine to persuade them and he did so in January 1992. Bishop Ablondi—a much loved and respected figure in Livorno—had played a significant role both in the UBS and in the Catholic Biblical Federation. He was a vice president of the UBS Europe-Middle East Region and president of the Catholic Biblical Federation. Hartberg reported requests for Bibles in quantity—for the Protestants, 100,000 Russian Children's Bibles and some Russian "Protestant Bibles"; the Orthodox Exarchate asked for 50,000 Russian Children's Bibles, but wanted them direct from UBS. Some effort was necessary to persuade the Orthodox churches and the Catholics to receive their Bibles through the Bible Society, which was in accordance with UBS policy.

With the help of the UBS, things began to move—office space and transport for which the UBS provided foreign currency; translation into Ukrainian of an interconfessional Bible (UBS translation seminar for March 1992). The church situation was tense, and Hartberg left the Ukraine after a short visit unclear and not too hopeful of its political future.

In July 1992, Hartberg suggested to John Dean who had been newly appointed to the Europe-Middle East Region that he should accompany Smaadahl on his next visit to the Ukraine and take over his contacts. The principal needs of the Ukrainian Bible Society were now for the setting up of an infrastructure, accounting, and training of new staff. This joint visit took place in September 1992 and from then on the main contact the Ukrainian Bible Society had was with Dean, who visited at regular intervals. He saw things move, slowly but surely, and on his second visit in March 1993, he could report, "On my first visit to Kiev, everywhere I looked I saw a problem; praise God, some solutions now seem to be emerging."

Translation made some progress after hesitation because of the expressed need to purge the Ukrainian language of Russian influence.

But that was soon overcome. In August, Dean went again, particularly to set up a branch office in Lvov, where the Greek-speaking Catholics were the major church and to select property in Kiev. He succeeded in both and had a profitable board meeting.

Dean was inevitably caught up in difficult church relations. With the Orthodox churches split into four, not all supported the Bible Society plan. Despite this the work looked promising, demand in excess of resources, and there were hopes that one day all the Orthodox churches would be included. In October 1993, Dean made his seventh visit to Kiev and reported sadly:

> Here is a new Bible Society, making good progress in establishing itself, a Society which over the last nine months has distributed over three quarters of a million Bibles (including Children's Bibles), a Society with a new Bible House, an enthusiastic staff and an active board—and yet a Society whose adopted budget will provide for only a tiny fraction of the Scripture needs in 1994.

Dean was deeply moved by this situation and asked, "What can be done?" He added, "Here is a country of 50 million people, scrambling out of a past of seventy years of atheistic communism, undergoing hyperinflation, and crying out for more Scriptures." He gave examples of the hyperinflation that was destroying so much business in the Ukraine and making Bible society accounting very difficult, but he wrote, "Anyone who is in any doubt as to whether people really want this strange old book should spend just twenty-four hours talking to Christians in any part of the Ukraine."[7]

UBS Cooperation with Other Bible Agencies

Bible work was undertaken by several organizations, not connected with the Bible Societies. Some of these organizations have had policies which made this difficult. As the "New Europe" opened up in the east and the demands for Scripture accelerated beyond the level that any organization could meet, cooperation to avoid duplication became essential. The 1990s saw the coming together in consultation and cooperative work of many organizations that had in the past been competitors for the limited amount of funds available. The first tentative meeting of the UBS with these "other" organizations took place in Horsley Green, England, October 1990. There were two areas in which cooperation seemed desirable—distribution and translation. The distribution agencies met with the UBS in Orlando, Florida, in July 1991 and the translation agencies in Dallas, Texas, in the October of that year.

After the two major areas of cooperation had been thoroughly discussed at the distribution and the translation meetings, a joint and all-embracing meeting was held at the global offices of the UBS, April 27–30, 1992. Then the UBS met with seventeen major Bible agencies. The list was impressive, including agencies engaged in translation and some with their own peculiar means of distribution: Bibles International, Bibles to All, Evangel Bible Translators, Every Home for Christ, Institute for Bible Translation, International Bible Society, Lutheran Bible Translators, Open Doors, Pioneer Bible Translators, Scripture Gift Mission, Scripture Union, The Bible League, Vida, Life Publishers International, WEC International, World Gospel Crusades, and Wycliffe Bible Translators. Dr. Lars Dunberg of the International Bible Society, which had recently merged with Living Bibles International, voiced the opinion of them all: "History is being made here today. This meeting couldn't have happened five years ago when some of our organizations were not even talking to each other. Now we have become friends."

At the meeting in April 1992 they found a name for themselves; quite simply the Forum of Bible Agencies and decided upon regular meetings. The work was divided into two groups—translation and distribution. This meant separate meetings, but those agencies which work in both fields were represented in both groups. The key goal of the Forum was defined as, "to coordinate ministries, avoid duplication, and plan cooperative programs."

Dr. John Bendor-Samuel of the Wycliffe Bible Translators was appointed chairman of the translation group and put the urgency clearly to the group: "When you consider the massive task facing the church in making the Scriptures available in hundreds of languages, our supporters will not tolerate any duplication of effort. They demand good stewardship."

The translation group meeting in Dallas the previous year had set one goal: "Translation in progress and at least some Scripture Portions published in all languages with more than 500,000 speakers in which there is not yet an adequate existing New Testament or Bible" by the end of 1996.

The Reading meeting in 1992 had before it the list of these languages and agreed upon which organizations should investigate what kind of Scripture was needed in each of these languages—Bible, New Testament, or Portion or a combination of these. A similar decision was taken about those languages spoken by more than 250,000 people. The assigning of translation to specific member organizations of the Forum was dependent, of course, upon agreement on a set of standard qualifications required of translation consultants. The careful work done by Nida, who started his Bible translation work with the Wycliffe Bible Translators, gave to the UBS the key role in determining those standards. In any case, this was going to be a delicate work and only close cooperation with churches and Bible agencies in the countries and regions concerned would make it possible. The distribution group put forward a practical plan for a joint program of Scripture distribution in Ethiopia, as a model for joint programs in other countries. This plan was a firm commitment to work together, and it came in response to an enthusiastic request from the Ethiopian churches.[8]

CHAPTER TWENTY

Looking Toward
the Third Millennium

———— ◇ ————

*I alone know the plans I have for you, plans to bring you
prosperity and not disaster, plans to bring about the future you
hope for.*   Jeremiah 29:11 (Today's English Version)

The Golden Jubilee of the UBS falls in the closing years of the Second
Millennium after Christ. Dates in themselves are of minor significance,
but they tend to trigger the imagination. When the First Millennium
ended, all Europe was agog with anticipation and fear at the prospect
of the return of Christ in glory "to judge both the quick and the dead."

The first Christians similarly waited for the return of Christ within
their lifetime. They could never look far ahead without taking into
account the coming of the Lord. Paul, however, chided the Christians
of Thessalonica for stopping work and waiting in idleness for the Second
Coming. He urged them to "settle down and start working, never to
grow tired of doing right." Within the context of the overriding plan
of God, the UBS will heed Paul's advice and "settle down to work."
Much has been achieved over these fifty years, but much remains to
be done. The year 2000 will be no time to "grow tired of doing right."
The Very Rev. Dr. Kenneth C. McMillan, after long years in the service
of the Canadian Bible Society and considerable involvement in the
committee structure of the UBS, looked forward to the future with
confidence:

There is every reason to believe that the greatest days of the Bible Society movement are in the future, not the past. Rapidly changing world events which made traditional work difficult can be new opportunities for the Bible Society. Look what happened in China. In recent years its iron broom cleared the way for Christianity to spread as never before and for the Scriptures to be provided. The painful revolutionary changes made way for a miraculous explosion of Christianity in China and for an enormous demand for the Word of God. This will be true in country after country.

Even in the post-Gutenberg age the printed page *will* communicate in a unique and distinctive way, *but* the Bible Societies will be involved also and increasingly in electronic publishing. . . . The greatest challenge the Bible Society movement faces is meeting the modern world with the same vision and faith the founders met their world.[1]

The Shifting Sands of Politics

The UBS now has a global structure which can be sensitive to political change anywhere in the world. It has a regional structure which can see national movements more closely. It has member Societies in touch with the political changes in each country. It has a global budget which can move funds and other resources to the points of opportunity and need. A network of information should enable the UBS to see new opportunities as they arise. The formation of the Forum of Bible Agencies, apart from enlarging the capacity to react, could widen the range of contacts, resources and expertise. It is most likely that this will grow in the future and chart new Bible work through the "shifting sands of politics."

Looking across the world at this time, the UBS watches with anticipation the change in South Africa to a multi-racial government; Israel, with hopes of peace between Arab and Israeli; and Cambodia, recovering from its horrific recent past. Many examples could be given of opportunities seized in changed political situations which offer some guidance into the future. Cambodia, with the largest number of disabled people in the world, is finding new life "beyond the killing fields." The churches are playing their part in this hopeful renaissance. On October 10, 1993, the new Khmer New Testament was dedicated in Phnom Penh. Along with UBS representatives from Hong Kong including Regional Secretary Jen-Li Tsai, was Rev. Serge Oberkampf de Dabrun, General Secretary of the French Bible Society. His Society had played a key role in supporting the translation during the years when few expected it to be allowed into the country.[2]

The UBS has shown its flexibility in the past and will be well equipped to identify needs as they arise in the future. It has the structure, if not always the resources, to meet these needs. The world of the future will be different from anything it has known in the past and the ability to recognize that a changing world requires different approaches will be crucial to its efficiency.

The Importance of the National Bible Societies

Dr. Basil Rebera, a UBS Translation Consultant, who was appointed UBS Translations Service Coordinator in succession to Dr. Philip C. Stine in January 1993, was insistent that in the future, national Bible Societies must take ownership of the translation program in their own country. Translation, which must continue to maintain the high standards set by Nida and continued by his successors, will have to be seen as the task of the national Bible Society and be included in its budget. "It can no longer be regarded as something remote," he said, "which is being taken care of by some translation consultant, who belongs more to the global level than the national." Already, the UBS has set up a task force which is called a Publishing Translation Programs Management Task Force. It does not make the UBS the publisher. What the Task Force is trying to do is to make sure that processes are in place and skills available within the UBS fellowship (including national Bible Society staff) to ensure that translations are done in such a way that they meet the needs of their target audience, and are published in such a way as to maximize their effective distribution.[3]

Electronic Publishing

Already in 1991 at the Triennial Translation Workshop at Victoria Falls, a major special interest group was the audio group. A translation project was developed with coordination, initiation, and encouragement by media consultants. Scripts were devised by national Societies, cooperating with various agencies who are working on audio programs, although each national Society will have to go at its own pace. Rebera comments:

> We are beginning to interact with what is happening on the TV screen and on video. We have to be ready for the time when people are going to be spending more and more time in front of their TV sets, but also with the computer alongside it, to link and interact with what is on the screen. That time is not far off. At first this can only be faced by *some* of the Bible Societies.[4]

There are already UBS New Reader and Audio Scripture consultants, like Dr. Mae Alice Reggy, appointed for Africa, who combine their interest in literacy and the provision of new reader material with audio cassettes. Reggy has done much successful work with the Mooré translation in Burkina Faso, where 9.5 million people speak Mooré, in addition to the 3 million in Côte d'Ivoire. The project has the support of local church leaders. The extent to which the German Bible Society is involved can be clearly shown by a quote from Meurer's "Report" of the Society to the General Assembly of the Society in 1991:

> Several years have passed since we first ventured into the area of Bibles on diskette (computer discs) and CD-ROM. The development of a new generation of computers has necessitated renewed efforts in this area. We now employ a computer specialist who concentrates on improving our computer products and keeps himself and us informed of the latest developments. With his help we will also be able to develop more effective means of product evaluation for use in the future. We cannot afford to ignore the demands of this new technology, as our rivals neither slumber nor sleep. There are developments within our fellowship also: The ABS is producing Bibles on CD-ROM with similar aims to our own; ie. to set source texts alongside national languages and to distribute the products internationally.[5]

For some of the European Societies, the ABS, the Bible Society of Canada, the Bible Society of Australia and others this is more or less, the "state of the art" already and developing still. For many other Bible Societies it is the future.

The Role of Women

David Ayi Hammond, the General Secretary of the Bible Society of Ghana, writes of the role of women in the senior positions of Bible Society work:

> I see the involvement of women in Bible work in Ghana as a welcome breakthrough both in the areas of distribution and fundraising.
>
> Speaking in the Ghanaian context there is no doubt that women make up more than 65 percent of regular church attendants. No wonder that in the Bible Society of Ghana four of the Standing Committees of the Society are chaired by women. In Rodrigues women play an active role in distribution.
>
> The importance of women cannot be over emphasized. One of Africa's greatest scholars, Dr. Aggrey is quoted as saying that to train a man is to train an individual but to train a woman is to train a whole nation or community.
>
> I am hoping that other Societies are seeing the need for definite inclusion and involvement of women on committees. This point came home forcefully to participants at a meeting held in October 1993 in Nairobi for Chairpersons of Boards and General Secretaries of selected Bible Societies in the Africa Region. It is my fervent belief that what now obtains on UBSEC namely that there is only one woman on a global committee of twelve people drawn from all the UBS Regions will soon become a matter of history and give way to a realistic approach to the question of gender balance in our global, regional and national committees and boards. The UBS stands to gain. In the coming years we should ensure that women have a good representation on the policy-making body of the fellowship.

Future Distribution to Non-Christians

In the WASAI subregion, Thomas was successful with the Muslims, because he recognized that not all non-Christians are to be approached in the same way. A three-year pilot project was necessary to discover how to approach and maintain the interest of Muslims. Based upon that experience he has now turned to the Buddhists, a very different group. In 1993 he was just at the beginning of a three-year pilot project in different countries. The same pattern will be followed with

Buddhists as with Muslims, putting out trial editions of various Selections and Portions and seeing what works and what doesn't. There are programs in Sri Lanka, Thailand, North India, and Nepal and among Tibetan refugees. Observations are going on also in Taiwan and in Korea.

This will be more complicated because of the many differences in Buddhism. Not only are there the major divisions between Mahayana and Hinayana Buddhism, but every nation seems to have developed its own variety. This is a necessary research if the Scriptures are to be circulated among Buddhists effectively. After Buddhism, there will probably be a study of approaches to Hinduism. In this work, it becomes necessary to involve Catholic, Orthodox, and Protestant. Some of the difficulties lying ahead are expressed by Thomas:

> We are beginning to see some results in Sri Lanka already, even from the trial program. The biggest problem, however, is working with the Christians! We are trying to open up the Christian minds to what can be done. We found (among them) the greatest difficulties when we were working with Muslim audiences. The ignorance, the suspicion, the dividing walls, and the barriers were there. Even when Muslims responded to the gospel, the established Christians did not want them in their churches. We had to build up support communities, who would be receptive and continue to nurture them. This required also the preparation of special material for building disciples, biblical material for new Christians.[6]

Serving All the Churches

Almost all the members of the Forum of Bible Agencies have their origin in the evangelical drive of Protestant churches or missions. Some would not welcome the participation of Roman Catholic or Orthodox, because they have a long tradition of conflict rather than cooperation with these churches. This is not true of the UBS which has striven to provide Bibles for all the churches. In order to do this it has been prepared to include the Apocrypha when the churches required it and to move away from "no note or comment" to "no sectarian doctrinal note or comment." The UBS as such has followed that principle, but not all of its members. The future should see the total application of the principle expressed in the words:

> The Bible Societies seek to enlist the support and welcome the counsel of all Christian groups in the country for the one purpose only: to encourage the wider distribution of the Holy Scriptures throughout the land without doctrinal note or comment. . . . Their sole concern is to recruit every believer, whatever his (her) private creed may be, to join in the most urgent task of our time—the proclamation of the Gospel in every land and in every tongue.[7]

The story of Roman Catholic cooperation with the Bible Societies has already been told. It is a success story, but there will be continuing need to keep the lines open and friendship fresh. The future will also see efforts to persuade the Roman Catholics to subscribe amounts of money commensurate with their demands. Despite some remaining problems and limitations, one can be confident that good relations will continue. A recent example is the acceptance of the Contemporary English Version, published by the ABS in 1992 as the "Bible for Today's Family," containing the New Testament with Psalms and Proverbs. This translation has been accepted by the Roman Catholic Church for use in the lectionary for children.

This relationship will be kept in good repair so long as it is desirable to the Bible Societies in their objective of "serving all the churches" and to the Roman Catholic Church so long as it continues to recommend "easy access to the Scriptures for all the faithful."

It is a much more difficult task with the Orthodox churches, although the future must see further cooperation here too. In some parts of Eastern Europe, this has been partially accomplished. The key lies in making it clear that the Bible Societies are seeking to serve the churches and that the churches recognize their need of the Bible Societies. Great sensitivity on the part of the Bible Societies has been called for, and there is no reason to believe that this will diminish in the future. The building of trust and understanding is a slow process, sometimes hastened by a crisis of need. There are two difficulties with the Orthodox churches which were not there with the Roman Catholic Church:

1. The Orthodox churches of the East have survived centuries of hostile rule with a form of self-protection. For most of their history they have been in the situation of the church of the New Testament and of the Age of Persecution. Many of them have never been in positions of power or favor except for a very limited period. They have known Muslim and Marxist regimes over most of their history and have seen their first priority as survival.
2. This has meant the development of self-governing churches in different countries. There is no central control, no unifying instrument. The Bible Societies will have to relate to them one by one.

   The Ecumenical Patriarch can, to a certain extent, be a point of coordination, but he does not have the authority over the Orthodox churches which the Pope, or the Vatican, has over the Roman Catholic churches.

Looking Into the Future

Those who have been involved in the work of the UBS, as committee members or officers, generally tend to think of the past as a good model for the future. They usually indicate some areas in which improvements can be made but there are few radical proposals for major change. Florin, first appointed as a representative of Europe on the Executive Committee in 1972 and subsequently first chairman and then regional secretary of the Europe Region, comments:

Depending on where one stands, a look into a different future might not be needed or wanted. It might well be that many in the UBS will be quite happy to go into our future with our present equipment and what we have achieved so far, which, by the way, is quite respectable. . . . If we all are satisfied that the UBS are on the right lines, that they perform at maximum potential and thus fulfill their calling, no "new vision" for beyond the second millennium is needed. In many ways I agree with this assessment.

But he adds a paragraph seeking a new vision:

As a pre-eminent member of the worldwide Bible movement, the UBS has offered and received cooperation from those agencies in the Bible ministry, which for various reasons cannot or choose not to be UBS members. It is my hope that this cooperation will hold and expand as in the future the UBS, true to their calling of "serving all the churches," will further develop and define and strengthen their servant ministry to all churches—particularly towards those two majority church groupings, Orthodoxy and Roman Catholicism.[8]

Payne, General Secretary of the Australian Bible Society from 1968 until his retirement, and the longest serving chairman of the UBS Executive Committee writes:

The single-mindedness of the Bible Society movement has been and remains the most impressive characteristic of its distinguished history. "This one thing I do"—*the wider circulation of the Holy Scriptures.* This policy has been reaffirmed many times and remains valid today. It is crucial that it continues as *the* hallmark of the UBS into the future.

He makes three points about possible changes of emphasis. In view of the competition for funds, "it is absolutely essential that the Bible cause be so persuasively presented to the Roman Catholic Church and to the Pentecostal churches that massive funds will become available from these sources. So far, support from the former has been token and from the latter absolutely minimal." About the recruitment of staff and officers, he says, "the UBS must continue to strive to attract persons of the highest caliber, with wholehearted Christian commitment, to serve in all aspects of its outreach." And as a third point, Payne stressed the need for the UBS to remain a fellowship, adding, "The keynotes of a fellowship are consultation and cooperation. There is a dangerous alternative, the multinational corporation approach. Any attempt to move the UBS in that direction must be strenuously resisted."[9]

Charles Baas, looking into the future of the UBS, noted that many of the present staff talked often of their concern that the UBS should keep "on the cutting edge of communication developments." This of course could hardly be questioned, but he expressed a concern about the possible neglect of the print medium and said,

Looking far back over Bible Society history I have gotten the feeling that the movement, if charted, would have the look of a continuous series of waves. For various reasons there would be a surge, a crest, then followed by a trough and eventually another crest—usually at a bit higher level than before. These surges seem to occur when some person, usually persons, became inspired and stimulates dramatic activity. The track record is such that it is obvious we have not been alone in what has happened. As for the future I look for more and higher surges as long as the Bible Society movement remains true to its calling.

Laton Holmgren

Holmgren has been at the center of the administration of the UBS for longer than any other senior officer. When he undertook to look into the future, he recalled the prophetic words of the young people at Budapest in 1988: "We are at the beginning of a new era." He affirmed these words with the conviction that major changes in all aspects of life throughout the world would mark the new millennium. The UBS then must change, and he listed the areas of change.

The challenge of relevance: The question likely to be asked by the growing, enlightened populations of the world will be, "Is the Bible relevant to life in today's world?" As the Bible is systematically and progressively dethroned by both the scholarly and sceptical communities, and as the poor, marginalized, and violated peoples of the world struggle to be emancipated, the UBS will be required to make the entire Bible cause—translation, production, distribution, fundraising, etc.—more effective and persuasive.

The challenge of resilience: The new era will certainly require the UBS member societies to offer the Word to the people in their communities in new and profound ways. Important changes and improvements in program and organization are likely to be called for to meet quickly the new situations in the world as they develop. The pace of change is likely to be more rapid and universal than anything we have seen in the past; organizational structures and procedures that were created for another period of time simply will not do. "Time makes ancient good uncouth!"

The challenge of resources: Obviously vast new funds will be required to meet effectively the vast new needs that are already arising in the world's exploding populations—calling for completely new approaches to global fundraising. Selective recruitment and training of personnel at all levels will become a top priority and should employ all the psychological and technological resources available in the process. Far more women should be brought into positions of responsibility in the new millennium. (Women outnumber men in the churches of the world, but are under-represented in leadership and decision-making roles in the UBS world outreach.) Above all, the new era will require new creative strategies touching all aspects of the work in all places throughout the world. The UBS speaks of itself as a global movement, but there are so far few global strategies in place, the principal concerns being on parochial programs and interests. Perhaps the phrase "A fellowship of Bible Societies" with its overtones of a congenial camaraderie—appropriate for our early beginnings—ought now to be changed to the more vigorous, creative, and aggressive phrase, "A partnership of Bible Societies," a reflection of our new commitment as we approach the Third Millennium.

Ulrich Fick

Fick was General Secretary for sixteen years and during that time had responsibility for coordinating the work of the UBS. He had some very definite things to say about the future, and he said them based upon both long experience of the past and his present involvement, under three headings:

First, Christianity today is shifting its center of gravity in a breathtaking way. The distribution of Christians over the globe is changing. Second, The movement which led to the decision of the Roman Catholic Church to aim at giving "easy access to the Holy Scriptures" to all believers can now be seen also within the Orthodox churches. Third, Marxist-Leninist governed countries now give Christians more opportunities for and freedom of expression; they are inviting Christians to participate in the life of the society and giving them a wider range of opportunities for witness and service than ever before in their history.

He goes on to say that all these developments have far-reaching consequences for the church of tomorrow; they also have directly and profoundly to do with the translation and distribution of the Scriptures. This he developed with three major points:

First, the importance of recognizing how the church has changed from being a western organization basically to a fully worldwide church. It is now we recognize that the church of the future will not be a white western church but will be a church that is throughout the whole world and not just appendages to Europe and North America. And he adds, "A Christianity which was reflecting such different contexts and responses to its surroundings can only collapse unless its members apply the same standard when it comes to determine what is 'Christian' and build their spiritual life and their witness on the same foundation. This can only be the Bible." The second concerns the use of the Bible as a partner in dialogue for all, not for a minority. He says:

> It can be predicted that from this wider encounter a wider platform of understanding results between Christians of various traditions. Those who read the Bible together find it hard to maintain inherited prejudices and misunderstandings. Once the Bible is available to all in all tongues its message can speak to all. The gospel—hitherto overshadowed, darkened, and conditioned by various dogmatic coloring—can show forth its light. A message which was hitherto distorted by various forms of folk piety and ideology can be heard in its original sound.

His third major point is the one that others have made, including Sverre Smaadahl and John Dean, about the significance of the former "communist" countries. When asked for something, "fresh and short," he emphasized his confidence in the future of the UBS:

> Nobody can greet the twenty-first century and the next millennium with a flourishing trumpet call of enthusiasm about trust in human abilities and technical progress. Even stronger than the surprise about the political restructuring which has occurred in recent years is a disappointment about the obvious inability of people anywhere and everywhere to make the world a place where all have enough scope to live. The generation now attempting to imagine its role in the coming century experiences resignation, escapist dreams and shortsighted solutions. For me, one thing is sure: tomorrow people will need the message in the Bible just as much as they will need air to breathe and food to eat. In a world becoming ever more constricted and poorer, people cannot live peacefully together in freedom and dignity without the liberation that comes from the Good News: All who see in Jesus Christ that God is powerful and merciful lose fears about their own life and thereby their fear of others. The Bible Societies have been entrusted with a treasure that will maintain its value as long as there are people, and as long as the earth turns.

The Founding Fathers

The UBS arose out of the vision and initiative of four Bible Societies: ABS, BFBS, NBS and NBSS. Senior executives of these four Societies today saw the UBS moving into the Third Millennium and described their view.

American Bible Society (ABS)

Through its President, Eugene B. Habecker, the ABS saw the future direction of the UBS under three distinct, but connected, headings:

1. We must find ways to continually reassess the mission (the "why" of our efforts together) and vision (where God is leading us in the future) of the UBS in positive and supportive ways.

   The UBS, in tandem with the efforts of its member societies, must consider the following type of question: If there were now no UBS, and several national Bible Societies came together to consider establishing such an entity, what might it now look like? What would be the similarities/differences given the multiple conditions/agenda of our time? Would our mission be the same, different, or modified? What would our future planning look like? What would be the shape of our vision?

   In brief, we must remember the words of Eric Hoffer: "The future belongs to the learning, not the learned." For the future, all of us must become first-rate learners in every area of our work and service for the cause of Christ and His Kingdom, and in the context of our mission and vision.

2. We ought to consider becoming much more strategic in our areas of emphases.

   We can't do everything we want because of the constraints of time, financial resources, and people. Do we consider all programs worthy of support or should we struggle, as difficult and as imprecise as our efforts will be, to develop criteria to help us better plan and strategize operational efforts given our limits?

   In these efforts, we need to consider the following types of questions: Are clear criteria in place for determining which countries/programs should receive the greatest amount of limited resources? What ought to be the relationship between the size of a UBS grant and a country's population, Christian population, commonly determined literacy rate, distribution (including free distribution), country infrastructure, etc.? How should what has been done in the past affect what happens in the future? And if changes are made, how quickly should those changes take place? Further, when the various UBS declarations/emphases are considered, the need for strategic operational thinking and planning becomes all the more imperative.

3. The UBS ought to identify more ways to empower all national Bible Societies so that as many as are able can achieve their full potential in line with their mission.

This may need to become the operative challenge of every Bible Society, large or small. And this may require a greater commitment to developing people and Bible Society leadership. We may need to have a better understanding of what it means to achieve full potential. Does it mean that meeting local needs, and only local needs, are the key operating priorities? Does it mean making a financial contribution to the needs of the global fellowship even though local needs remain unmet? Simply put, it may be necessary to consider criteria that a national Bible ought to aspire to if it is to achieve its full potential.

In sum, all of us may need to offer fewer "prescriptive" solutions and pay greater attention to more "listening" solutions. And we must somehow learn how to hold in tension multiple global mandates while at the same time we respect changing national contexts and needs. We have made many positive strides in past years, we have many more to make.

British & Foreign Bible Societies (BFBS)

Through its Executive Director, Richard Worthing-Davies, BFBS saw the need for the UBS to become more flexible in certain clearly defined areas:

1. Support much more variation in how individual national Societies and Regions interpret and pursue the overall UBS purpose. A three-fold division of the world might be helpful in articulating different visions for the future:

- The Western world, where Bibles are readily available and the Church is static or in decline. The focus will be on Bible use.
- The world where the church is growing—Africa, Latin America, etc. The focus will be on making the Scriptures available, with good basic helps for the reader.
- The so called 10–40 window (an area bounded by the Atlantic and Pacific Oceans and by ten degrees and forty degrees north latitude). Here 40 percent of the world's population lives, where the greatest resistance to the Gospel is found, and a tiny minority of Christian missionary effort is channeled. Here the focus needs to be on contextualization—the WASAI translation is a good example of this.

   Overall, I am sure we need to bury the idea of UBS as a centralized multi-national organization once and for all.

2. Allow much greater variation in the organizational forms that Bible work will take in future in different parts of the world. For example, given the different cultural contexts within which UBS operates, it is surprising how alike national Bible Societies and Regional Centers look. I believe that will change in the future. Secondly, as the concept of the nation state disintegrates in, for example, Africa, "national" Bible Societies will cease to have relevance. Regional or even ethnic societies will develop. Perhaps "temporary Societies without boundaries" will be needed in parts of the world to cope with shifting/migratory populations.

3. Deliberately foster a variety of temporary and semi-permanent working alliances and partnerships with other agencies and churches. I am not sure that the "Forum" in itself will be terribly significant—because of the range of organizations involved. But I am convinced that the various working alliance of different members of the Forum plus other organizations will be increasingly significant in future.

National Bible Society of Scotland

Through its General Secretary, Fergus Macdonald, the NBSS saw the importance of the Forum of Bible Agencies and commented:

It is true that more Scriptures are slowly becoming available—the member societies of the United Bible Societies were able in 1993 to increase their total distribution of Bibles by one million. But, sadly, we remain far short of the quantum leap required—a leap that could come if the western churches, which have over 90 percent of the total material resources of the church worldwide—were to recover the priority of Holy Scripture.

What then are the missing links? I suggest there are five.

1. The need for prayer. Too often we expect the Bible to do it all! We sow the seed, but don't water it with our prayers.

2. There is the need for witnesses. God's normal way of using his Word is in the hands and on the lips of his people. The Scriptures are the Father's witness to Jesus Christ (see John 5:37–40) and all of us who are followers of Jesus are called to add *our* witness to this divine witness. In the Acts not only the apostles, but the believers also "went from place to place announcing the word" (Acts 8:4). God does not send out the Word by itself; he sends it in the mouth of witnesses who, as they announce it, commend it from their own experience.

3. There is a growing need to multiply the media in which the Scriptures are available. Today in the U.K. four out of ten young people ages 16–20 rarely or never read books. If these nonbook readers are to be reached then the Scriptures must be translated on to audio tape, video cassette, computer disk, and graphic format. On the other hand, it seems highly unlikely that print is about to disappear—in fact the computer screen is helping it to stage a partial recovery. The role of the other media is not to supplant print, but to supplement it.

4. There is an urgent need for churches to mount campaigns of biblical literacy. The object of these campaigns will be to get a majority of church people into reading and sharing the Scriptures regularly, looking at life through what Calvin calls the "spectacles" of the Word of God, and working out the values of Scripture in their daily living. The regular distribution of Scripture selection leaflets to members will encourage them to share the Gospel with others. In addition, periodic training courses in personal witnessing out of their experience of the Word of God will be necessary.

5. A determined effort needs to be made to enable the western churches to recover a high view of Scripture. We cannot overlook the fact that the marginalizing of the Scriptures affects evangelical as well as the more liberal churches. The uncritical adoption of

marketing techniques in evangelism has downgraded the text of Scripture to a manipulative tool; the emergence of magnetic authority figures is robbing believers of the right to interpret Scripture by Scripture as the Holy Spirit guides them; an extraordinary emphasis on "prophecy" is leading to Scripture taking second place in the authority structure of local congregations; and the emergence of "prosperity teaching" is reducing the Bible to an adjunct of modern consumerism.

Netherlands Bible Society

Through its General Secretary, Dr. Cock van der Hoeven, the NBS is most aware of creative tensions which could be fruitful in the future. Five of these are listed:

1. The Holy Word (original text) and helps to the use of the Bible (intrinsic base): Between the churches and the wider mass of believers, the Bible Societies have a significant role to play.
2. Word and Image: The future will see higher quality demand for illustrations which will require different standards for different target groups. It will become increasingly necessary to see that the text is elucidated by the illustrations and not lost in them. As media like television are used this will be a sensitive area.
3. Spirituality and Technique: The UBS, at all levels, regional and national as well as international, will be credible to the extent of its spiritual commitment. An internal lapse amidst highly efficient techniques could be a greater threat to the future than anything else.
4. Centralization and Decentralization: The UBS will remain as a provider of services, but not in a regulatory way. The work is the work of the national Bible Societies. But the UBS has an important role to fill as it follows the Spirit moving across the face of the earth.
5. Professionalism and Grassroots Support: As the UBS becomes more professional and efficient, it will become more important to keep contact with grassroot support. Voluntary workers will need to be involved at every level. For this, training programs

and financial arrangements to cover the expenses of volunteers will increase. A highly efficient UBS will need to do more than keep its supporters in the picture. There is need for involvement in policy guidance.

There is a sixth point, but it is less a tension than a plea for cooperation:

> In the perception of its partners, the role of the UBS will have to become more apparent. What do we stand for and what is the target of those (most essential) groups with whom we are in alliance? For Bible Societies, this cooperation is of vital importance, but in this context the ideal of solidarity is needed, and this must be made concrete. This need not always be expensive international gatherings, where costs are enormous and sometimes spiritual effects are limited and disappointing. It will be better to strive for meaningful, responsible, and ordered contacts addressing country or region assuring restraint and relevance.

The Continuing Leadership

The UBS is a living and growing organism. As it comes to its fiftieth birthday and approaches the Third Millennium, its present staff and officers have clear ideas about where it should be developing. The UBS President, appointed at Budapest in 1988, Prof. Dr. Eduard Lohse, gave his view briefly under five headings:

1. *New Translations*—As well in our western countries to strengthen the ecumenical cooperation as also in the so-called developing countries in order to enlarge the number of languages in which the Bible is to be read and heard. . . . This result could only be achieved by the cooperation of all Bible Societies in the solidarity of the UBS.
2. *Wider Distribution*—In the fellowship of 111 Bible Societies in more than 200 countries and territories it will be possible to fulfill the new tasks we are confronted with not only in Africa and Asia, but also in Eastern Europe. The good experience we have made

in China with Amity Press will help us to develop new ideas and find new solutions in other parts of the world.

3. *Serving the Churches*—Since Vatican II the cooperation with the Roman Catholic Church has led to quite a few new translations produced in ecumenical cooperation. Now we are faced with new chances of brotherly relations with the Orthodox Churches. We are quite hopeful that these ties will become as close and strong as those with the Roman Catholic Church.

4. *Scholarly Editions of Old and New Testament*—The Biblica Hebraica and the Greek New Testament are needed in all the churches for theological teaching and scholarly research. By the work of the Bible Societies, the same editions are used in all parts of the world. The Bible Societies will encourage all theological schools to make use of these editions in their training of the clergy and in producing new translations.

5. *Interpretation*—In producing new editions of the Bible, the UBS will have to think about interpretation, exchanging experiences the regional Societies have had with interpretation, and helps for understanding the meaning of the Scriptures. This will be done in the worldwide family of the UBS.[10]

The General Secretary—Rev. Dr. John D. Erickson

By nature of his office, the General Secretary has the greatest difficulty in putting down on paper any plan for the future. He has to be aware of movements within the UBS and react to them in his thinking about the Third Millennium. To know what his views are you must catch him like a bird in flight!

One such moment was in China, when the UBS Executive Committee met at Nanjing, towards the end of September 1994. Erickson chose as the title of his address "Where do we go from here?" He focused his sights on 2004, the 200th anniversary of the modern Bible Society movement. The question then became, "Where do we want to be in 2004?" But he would not attempt an answer, so much as "the way in which we can approach the development of an answer." For this approach he had six steps, and with them he took the UBS into the Third Millennium.

1. State precisely what our common vision or mission is in every aspect of UBS work. And he suggested a vision/mission:

   • That our mandate is to reach every person, man, woman, child, and youth with the lifegiving Word of God.
   • That each might have the right Scripture at the right time, provided and shared in the right way, and in the right format, and at the right price, so that each person can be confronted with the claims of Christ on his or her life, and if necessary repeatedly.
   • With this as a single common vision, all that we do in the Bible cause will be done:

     —in order that the already committed can be strengthened, comforted, encouraged, edified, stimulated, and guided;
     —that those who do not yet know the Lord Jesus Christ as their Savior can be led to know Him as their Life, Hope, and Fulfilment;
     —and that each person may know the joy of fulfilling God's destiny for them.

   It was this particular expression of a common vision/mission that Erickson called upon the UBS to adopt for the coming millennium.

2. Research must then be done into the three obvious questions:

   • What have we done and what have we accomplished?
   • Where are we now?
   • Where ought we to go?

   Such research, he maintained, should be done "within the framework of the Hakone statement of our goals and the Burundi Exercise." The former is "at least a Bible in every Christian home; a New Testament for every literate Christian believer; and ample supplies of Portions and Selections for Christians to share." The latter is a careful assessment of the numbers required, if necessary auxiliary by auxiliary, Society by Society. That exercise involves noting population, literacy rate, Christian percentage, etc.

3. This should not be centralized, but each region take responsibility

for developing its own program. This means seeking agreement regionally and nationally, establishing plans and programs necessary to do the job, and then setting specific roles relevant to the region or nation. "Without a vision the people perish," but "without goals, movements languish and linger and fade away."

4. Having accepted the vision/mission, develop the resources that are needed. That is the right order. Determine responsibilities and then, "mission drives money." The other way around is doomed to failure.

5. Review progress and make adjustments. "Further, it must be emphasized that all these resource development efforts must be undergirded by continuing, informed prayer to God, so that we are guided by the Holy Spirit and strengthened by the power that God has promised to make available to His people."

6. A timetable must be set.

The General Secretary did not hesitate to set one:

1. The period from 1994 to 1996 (World Assembly) should be the time for each and every part of the fellowship to agree on the vision, refine their focus, do the research, and begin the preparation for the work to come.

2. At the Assembly, and for the period 1996 to 2004, the specific outcome of the Assembly might be the launching of a Great Plan of Advance which could encompass two four-year periods (1996–2000; 2000–2004) with a significant review of developments during the first period to take place in the year 2000 (whereby the plan of advance would be reviewed, revised, corrected, and strengthened) followed by a "pressing on" with the plan until the year 2004. At that point a comprehensive report of accomplishments would be presented to the 2004 World Assembly meeting in England.

Endnotes

Prologue

1. Laton Holmgren, "Bible Societies," in *The Oxford Companion to the Bible*, (New York: Oxford University Press, 1993), 80.
2. Ibid., 80.
3. The NBSS was formed from the Bible Society of Edinburgh and that of Glasgow, which already had many years of Bible work before 1861.

Chapter 1—How It All Began

1. ABS, Bible Society Record, July 1930, 119.
2. ABS, ABS History—Essay No. 24 (III), 51.
3. Hendrik Kraemer, "The Place of the Bible in the Work of the Church as Seen in the Madras Conference," 7–11. (An appendix to the minutes of the Conference of Bible Societies, July 24–27, 1939, Woudschoten, Netherlands.)
4. Minutes of the Conference of Bible Societies, Woudschoten, Netherlands, 24–27 July, 1939, 8.
5. Ibid., 11–12.
6. "Elfinsward" Conference of Bible Societies, Haywards Heath, England, 6–9 May 1946, 9.
7. ABS, ABS History—Essay No. 24 (IV), 136–137.

Chapter 2—"Elfinsward"

1. Eugene Nida, "'Elfinsward' Changed Us All," an address given to the Netherlands Bible Society, December 1991.
2. BFBS, "Elfinsward," 1946, 9–10.
3. Ibid., 10–11.
4. Eugene Nida, 3.
5. Rt. Rev. George Bell, "The Church and Humanity," 179–180.
6. BFBS, "Elfinsward," 1946, 15–17.
7. Ibid., 17–19.
8. Ibid., 21.
9. Ibid., 12–13.

Chapter 3—The First Crisis

1. W. J. Platt, Private Papers.
2. Olivier Béguin, Report to Officers of UBS Council (Reading), April 1949.
3. Olivier Béguin, Report of Bünde Conference (Cambridge Archives).
4. Béguin, Bible Society Record (ABS), March 1942.
5. Béguin, Report to ABS, presented in "The Bible Society Record" 1947.
6. W. J. Platt, "The Future of the United Bible Societies" (Archives, Cambridge) New York, 22 February 1949.
7. W. J. Platt, "The Bible for the World" sermon preached at Fifth Avenue Presbyterian Church on the occasion of the meeting of UBS Council in New York, 12 June 1949.
8. Olivier Béguin, UBS Bulletin, No. 2, Second Quarter, 1950, 41–46.

Chapter 4—The Bible in Evangelism

1. Norman Goodall, "International Review of Missions," July 1949.
2. Olivier Béguin, UBS Bulletin, No. 4. Fourth Quarter, 1950, 1–2.
3. Arthur M. Chirgwin, Appendix IV to the Minutes of the Standing Committee, Sarpsborg, June 1951, 40–45.
4. Arthur M. Chirgwin, "Facing Our Task Together," Report of Conference, UBS Eastbourne, April 1954, 31–34.
5. W. A. Visser 't Hooft, ibid., 11–15.
6. Eric North, ibid., 15–25.
7. Berggrav, UBS Bulletin, No. 28, Fourth Quarter, 1956, 143–149.

Chapter 5—First Steps in Translation Together

1. James Roe, History of BFBS: 1905–1954, 417.
2. Eugene Nida, *The Bible Translator*, No. 1, 2.
3. Minutes of UBS Subcommittee on Translation, March 3–5, 1955.
4. Ibid.
5. Eugene Nida, Resolution 209, Minutes of UBS Council, Brazil, July 1957, 26.

Chapter 6—The Place and Use of the Bible

1. Full text of Questionnaire in UBS Archives, Cambridge.
2. *UBS Bulletin*, No. 49, First Quarter, 1962, 1–21.
3. Minutes of Standing Committee, Stuttgart, November 1962.
4. WCC, Department Studies Report of "The Responsible Society," 1956.
5. Faith and Order, Louvain 1971, No. 59, 9–23; 212–215.

Chapter 7—A Renewed Vision

1. Appendix I to Standing Committee Meeting, Stuttgart, November 1962, 29.
2. Ibid., 30.
3. Ibid., 31.
4. Appendix IV to UBS Council Meeting, Grenoble, May 1960, 68.
5. Ibid., 66.
6. Minutes of the Standing Committee Meeting, Eastbourne, December 1961, 48.
7. Minutes of the UBS Council, (Resolution 269A) Hakone, Japan, 1963, 38.
8. *UBS Bulletin*, Third Quarter, 1963, 103.
9. Appendix II to the Minutes of Council Meeting, Hakone, 1963, 52.
10. "Bible Societies and Churches," Report of the Driebergen Conference, 4.

Chapter 8—The Bible Societies and the Roman Catholic Church

1. Documents of Vatican II, Chapter 6, paragraph 21. (In Walter Abbott's English Edition, 125).
2. *UBS Bulletin*, No. 34, Second Quarter, 1958, 56
3. Cardinal Martini, "La Parolu di Dio alle Origini della Chiesa."

4. Walter Abbott, "The Documents of Vatican II" Chapter 6, paragraphs 21, 22, 125–126.
5. Ibid., 129–132.
6. Minutes of UBS Council Meeting, May 1966, 26–27.
7. Laton Holmgren, Personal Communication.
8. Minutes of UBS General Committee, Appendix V, September 1969, 81–83.

Chapter 9—"All Things in Common"

1. Olivier Béguin, Minutes of UBS Council Meeting, Appendix II, 1963, 47–53.
2. "Financing the Work" (One of six booklets prepared for the UBS Council meeting in 1988) 5–6—quoted from "Asia and her Global Obligation" (Malelu).
3. UBS Bulletin, No. 66, Second Quarter, 1966, 68–73.
4. Olivier Béguin, Minutes of UBS Council Meeting, Appendix I, 1966, 50–55.
5. Ibid., 55

Chapter 10—The Jewel in the Crown

1. Minutes of UBS Standing Committee, Stuttgart, 1962.
2. The Prefaces, printed at the beginning of The Greek New Testament: Fourth Revised Edition, (Germany: Deutsche Bibelgesellschaft, United Bible Societies, 1993).
3. Eugene Nida, "The Role of the Translation Consultant," ABS paper, New York.
4. Interview with Philip C. Stine, UBS Reading, 1994.
5. The Bible Translator, Vol. 24, 1973, 221.
6. Letter from Nida to Erickson, 21 February 1995.

Chapter 11—The General Secretary

1. A. H. Wilkinson, "Tribute to John Temple," BFBS Archives, Cambridge, 1948.
2. W. J. Platt, "The Future of the United Bible Societies," paragraph 2, (UBS Archives, Cambridge), New York, 22 February 1949.

3. John Temple, Letter from Shanghai to his son, James, 6 October 1948.
4. Minutes of UBS Standing Committee, Sarpsborg, Norway, June 1951, 35.

Chapter 12—The Growth of a Regional Structure

1. Minutes of UBSEC, London, February 1969, 90.
2. Minutes of the UBS Council, Addis Ababa, October 1972, 56–59.
3. Ibid., 62.
4. UBSEC, Brazilia, September 1973, 126–127.
5. Ype Schaaf, *On Their Way Rejoicing: The History and Role of the Bible in Africa* (Carlisle, UK: Paternoster Press, 1994), 139.
6. Ibid., 134–36.
7. "World Summary" taken from *UBS Bulletin*, No. 91, First Quarter, 1973. The summary is for the year 1972.
8. Report of Americas Regional Conference, Oaxtepec, 1968.
9. UBSEC, Resolution E, 1972.32, Addis Ababa, 1972, 11.
10. *UBS Bulletin*, No. 83, First Quarter, 1969.
11. UBSEC, London, September 1976, 222–223.
12. Letter from Béguin to Smaadahl on his appointment, 1967.
13. UBSEC Brazlia, September 1973, 104–105.
14. *UBS Bulletin*, No. 95, First Quarter, 1974, 5–8.
15. UBS Council, Addis Ababa, October 1972, 55–56.

Chapter 13—Europe and China

1. "Survey of the History of Developments Which Led to the Set-up of the Continental European Production Fund," UBS Working Paper, 17–18 February 1969, (Archives, Stuttgart).
2. Sverre Smaadahl, "The Development of Bible Work in Eastern Europe," a paper delivered to the meeting of European Region, February 1990, 1.
3. Willy Brandt, "People and Politics," Collins, London, 1978, 426.
4. Sverre Smaadahl, 2–3.
5. Ibid., 4–5.
6. Ibid., 6.
7. Minutes of UBS Executive Committee, Crete, September 1979, 178.
8. Limited Circulation Report, UBS Global Offices, Reading, England.
9. Ibid.

Chapter 14—Global Distribution and Fundraising

1. Interview in Toronto, August 1992.
2. Minutes of the UBS General Committee, Addis Ababa, September 1972, 43–44.
3. Minutes of the UBS Executive Committee, Santo Domingo, March 1977, 52–53.
4. Minutes of UBSEC, Nairobi, September 1977, 77–79.
5. Ibid., Appendix I, 93–98.
6. Minutes of UBSEC, Hong Kong, September 1978, 137–138.
7. Ibid., 137.
8. Ibid., 136–137.
9. Ibid., 116–117.
10. Minutes of the UBS General Committee, Appendix II, Chiang Mai, September 1980, 225–231.
11. "Report on a Symposium on Fund Raising by Direct Mail for Bible Societies," Breda, Netherlands, Confidential, ABS, 1972.

Chapter 15—Dressed for Action with Lamps Lit

1. Minutes of the UBS Council, Chiang Mai, 28 September—5 October, 1980, 232–239.
2. Ibid., (Appendix V), 275–279.
3. Ibid., (Appendix VI), 280.
4. Ibid., (Appendix III), 258–259.
5. Minutes of UBS Europe Region, Budget Workshop, 1980.
6. Minutes of Fundraisers Meeting, Lisbon, February 1984.
7. "A Guide to Scriptures Prepared by the Bible Societies in West Asia, South Asia, and Indonesia" UBS Bulletin, Third-Fourth Quarter, 1979, No. 116–117.
8. Ulrich Fick, "The Promise of a Beginning," UBS Bulletin, No. 134–135, First-Second Quarter 1984, 6.
9. Letter sent from Haywards Heath, England, all Bible Societies on the occasion of the fortieth anniversary celebration of the founding of the UBS at "Elfinsward" on May 9, 1946.
10. From the archives of the Netherlands Bible Society, Haarlem, Holland.

Chapter 16—Coordinating the Advance

1. Minutes of the UBS Executive Committee, Guatamala, February 1981, 6–8.

2. Ibid., 9.
3. Ibid., 12–13.
4. Ibid., 18–19.
5. "What Are the Main Tasks Ahead in Our Part of the World," from the Minutes of the UBS General Committee, Cuernavaca, October 1984, Appendix I, 216–221.
6. Ulrich Fick, "The World and the Work of the Bible Societies in the Second Part of the Eighties," Minutes of UBS General Committee, Appendix II, 228–235.

Chapter 17—God's Word Open for All in the Eighties

1. Minutes, UBS Executive Committee, Canberra, September 1983, 136–140.
2. Quoted by Ellingworth in his paper for the Conference on Study Bibles, held in Majadahanda, 1989, which surveyed the history of Readers' Helps and Study Bibles, 1939–1989, 8.
3. "Guidelines for Bibles with Study Notes," UBS publication, 1986.
4. Interview in New York, October 1993.
5. *UBS Bulletin*, No. 140–141. 6.
6. Interview in Reading, March 1994.
7. *UBS Bulletin*, No. 132–133, 1983, 63–65.
8. German Bible Society, Stuttgart.

Chapter 18—Budapest—1988

1. *UBS Bulletin*, No. 152–153, Third-Fourth Quarter 1988, 3.
2. Ibid., 5
3. Ibid. ("Presented with hope by the youth delegation."), 87–89.
4. Ibid., ("What have we done since Chiang Mai?"), 21–30.
5. Appendix I (The Budapest Declaration), *UBS Bulletin*, No. 152–153, 107–109.
6. Ibid., 105–106.
7. Domini M. Torrevillas, "A Small-Town Boy who made Good," from *Starweek* (the Sunday magazine of the *Philippine Star*), 16 July 1989.
8. From UBS papers circulated at the time of his nomination.
9. "Facing the Future, *UBS Bulletin*, No. 152–153, 71–78.
10. Ibid., (Closing Sermon), 102–104.

Chapter 19—The UBS in the Nineties

1. Minutes of UBSEC, Hong Kong, October 1986.
2. UBS Manual for Policy Making and Administrative Procedures, 16.
3. UBS World Report 232, December 1989, 22.
4. UBS Executive Committee, Reading, 4–6 April 1990.
5. Ibid.
6. Ibid., Report, 52.
7. From Confidential Reports on his visits to the Ukraine throughout 1993. Europe-Middle East Regional Service Center.
8. Minutes of Meeting of the Forum of Bible Agencies, UBS General Office, Reading, April 1992.

Chapter 20—Looking Toward the Third Millennium

1. Letter from McMillan, 9 August 1993.
2. UBS World Report, No. 282, February 1994, 10.
3. Interview in New York, October 1993.
4. Ibid.
5. Meurer, Report to the General Assembly of the German Bible Society, May 1991, 5.
6. Interview in New York, October 1993.
7. Minutes of the Meeting of the Forum of Bible Agencies (Joint Groups), Colorado Springs, U.S., 31 March—1 April 1993, 2.
8. Letter from Florin, 19 April 1994.
9. Letter from Payne, 18 April 1994.
10. Letter from Lohse, 2 May 1994.

Index

Chirgwin, A. M., *45–53*, 79, 82, 95, 328
Chisholm, R. S., *9*
Cline, E. A., *180–182, 214*
Cock van der Hoeven, *321*
Cockburn, Norman, *45, 93*
Coggan, Donald, *74, 77–78, 89, 94, 96–100, 151, 186–189, 235, 272, 281, 283*
Coleman, N. D., *32, 58–59, 63*
Culshaw, W. J., *114*

Darlington, *89, 275*
Dean, John, *186, 194, 210, 219, 276–277, 288, 296–301, 316*
Driebergen, 1964, *99–101, 121, 166, 188, 228*
Dunblane, 1948, *32, 39, 153*

Eastern Europe, *vii, 183–184, 195–201, 232, 248, 265, 290–291, 311, 322*
Elfinsward, 1946, *1, 15, 17–20, 22–23, 26–28, 31, 35, 58, 83, 92, 106, 152, 155, 159, 163, 235, 273*
Ellingworth, Paul, *60–61, 199*
Enholc, Alexander, *13, 18–19, 190, 198*
Erickson, John, *180, 186, 202, 204, 213, 222–226, 277–278, 291–292, 297–298, 323–324*
Europe-Middle East Region, *295–296, 299–300*
European Production Fund, *193–194, 216, 220, 237, 264*

Fenn, Eric, *71*
Fick, Ulrich, *151, 163–165, 167–169, 171, 183–186, 188, 195, 197, 202, 204, 215, 218, 220–221, 229, 239, 243, 249–253, 258, 267, 270, 273, 281, 285, 315*
Florin, Hans, *169, 197, 232, 312*
Forum of Bible Agencies, *302, 306, 310, 319*
Fundraising, *xii, 2, 28–29, 125, 134, 167, 180, 190, 203, 207, 221–224, 235, 243–244, 280, 309, 314*

Geneva Office, *19, 28–29, 37, 48, 155*
Germany, *vi, x, 1, 9, 12, 14, 18–23, 25, 28–31, 34, 42, 73–76, 93, 105, 129, 132, 156, 164, 169, 183, 193–198, 223, 237, 242, 258, 284, 290, 293*
God's Word for a New Age, *95–96, 98–101, 120, 130–131, 135, 160, 165, 188*
Gulin, Eeelis G., *74*

Habecker, Eugene B., *297–299, 317*
Haig, A. L., *18, 25–26, 30*
Hakone Formula, *97*
Hawthorn, Tom, *90*
Hoffmann, Oswald, *188, 204, 283*
Hogg, Gilbert, *26*
Holmgren, Laton E., *x, 74, 93, 95–96, 115, 117–118, 123–125, 133, 146, 151, 159, 165, 169–170, 172, 181, 188, 190, 194, 210, 216, 218–219, 221, 235, 237, 273–274, 277, 288, 298, 314*
Hughes, J., *2*
Hungary, 1949, *42–43*
Hutchinson, W. A., *160, 180, 186, 202, 211–212, 297*

Inbanathan, A. E., *75, 79, 96, 120, 130, 170, 208, 214, 277*

Joint Agencies, *124*

Kindt, Dorothea, *195, 262–265*
Koren, L., *9*
Kraemer, Hendrick, *9–10, 22, 41*

Lacy, Carleton, *8*
Larson, Carl, *75*
Laubach, Frank, *40*
Lilje, Hanns, *19, 22–23, 284*
Lohse, Eduard, *283–284, 292, 322*
London Office,
Loomis, Henry, *6*
Lukl, Jiri, *293*

Macdonald, Fergus, *319*
Mahanty, Premanand, *89, 96, 125, 127–128, 130, 208–209*